PRESSU

PRESSURE COOKING

Day by Day

K. F. BROUGHTON

Queen Elizabeth College, London University
National Society's Training College
Fellow of the Association of Home Economists
Formerly Home Economist, The Prestige Group Ltd

KAYE & WARD · LONDON

First published by
Kaye & Ward Ltd
21 New Street, London EC2M 4NT
1970

Eighth impression (with minor revisions) 1976
Twelfth impression 1978

ISBN 0 7182 0828 5 (Cased edition)
ISBN 0 7182 1146 4 (Paperback edition)

Filmset in Photon Times 12 on 13 pt by
Richard Clay (The Chaucer Press), Ltd, Bungay, Suffolk
and printed in Great Britain by
Fletcher & Son Ltd, Norwich

ACKNOWLEDGEMENTS

I wish to thank sincerely my colleagues, friends and family for their help in the preparation of this book.

CONTENTS

FOREWORD

Perhaps as you pick up this book you are still one of those who has not yet made up their mind about pressure cookers and whether they really are as useful and essential to the modern housewife, career woman and bachelor-cook as they are claimed to be. Of course, you will have heard of this quick and easy way to make light of cooking, while serving even more delicious, varied and nourishing meals but there are still so many things you want to know about it. How do pressure cookers work; are they safe; can they really keep and improve the flavour, appearance and goodness of food; would it be worth while to change one's way of cooking and above all, would it be money well spent?

On the other hand, you may know someone who has a pressure cooker which has never been used or which she could not get along with when she tried it, and now it languishes up on a shelf or tucked away in a cupboard. Or it could be you are one of those who has had a pressure cooker in use for so long that you cannot imagine life without it, particularly when you think back on those long unnecessary hours you had to spend in the kitchen and over the stove which happily are now a thing of the past.

Whichever you may be, it is hoped you will find pleasure in this book; that with its help you will be able to take advantage of all that a pressure cooker can mean in these busy, rushing days; that it will answer all your questions and provide new ideas to give you added interest and satisfaction in the preparation and serving of meals, not only every day for your family but also when entertaining friends and those special-occasion guests for luncheon and dinner parties. It will have served its purpose if, with its help, your pressure cooker becomes both a servant and a friend.

INTRODUCTION

The Advantages and Principles of Pressure Cooking

THE ADVANTAGES

Food and nutrition in relation to methods of cooking have, in recent years been the subject of much discussion. Pressure cooking, a method by which foods are cooked in super-heated steam, has a definite role to play now that the necessity of conserving food values is recognised along with the advantages of speeding up cooking times for the busy, working housewife. It is therefore natural that a pressure cooker should find a place in the modern kitchen as an essential basic article of kitchen equipment.

Correctly used, a pressure cooker has everything to recommend it to those of us who are interested both in economy and obtaining the best results when preparing and serving meals. With it, most foods require no more than a third of the normal cooking time. This must lead to a noticeable reduction in the fuel bills, less steam in the kitchen for a shorter time so that the condensation problem will be less and cooking smells through the house will not be so apparent but above all, the retention of food values, especially of the mineral salts which are usually wasted away into the cooking liquid, will be improved.

The question of the effect of pressure cooking on these food values is one which should be especially considered. When pressure cookers were first introduced careful experiments were carried out and the reports were later issued by the then Ministry of Food and printed by the British Medical Journal. These confirmed that an increased conservation of Vitamin C in fresh vegetables, particularly cabbage, cauliflower and spinach, and of B1 in meat and pulses could be achieved over that by normal cooking methods, if the correct times were adhered to and the small amount of liquid needed for the cooking was included in the finished dish. In addition, all such tests confirmed a higher retention of flavour and colour so that the food when presented, was both more appetising and attractive in appearance.

A pressure cooker is of course not meant to be used always on its own: it will work well in harmony with the frying pan, the grill and the oven, and can save countless kitchen hours in the preparation of those foods which do not in themselves constitute a meal but which often require the longest cooking.

In every way then and for everyone, the growing, the healthy and those with stomach and duodenal complaints, the economy in time and fuel and the higher retention of food values means that a pressure cooker is an asset in every home. It achieves that which is the ultimate aim of all cooking—to maintain the natural goodness of the food while increasing its attractiveness, flavour and digestibility.

THE PRINCIPLES

Cooking is merely the application of heat to food, and the higher the temperature, the quicker the food will cook. With nearly all liquids the highest temperature that can be reached at sea-level is 212° F (100° C), and it does not matter how fast or how slowly they boil, the temperature will not rise above this and nor will that of the steam into which the boiling liquid turns.

A pressure cooker however, is designed to harness and control this steam, which in an ordinary saucepan escapes and is wasted. The sealing-in of the steam which leads to a rise in pressure also causes a rise in temperature, and it is this, coupled with the fact that the steam under pressure is actively being forced through the food to soften and tenderise it, which explains the rapid cooking which results.

The relation between the rise in pressure and temperature is a simple one, and below 2,000 feet above sea-level can be taken as follows:

PRESSURE	TEMPERATURE	
	Fahrenheit	*Centigrade*
Atmospheric	212°	100°
5 lb	228°	109°
10 lb	240°	115°
15 lb	250°	121°

Exposed to these high temperatures, the fibrous tissues of meat and fish are quickly tenderised, starch grains are softened, the colour and flavour of green vegetables are retained and the safe sterilisation of milk, bottles, fruit, vegetables and meat is assured. While it is true that exposure to any heat leads to a partial loss of certain vitamins, the length of time that foods containing them take to come to the boil and are then boiled are important factors and here a pressure cooker has the advantage, as these times can be cut down, in many instances, by as much as seventy-five per cent. Again, as different foods and cooking processes attain the best and safest results at specific temperatures and pressures, a cooker fitted with a variable control can be easily adjusted so that these results are obtained in the shortest possible time.

When three pressures are available, **High** (15 lb) should be used for day-to-day cooking; **Medium** (10 lb) would be recommended for softening fruits for jams, jellies and marmalade and for bottling vegetables; **Low** (5 lb) for steaming mixtures with raising agents, for fruit bottling and the blanching of most vegetables before deep-freezing. When only one pressure is available, this may be 15 lb or 10 lb or with a low-pressure pressure cooker an approximate value of 8 lb.

As pressure cooking is accomplished in a sealed pan and in 'minute' cooking times, only a very little liquid has to be added to provide the steam and so there need be no wastage of the stock or cooking liquor from vegetables, fish and meat, which will always contain a certain amount of the flavour and goodness of the food.

Ideally, cooking, particularly of vegetables, should be done in the absence of air and light and with as little liquid as possible; a pressure cooker fulfils these conditions exactly.

About Pressure Cookers, their Use and Care

ABOUT PRESSURE COOKERS

Many models of pressure cooker for domestic use are now available. These may be made from high-quality aluminium alloy of a drawn or spun manufacture with a mirror finish polish or from various qualities of stainless steel. The two most popular types of pressure cooker are the casserole version with 2 short side handles, particularly suited to small stoves and where storage space is limited and the more versatile saucepan-type with a conventional long handle to both cover and base. Capacities are from 7 pints (3½ litres) upwards, but when making one's choice it is perhaps wisest to buy the largest one can afford, as a small amount can always be cooked with the same economy of time and fuel in a large pan, but it is disappointing to find that a small one cannot be stretched as the family increases or when entertaining guests.

Pressure cookers can be used on any kind of heat, gas, all types of electric hotplates, oil, pressure stoves and solid fuel ranges though with the latter of course, no saving of fuel will result.

The component parts of a pressure cooker are the **cover** and **body** and may be of varying design according to the make; the most familiar types are those with an insert rigid cover, opening and closing by a centre knob with an internal spring or screw action and those with an outside closure in which the cover fits on to the body with matching notches, the closure of the cover handle over the body completing the locking device.

The **cover** of each cooker will be fitted with a pressure control or valve, those in most general use being:

A lever type, fitted with a spring valve.

A control valve or weight giving a fixed pressure only.

A variable control with a sliding centre stem calibrated to register 2 or 3 pressures.

A variable control consisting of 3 pieces: an inner **L** (5 lb) weight, a sleeve screwing on to give **M** (10 lb) pressure and an outer sleeve to complete the maximum **H** (15 lb) pressure.

In addition, each pressure cooker conforming to British Standard Institute standards, must be fitted with a safety device that will come into action automatically should excess pressure be built up. The types most commonly fitted are:

A rubber plug with a movable centre pintle which combines two safety factors. The pintle, which will pop up should excessive pressure be built up so that this will be released and can then be reset for further cooking, and the crosspiece of the pintle made of a fusible alloy which will melt at an excessive temperature to warn that the cooker is boiling dry.

A solid rubber excess pressure plug which can be reset, with a separate rubber plug with fusible core to come into action with excess temperature.

A rubber plug with fusible core only.

The cover will also be fitted with a gasket or sealing ring made from a rubber compound, to ensure that no leakage of steam will occur at the join between the cover and base.

The design of a pressure cooker must always incorporate a locking device to ensure that the method of joining the cover to the base will prevent its removal during cooking or while any pressure at all remains inside the cooker.

Varying accessories are made available by the manufacturers, either at the time of purchase or as additional separate items, but each pressure cooker must come complete with a trivet or perforated tray on which certain foods should be put to keep them out of the cooking liquid. In this way several vegetables or foods can be cooked at the same time without mixing them together or causing any transference of flavour from one to another. A set of three containers or separators, which may be perforated or solid or a container fitting the cooker which can be divided to hold two different foods are among the extras which can be supplied.

THEIR USE

Using a pressure cooker is basically the same in all models, varying only in the practical method by which pressure is attained in a particular type. The various steps must always be followed through and are simply to bring the liquid put into the cooker to the boil so that the pan fills with steam which will drive all the air from the pan. This steam is then sealed in by closure of the valve when the pressure within the cooker will rise to that required and can be maintained over a low heat throughout the cooking time. Before opening the cooker, the steam pressure has to be allowed to fall back to normal, either immediately with cold water or by gently lifting and tipping the weight (not by pulling it off completely) to allow the steam to escape or else, allowing the cooker to stand at room temperature for a few minutes.

Each pressure cooker comes with the manufacturer's recommended instructions for its correct use and these should be studied and followed; only when you get to know your cooker and become completely confident in its use is this precision item going to be the real asset to you that it can and should be.

IMPORTANT THINGS TO REMEMBER WHEN USING A PRESSURE COOKER

√ that the liquid being used for the cooking must be one which will give steam when it boils—fat alone is suitable, only with low-pressure pressure cookers when recommended by the manufacturers.

√ that, when browning or frying with fat before pressure cooking, the base should be used as an open pan.

√ that the amount of liquid required for the entire cooking must be put in at the start.

√ that the quantity will depend on the length of the cooking time and not on the amount of food being cooked, as sufficient must be put in to turn into steam and keep the pan filled with steam while it is under pressure.

√ that sufficient space must always be left in the cooker for the steam to circulate and do its work. This means that the complete cooker, taking into account the base and cover, must not be more than two-thirds full of solids.

√ that, as most liquids such as stocks, soups, milk, fruit juice or those in which cereals and pastas are being cooked tend to boil up and over, sufficient space must be left to prevent this happening, so for these the cooker base should never be more than half full.

√ that the cover must always be in the fully closed position before attempting to bring the cooker to pressure.

√ that recipes should be checked to see whether the cooker is to be brought to pressure on a high, medium or low heat. A good reason will always be given for this.

√ that the first stage in pressure cooking is the expulsion of all the air in the pan as the liquid comes to the boil and turns to steam. If the control valve has to be left open to allow for this, close it when you SEE the steam.

√ that the second stage is the building up to pressure which occurs, as the steam will now no longer be able to escape through the control until the required pressure is reached.

√ that this will only be when a LOUD hissing sound is heard or the indicator on the calibrated stem type of control shows, accompanied by an escape of steam which will be the signal that the actual pressure cooking time can begin.

√ that once timing the cooking, the heat should be lowered to the point where the loud hissing stops yet a gentle and definite muttering sound continues and there is a gentle escape of steam. If the cooker is left hissing loudly it will not cook any faster, fuel will be wasted and sooner or later the cooker will run short of steam and liquid and boil dry. If, on the other hand, the cooker goes silent, then the pressure will be dropping and at the end of the cooking time the food will not be cooked.

√ that, when the cooking time is up, pressure should only be reduced according to the recipe instructions. These will be to do this immediately by standing the cooker in a bowl of cold water or under the cold-water tap, by gently lifting and tipping the pressure control, without taking it right off, until no further steam escapes or, by leaving the cooker, away from the stove, to stand in the room temperature for a few minutes.

√ that before removing the cover at any time, the valve should be opened by raising the lever or removing the set of weights.

√ that the liquid in the base of the cooker, unless it has been used only for steaming puddings, cakes, for bottling and so on, should never be wasted but used as stock or for adding to soups, stews, gravies and sauces.

√ that the recommended cooking times should always be scrupulously kept to. Providing the pressure cooker is in good working order and that it is being used correctly, the methods and times given for these tested recipes will be those that will ensure the best results in every way.

√ that foods will always cook more quickly if loose in the cooker, either in the liquid or on the trivet, according to the recipe. Perforated or solid containers need only be used when recommended in the instructions.

√ that only foods requiring the same pressure and cooking time should be put into the cooker together, otherwise those requiring a shorter time will be overcooked losing their colour, flavour and too much of their goodness. It is often possible to adjust cooking times by cutting larger vegetables for example, into halves or quarters or by packing small or quicker cooking vegetables into the separators where, cut off from the full force of the steam they can afford to be given a little longer.

√ that otherwise it is always possible to open the cooker towards the end of the cooking time by reducing the pressure, opening the valve and adding in those foods requiring a shorter time. A simple example of this would be Braised Steak taking 10 minutes and accompanying vegetables requiring 5. After the first 5 minutes of the cooking, the cooker would be opened and the vegetables added for the last 5 minutes so that, when the cooking time was up, the meat would have had its full 10 minutes and the vegetables their correct 5.

THEIR CARE

Like any new piece of kitchen equipment the pressure cooker

should be washed in hot, soapy water, be well rinsed and then dried before first using. Soda in any form should never be used to boil up the cooker or in the washing-up water, as it reacts with aluminium and will discolour it and can lead to pitting of the material.

Any staining or darkening which may occur from cooking certain foods is not harmful in any way to the food which will be subsequently cooked and eaten or to the cooker itself. In hard-water areas, staining can be avoided by the addition of acid in the form of vinegar or lemon and this is why it is always recommended when foods are being steamed in containers as it prevents the base and the trivet from turning black.

For daily cleaning after use, the pressure cooker, trivet and containers should be treated like any other aluminium utensil —washed, rinsed and dried and should as necessary, be cleaned with a cleansing powder on a cloth, with any type of pot scourer or with soap pads.

The cover may need to be rinsed and the gasket to be lifted out and washed if any food can be seen to have boiled up, but otherwise a wipe over inside and out, after lifting off, while still warm, should keep both in good condition. The vent however, must be looked through each time after use to make sure it is clear, and a check made that the safety plug is in the correct, closed position.

To retain the high mirror polish given to the outside of the cover and body the pressure cooker should not be left standing in water and then should never really need to be scoured which would spoil its appearance.

For storage, the lid of a pressure cooker should not be left in the closed position. Open or with the lid reversed and tipped according to the model, the air can circulate through the cooker and this will avoid any retention of cooking smells.

For more specific instructions for the care and cleaning of your pressure cooker you should check in the book of instructions.

The gasket and safety plug will need replacing from time to time as a rubber compound is bound to deteriorate with continuous exposure to steam and heat. This will be when steam or water is seen escaping around the cover or around the plug itself or if steam is seen escaping anywhere but through the valve or vent. A replacement should be bought and fitted at once, otherwise the cooker cannot continue to work efficiently and an uncontrolled escape of steam will almost certainly lead, sooner or later, to the cooker boiling dry.

It is only 'dry' heating when all the liquid has had to turn into steam to keep up the pressure which will cause the distortion or bulging of the base. Once this has happened, the cooker must be returned to the manufacturer for servicing, otherwise it will only continue to boil dry, will not make correct contact with a flat plate and so the distortion will worsen, spoiling the cooking and making it impossible in the end to use the cooker efficiently at all.

The cooker will also boil dry if it is left boiling away on too high a heat with the valve or vent open or again, on too high a heat after pressure has been reached. Even if a little liquid is found in the bottom of the cooker on opening it, if this is brown or if the base is bulged it must mean that the cooker was dry and the liquid will be only the steam condensed as pressure was reduced. Should you at any time smell the cooker burning, turn off the heat and lift the cooker away but do not put it into cold water. Let it cool of its own accord. You should then check if the base has bulged and, if it has, the cooker should be returned for servicing. To test whether the gasket or safety plug has shrunk or hardened due to exposure to the 'dry' heat, just put a little water with acid into the cooker and bring it up to pressure and should any leakage of steam be seen, then replacement parts should be bought from your local stockist and fitted at once.

The safety plug comes into action if the vent or valve gets blocked because the cooker is too full, or because food is boiling up into it or if the cooker is left too long boiling dry. The noise this causes may be a little unnerving, particularly if liquid is also expelled with the steam, but just take the cooker away from the heat and if the liquid continues to boil out put it in the sink or outside the back door. You should then check your method of using the cooker for that particular recipe to find out where you went wrong, for a safety plug will not blow of its own accord—unless of course, it was in need of replacement and you either did not notice this or put off getting a new one.

Manufacturers of pressure cookers offer a complete reconditioning and repairing service, and an estimate of the cost of this can always be obtained before the work is put in hand. The various replaceable parts—gaskets, safety plugs, control valves, handles and instruction booklets—are available or can be ordered through your local stockist or direct from the manufacturer. Always remember that the manufacturer will be as interested and keen as you are that you should use your cooker and be pleased with it and be prepared to help you in any way he can to achieve this.

CONCERNING THE RECIPES

The recipes given in this book are for use with a **High** (15 lb) pressure except where a lower pressure is recommended to obtain the best results. If the model you are using does not have a variable control or you are not sure what the pressure is then you can still follow these recipes by taking the cooking time for the principal ingredient as shown in the handbook given by the manufacturers of your cooker.

For example BEEF STEW	High (15 lb) pressure	15–20 minutes
	Low pressure	45–60 minutes
CHICKEN À LA CRÊME	High (15 lb) pressure	4 minutes
	Low pressure	15 minutes

When you wish to adjust recipes from other books or just your own favourite ones again consult the timetable or a recipe given here using the same basic ingredient, then remember that the quantity of liquid must be adjusted according to the cooking time.

A conversion table for weights, measures, pressure and temperatures will be found on p. 303.

Because water boils at a lower temperature as altitude increases and therefore the atmospheric pressure decreases, allowance must be made for the height at which a pressure cooker is being used if this is over 2,000 feet above sea-level.

For day-to-day cooking the adjustments are as follows:

L (5 lb) pressure—use **Medium** pressure and do not increase cooking time.

M (10 lb) pressure—use **High** pressure and do not increase cooking time.

H (15 lb) pressure—increase cooking time by one minute for every 1,000 feet.

Quantities for thickening gravies and stews, making sauces, stuffing ingredients and so on, where absolute accuracy is not essential, have been given in spoonfuls rather than ounces as this will save having to weigh small amounts. For this purpose, a spoonful is taken as being as much above as is in the bowl and a half spoonful is level with the bowl.

For flour and powder ingredients	1 ounce = approx. 1 tablespoon
For shredded suet	1 ounce = approx. 1½ tablespoons
For sugar, fruit and heavy ingredients	1 ounce = approx. 1 level tablespoon
For syrup, jam	1 ounce = approx. 1 level tablespoon
For dry rice	1 ounce = approx. 1 tablespoon
For breadcrumbs, grated cheese coconut	½ ounce = approx. 1 tablespoon
For butter or margarine	1 ounce = approx. 1 tablespoon levelled along the bowl with a knife

One teacup of liquid	= ¼ pint approx.
One teacup of dry rice	= 6 oz approx.
One teacup of dry powder ingredients	= 4 oz approx.

For most recipes, butter and margarine are interchangeable; for small quantities and for sauces particularly, the difference in cost would not be noticeable and the improvement in flavour would make the use of butter well worth while.

For brown sauces, preliminary frying of ingredients for stews, braises, pot roasts, dripping can be used if available.

For steamed puddings and cakes where it is important that quantities are exact and for larger amounts as in jams, marmalades and so on, the measurements are given in ounces.

Here is a list of items for you to choose from which will help you to get the best results from your pressure cooker and the following recipes:

A soufflé dish, 6 inches or 7 inches, depending on your cooker size but leaving enough room to allow it to be put in and lifted out easily, holding it on one side: for milk, egg and miscellaneous sweets, for stewing fruit.

A casserole dish as above but make allowances for the side grips with which a casserole is provided; for use as above.

4, 6 or 8 teacups which can be kept specially for pressure cooking or be those which you have in daily use: for sweet and savoury custards, for infant and invalid cooking.

A stainless steel or aluminium bowl, 1–1½ pints capacity for steamed puddings of all kinds and for cooking rice.

Boilable plastic or china basins for Christmas puddings. If your cooker is a tall one and you choose wisely you will be able to cook 2 × 1½ lb puddings one on top of the other and at the same time.

Individual boilable plastic bowls: you may prefer these to teacups particularly when you are camping, caravanning or boating as they are light and unbreakable.

A second trivet which is always available from your local stockist or the manufacturer and which you may find useful to rest on top of other foods, for example when putting in a container of vegetables, rice, etc, or, instead of just greaseproof paper, to lay fish on for easy handling.

A long-handled straining spoon for serving vegetables and for hooking into the trivet to lift it out.

A long-handled fork for turning meat, tossing pastas.

A potato masher for potatoes, swedes, turnips, apples, for dried vegetable soups which do not need sieving, for pressing the water from spinach before lifting out of the cooker, for mashing, in the cooker, the mirepoix vegetables to make a thick gravy.

A long wooden spoon for stirring milk puddings, soups, jam, marmalades.

A small ladle for filling jam, etc, into the jars.
A 5–6-inch strainer for soups, purées, pulps.
A pair of lifting tongs for bottling jars.
A seamless loaf pan or round cake tin for cakes, bread puddings, galantines.

SECTION I

Stocks and Soups

This is the first section you will come to in the cookery part of the book, and you may think that it will not interest you as, up till now, you have not been a great soup-maker; too much time and trouble you have always thought perhaps, particularly as there are so many ready-made soups from which to choose. But now you have a pressure cooker you can see how easy it is to obtain delicious nourishing soups in minutes instead of hours, with all the fresh taste and flavour—and that individual touch—which distinguishes a home-made soup. From now on, no odds and ends, no left-overs should or need be wasted—just a few minutes pressure cooking and you can have a rich stock to serve as the basis for meat, chicken, fish or vegetable soups, to add to sauces and gravies, stews and so on. Again, when so many of the family now have their midday meal away from home, a well-made pressure cooked soup, full of flavour and goodness and served with fried croûtons, toasted French bread, fingers of toast, can often be sufficient for an evening round the fire and the television, after evening classes, or when the children bring their friends home from the cinema, the youth club, a football match. Even if you decide soup-making is not for you, be sure to use every last little bit from the joint, the fish, the chicken, the vegetables, so that you always have a bowl of stock on hand—nothing wasted, all the goodness preserved to give extra nourishment to all your other cooking.

Of course, there are certain things to be remembered when making stocks or soups in your pressure cooker:

Any bones should be broken up as small as possible so that all the goodness will be extracted from them.

Cooked vegetables, potatoes, bread or thickened sauces or gravies should not be added to stock as then it will not keep.

Stocks and some soups may require to have the scum removed as they come to the boil. Lift this off carefully with a metal skimmer or straining spoon. All fat should be carefully taken off stocks and soups before these are used and served. This may be done when cold and the fat solid enough to be lifted off with a spoon; when hot, the best method is to use pieces of soft, absorbent paper such as a kitchen towel, tearing off small pieces and using each once only, to 'blot' up the fat by drawing it across the surface of the liquid.

The water with which any green vegetable has been cooked cannot be used for stock as it may ferment; it should, in fact, never be recooked.

Every time other vegetables are pressure cooked, you will have made a concentrated vegetable stock and this can be used in making any soup, meat or fish dish. Only turnips are not always suitable as they can have too strong a flavour and they should be used only very sparingly when making a basic stock —and not at all in hot weather. If you do not find the particular recipe you are looking for here just remember that the pressure cooking time of the soup will depend on that required by the principal ingredient, which will be found in the time-table given in the appropriate chapter.

Be careful, until you are a little more experienced, with the amount of seasoning you add. Because everything is more conserved and concentrated in a pressure cooker, the seasoning required is very much less, the ingredients retaining far more of their own mineral salts.

The trivet is not used when making soups or stocks as all the ingredients must cook in the liquid so that their flavours mingle and the goodness is extracted.

Your cooker must never have the base more than half full when all the ingredients and liquid have been added. This is to leave room for the liquid to boil up—as it will do during the cooking—without boiling over, to leave plenty of room for the steam that will form and to ensure that the vent in the cover does not get blocked up. As there is little loss of liquid by evaporation during pressure cooking, the result is always a very concentrated soup. Therefore, if more soup were wanted for serving but it would more than half fill the cooker base, extra liquid could always be added after the pressure cooking.

For stock or soup which is to be stored for another day, it is useful to be able to make it so concentrated as it will take up less space in the refrigerator. For serving, hot water, vegetable or other stock or milk can be added to obtain the required amount. If you have not all the ingredients mentioned in a recipe just when you decide to make a particular soup do not let this deter you. You are sure to have a suitable substitute in the cupboard and this is when your soup-making experience will stand you in good stead. For instance, a spoonful or two of sweet-corn, cooked peas, sliced cooked beans heated and put into the serving dish before a soup is poured in, the addition of an unusual herb such as basil, or fennel, a pinch of saffron or nutmeg, a garnish of chopped sorrel or watercress may be just the touch you were looking for.

The following recipes are proportioned to serve up to six helpings for soup as a first course or four helpings as a meal in itself. Use High (15 lb) pressure.

FOUNDATION STOCK

Pressure Cooking Time: 45 minutes

This recipe will give approximately 2 pints of a very concentrated jellied stock which can be diluted with an equal quantity of water, vegetable water, etc, before use and which will give extra richness and goodness when added to packet or tinned soups, gravies, meat and cereal dishes.

2 lb meat bones—fresh or from the cooked joint; 2½ pints cold water; 2 large onions; 2 sticks of celery; 2 medium carrots; 1 teaspoon salt; pinch of pepper or 3 peppercorns; as available, sprig of parsley and thyme, bay leaf, blade of mace, pinch of mixed herbs.

Wash the bones well and break or chop as small as possible. Put them into the cooker with the water and bring to the boil over a high heat. While waiting, wash and scrape or peel the vegetables and cut them into rough pieces. When the stock is boiling, carefully lift all the scum from the top. Add the rest of the ingredients, turn the heat to **medium**, bring the cooker to pressure in the usual way and cook for 45 minutes. Allow the pressure to reduce at room temperature. Strain the stock, leave until cold then remove the fat before use.

If a marrow bone is used, add sufficient water to half fill the base, omit the vegetables, add the herbs and seasoning, and pressure cook for 2 hours. Continue as above.

If a **brown stock** is required, the onions must be fried first in hot fat either in the base of the open cooker or in a frying pan.

CHICKEN SOUPS

CHICKEN SOUP STOCK

Pressure Cooking Time: 20 or 30 minutes

The carcass and any left-overs of chicken should never be wasted. This stock is quick and easy to pressure cook, and will serve as a basis for a delicious home-made soup or for adding to packet or tinned soups.

The carcass, bones, skin and left-over scraps of a boiled, roasted or uncooked chicken; 1–2 pints of cold water; 1 peeled onion stuck with 2 cloves; 1 sliced carrot and leek; ½ teaspoon salt; pinch of pepper; as available, sprig of parsley and thyme, small bay leaf and piece of mace, ¼ teaspoon celery salt.

Break the carcass and bones of chicken as small as possible, roughly cut up any meat and put with all the other ingredients into the cooker. (The amount of water added should depend on how much chicken there is and how concentrated one wants the stock to be.) Bring to the boil in the open pan and skim if necessary. Bring to pressure in the usual way and allow 20 minutes if the chicken has been cooked before and 30 minutes if uncooked. Allow the pressure to reduce at room temperature, strain and when cold remove the fat from the top.

To use, dilute with an equal quantity of water.

CHICKEN CONSOMME REINE

Pressure Cooking Time: 30–40 minutes

1 Chicken or boiling Fowl (3–4 lb); 2 pints water; 1 onion stuck with 3 cloves; 2 sticks of celery; 1 carrot sliced; as available, sprigs of parsley, thyme; 1 bay leaf; 1 teaspoon salt; ½ teaspoon pepper.

Clean the chicken well, inside and out. Wash the giblets thoroughly in salted water. Put the chicken, giblets and all other ingredients into the cooker and, when boiling, remove all the scum. Bring to pressure in the usual way and cook for the required time, allowing 10 minutes per pound. Allow the pressure to reduce at room temperature. Lift out the chicken, carefully strain the stock and remove the fat from the top by passing small pieces of soft, absorbent paper across the surface. Remove the legs from the chicken, take off the skin and cut the meat into fine slices. Return this and the stock to the open cooker, boil, taste and correct the seasoning and serve piping hot.

The rest of the chicken can be eaten cold with fresh vegetables or salad, in a Chicken Pie, in a white sauce to fill pastry cases or to serve as a supper dish with a border of mashed potatoes, sprinkled with cheese and grilled, or in a border of cooked, savoury rice.

CHICKEN AND RICE SOUP

Pressure Cooking Time: 7 minutes

1 pint chicken stock; pinch of nutmeg; 1 finely diced onion; ½ teacup of long rice—for garnish, chopped parsley.

Dilute the chicken stock with 1 pint of water in the cooker, add the onion and nutmeg and bring to the boil in the open pan. Throw in the washed rice, bring to pressure in the usual way and cook for 7 minutes. Allow the pressure to reduce at room temperature and just before serving, piping hot, taste to correct the seasoning and sprinkle thickly with chopped parsley.

CHICKEN NOODLE SOUP

Pressure Cooking Time: 3–4 minutes

1 pint chicken stock; 4 oz fine noodles—for garnish, 1 hard boiled egg, parsley or watercress.

Dilute the chicken stock with 1 pint of water in the cooker and bring to the boil in the open pan. Add the noodles broken into 2-inch lengths, bring to pressure in the usual way and cook for 3–4 minutes according to the thickness of the noodles. While allowing the pressure to reduce at room temperature, prepare the garnish by chopping the hard-boiled egg and mixing with the chopped parsley or watercress. Just before serving, piping hot, taste to correct seasoning and sprinkle with the garnish.

CREAM OF CHICKEN SOUP

$1\frac{1}{2}$ pints chicken stock; 2 tablespoons margarine or butter; 2 tablespoons flour; $\frac{1}{2}$ pint milk; salt and pepper; chopped parsley or chives.

Melt the margarine or butter in a large saucepan, add the flour and cook gently for 2–3 minutes, stirring all the time and without allowing it to colour. Lift from the heat, gradually add the milk, then stir and cook until thick. Add the chicken stock, taste and correct the seasoning and just before serving, piping hot, sprinkle thickly with chopped parsley or chives.

For a complete supper dish, serve with fried croûtons.

MULLIGATAWNY SOUP

Pressure Cooking Time: 7 minutes

2 pints good stock made from carcass of cooked chicken; 2 tablespoons long rice; bouquet garni; 2 tablespoons margarine; 2 tablespoons flour; 1 cooking apple; 1 medium onion; 1 tablespoon curry powder (less or more according to taste); juice of $\frac{1}{2}$ lemon; 2 tablespoons cream; seasoning.

Before making the stock, take any remaining meat from the chicken carcass and put on one side. Lift the trivet from the cooker, put in the stock, washed rice and bouquet garni, bring to pressure in the usual way, cook for 7 minutes and allow pressure to reduce at room temperature. During the cooking, melt the margarine in another saucepan and gently fry the finely chopped onion, sliced apple, flour and curry powder for 10 minutes without discolouring. Lift the bouquet garni from the stock, strain the rice and keep warm. Gradually add the stock to the saucepan, stirring all the time, add the diced chicken meat and the lemon juice, bring to the boil and skim if necessary. Taste and add seasoning, throw in the rice and reheat. Add cream and serve piping hot.

FISH SOUPS

FISH SOUP STOCK

Pressure Cooking Time: 15 minutes

This stock should be made and used on the same day.

Cod's head, trimmings of white fish heads, tails, bones, skin left after filleting and so on—sufficient water to just cover; 1 sliced onion, carrot, leek; 12 peppercorns; 2 thin slices lemon peel; bouquet garni (p. 297); 1 small teaspoon salt.

Wash the fish well, put into the cooker with all the other ingredients and bring to the boil in the open pan. Carefully remove all the scum, then bring to pressure in the usual way and cook for 15 minutes. Allow the pressure to reduce at room temperature, strain at once.

Use as the basis for fish soups, sauces, curries and other dishes.

FISH TOMATO SOUP

Pressure Cooking Time: 5 minutes

2 cutlets of cod or fresh haddock; 1½ pints of fish stock; 1 small glass of white wine; 3 tablespoons tomato purée; 2 tablespoons flour blended with ¼ pint milk; salt, pepper; 2 tablespoons coarsely chopped parsley; toasted French bread when serving (p. 298).

Put the fish, stock and seasoning into the cooker, bring to pressure in the usual way, cook for 5 minutes, allow the pressure to reduce at room temperature. Carefully lift out the fish, remove skin and bone and divide the fish into portions. Strain the soup, stir in the wine, tomato purée and blended flour, return to the heat, bring to the boil and cook for a minute or two stirring all the time. This soup should be very smooth and not too thick; thin if necessary with a little more fish stock or milk. Taste and correct seasoning. It is best served in individual cups. Put a portion of fish into each, pour over the soup, garnish thickly with the parsley. Serve with slices of toasted French bread.

LOBSTER BISQUE

2 tablespoons butter, 2 tablespoons flour, ¼ pint milk; 1½ pints fish stock; 3 tablespoons crushed cream crackers; 1 small glass of white wine; 1 tablespoon lemon juice; 1 small tin of lobster; 2 tablespoons single cream; salt, pepper.

Melt the butter in a large saucepan, add the flour and cook for a minute or two over a low heat without allowing to colour. Lift from the heat, gradually add the milk, then stir and cook until thick. Add the fish stock and the juice from the strained lobster, then, when again boiling, stir in the crushed biscuits and leave to stand on one side for 2–3 minutes until the biscuits are softened. Stir in the wine, lemon juice and the finely chopped lobster, reserving a little for garnish. Bring to the boil rapidly, taste and correct for seasoning, lift from the heat, stir in the cream and serve at once, garnished with the rest of the lobster.

If a fresh-boiled lobster is available, pressure cook the fish stock for 10 minutes with the shells, then continue as in recipe.

MEAT SOUPS

BEEF AND MUSHROOM SOUP

Pressure Cooking Time: 7 minutes

2 tablespoons margarine; 1 sliced onion; ½ lb lean, minced beef; ¼ lb very thinly diced mushrooms; 2 pints brown stock; salt, pepper; chopped parsley; fingers of dried toast when serving.

Melt the margarine and fry the onion and meat until golden brown stirring to prevent any sticking or burning. Add the mushrooms and fry gently for a further minute or two. Lift the cooker from the heat, stir in the stock (use a meat cube dissolved in water if stock is not available) and add seasoning. Bring to pressure in the usual way, cook for 7 minutes, reduce pressure with cold water. Taste and correct seasoning, serve piping hot, sprinkled with chopped parsley. Hand the fingers of dried toast separately. Three tablespoons of tomato purée, dissolved in the stock, may be added for extra flavour.

For a complete supper dish, rice may be added. When the stock is boiling in the open cooker, throw in 3 tablespoons of washed rice and continue as in recipe.

KIDNEY SOUP

Pressure Cooking Time: 7 minutes

½ lb ox kidney; fatty rinds of 3 bacon slices; 2 pints brown stock; 1 small onion, carrot; bouquet garni; 1 tablespoon margarine, 1 tablespoon flour, ¼ pint milk for thickening; 1 teaspoon redcurrant jelly; 1 teaspoon Worcester Sauce; salt, pepper.

Remove the fat then wash, dry and cut the kidneys into thick slices. Cut the fatty bacon rinds into small pieces and heat gently in the open cooker until the fat runs out, then quickly fry the kidney and sliced onion until golden brown. Lift out on to soft kitchen paper and strain remaining fat from cooker. Put in the stock, kidney, onion, sliced carrot, bouquet garni and seasoning, bring to pressure in the usual way, cook for 7 minutes and reduce the pressure with cold water.

While the soup is cooking, melt the margarine in a large pan, add the flour, stir and cook for a few minutes allowing it to brown very lightly. Lift from the heat, gradually add the milk, bring to the boil and cook for 2–3 minutes stirring all the time. Strain the soup, lift out the kidney slices and chop very finely. Add the strained soup, chopped kidney, jelly and a dash of Worcester Sauce to the thickening, bring to the boil while stirring, taste and correct seasoning and serve piping hot.

For a special occasion, add a wine glass of sherry instead of the Worcester Sauce just before serving.

OXTAIL SOUP

Pressure Cooking Time: 40 minutes

This soup should be made the day before as it is necessary to remove all the fat which is extracted from the oxtail during the cooking. If a large oxtail is bought there will be enough meat left over to make a delicious Oxtail Stew for another day.

1 oxtail; 1 tablespoon dripping; 2 pints of water; 1 sliced onion, carrot, turnip; 2 sticks celery; bouquet garni; 1 tablespoon margarine, 1 tablespoon flour for thickening; 1 tablespoon redcurrant jelly; 1 teaspoon Worcester Sauce.

Wash the oxtail, cut into joints, fry with the sliced onion in the heated dripping in the open cooker until well browned all over. Add the water, sliced vegetables, bouquet garni and seasoning, bring to pressure in the usual way, cook for 40 minutes, allow the pressure to reduce at room temperature, then strain the soup into a bowl. Lift out the oxtail joints, take away any fat, then remove the meat from the bones while still hot and leave pressed between 2 plates (if it was a large oxtail, remove the meat from 3 or 4 joints only, using the rest for an Oxtail Stew. The next day, lift all the fat from the soup and cut the pressed meat into small dice. Melt the margarine in a large saucepan, add the flour and cook, stirring and allowing it to turn a good brown colour but without burning. Lift from the heat, gradually mix in the soup, then stir until boiling. Add the diced meat, the redcurrant jelly, the Worcester Sauce, taste and correct seasoning and serve piping hot.

For a special occasion, leave out the Worcester Sauce and add 2 tablespoons of a dry Madeira or port wine.

SCOTCH (MUTTON) BROTH

Pressure Cooking Time: 7 minutes

This soup is a meal in itself, excellent for children who need feeding up after illness and for filling up the energetic members of the family. It is best made the previous day so that all the fat can be easily removed.

1 tablespoon pearl barley; $\frac{1}{2}$ lb middle or best end of neck of mutton; 2 pints water; 1 leek, onion, carrot, stick of celery, small piece of turnip; bouquet garni; salt, pepper; chopped parsley.

Wash the barley well, put into a small pan of cold water, bring to the boil and strain. Remove all the fat from the meat. Put the water, the diced vegetables, the bouquet garni, the meat and seasoning into the cooker and bring to the boil in the open pan. Throw in the prepared barley, bring to pressure in the usual way, cook for 7 minutes and allow the pressure to reduce at room temperature. Lift out the meat and cover when cold. Turn the soup into a basin and remove the bouquet garni. Next day (or when cold) lift the fat off the soup, put back into the cooker and bring to the boil in the open pan. Take all the meat off the bones, cut into small dice, add to the soup, taste and correct seasoning. Serve piping hot, sprinkled with parsley.

GAME SOUP

Pressure Cooking Time: 30 minutes

As game is expensive and rather a luxury it is a pity to waste any of it and this delicious soup will make sure that the last ounce of goodness and flavour is extracted.

Carcass and left-over meat of game birds; 1–1$\frac{1}{2}$ pints water; 1 small onion stuck with 2 cloves; 1 sliced leek; 2 sticks of celery; bouquet garni; 2 tablespoons rice; 3 cooked and skinned chipolata sausages; 1 glass red wine; salt, pepper.

Break up the carcasses, put into the cooker with the water, vegetables, bouquet garni and seasoning, bring to pressure in the usual way, cook for 25 minutes and allow the pressure to reduce at room temperature. Strain the soup, return to the open cooker, bring to the boil, throw in the washed rice, pressure cook for a further 5 minutes, allow the pressure to reduce at room temperature. Add the finely sliced sausages, reboil, taste and correct seasoning and just before serving piping hot, add the red wine.

If there was any gravy left over from the previous cooking of the birds this may be used to give a thickened soup; leave out the rice and, after 30 minutes cooking, gradually add the strained soup to the gravy, then continue as in recipe.

FRESH VEGETABLE SOUPS

CLEAR VEGETABLE SOUP

Pressure Cooking Time: 5 minutes

3 rashers of streaky bacon; 2 small onions, carrots, turnips, finely sliced; 1 tablespoon flour; 2 pints of brown stock (or a stock cube); 2 sticks of celery, 2 skinned tomatoes finely chopped; 1 bay leaf; salt, pepper.

Cut the bacon into very small pieces and cook gently in the open cooker until all the fat has run out. Add the onion, carrot and fry until golden brown. Put in the flour and continue browning slowly, stirring frequently to prevent sticking. Lift the cooker from the heat, gradually add the stock, then the rest of the ingredients. Return to the heat, stir until boiling, skim if necessary, bring to pressure over a **medium** heat, cook for 5 minutes, allow pressure to reduce at room temperature. Remove the bouquet garni, taste and correct seasoning and serve piping hot.

If a thick soup is required, strain, sieve the vegetables, combine again with the liquid and reheat before serving.

SUMMER SOUP

Pressure Cooking Time: 5 minutes

A selection of any fresh, young vegetables available such as 4 oz shelled green peas; 2 oz each finely diced french beans, young carrots, young turnips, spinach; 2 pints white stock; 2 tablespoonfuls fine sago; sprig of mint and parsley; shredded lettuce; watercress, chervil; small knob of butter; salt, pepper.

Put the stock into the cooker and bring to the boil. Add all the diced vegetables, the sago, mint and parsley, seasoning, stir until reboiling, bring to pressure on a **medium** heat, cook 5 minutes and reduce pressure immediately with cold water. Lift out the mint and parsley, taste and correct seasoning, throw in the lettuce, watercress, chervil, reboil and serve at once, adding the butter at the very last moment.

FRENCH ONION SOUP

Pressure Cooking Time: 4 minutes

Use full quantity for a complete supper dish, half quantity as a course of a meal.

4 large onions, thinly sliced; pepper; 2 tablespoons butter; 2 pints of good brown stock; salt; 1 thin slice of toast per person; grated parmesan cheese.

Lift the trivet from the cooker, heat the butter and fry the well-peppered onion slices slowly until golden brown. Add the hot stock (if cold, allow the cooker to cool) and salt, bring to pressure in the usual way, cook for 4 minutes and reduce the pressure with cold water. During the cooking, make the toast and keep the grill hot. Pour the soup into individual heat-proof soup bowls, dividing the onion rings evenly among them, put a piece of toast on top of each, sprinkle thickly with the cheese and brown quickly under a hot grill. Serve at once.

Variations. For added richness, a little fresh or sour cream can be stirred in and the soup reheated but without allowing it to boil.

An added piquancy can be given with a dash of Worcester Sauce into each bowl before adding the toast and cheese.

TOMATO SOUP WITH RICE

Pressure Cooking Time: 7 minutes

1 tablespoon margarine; 1 medium onion, finely chopped; 1 lb skinned and sliced fresh tomatoes (or a large tin); 2 pints white stock (if tinned tomatoes are used, make juice up to 2 pints); pinch of sugar; 1 bay leaf; 2 tablespoons washed rice; salt, pepper.

Melt the margarine in the open cooker, add the onion and cook until transparent but do not allow to brown. Add the tomatoes, stock, sugar, bay leaf and bring to the boil. Throw in the rice, bring to pressure on a **medium** heat, cook for 5 minutes, reduce pressure with cold water. Lift out the bay leaf, taste to correct seasoning and serve piping hot.

To add extra interest to this soup, a dash of Worcester Sauce or 2 tablespoons of sherry may be added just before serving.

Cream Soups are those made from fresh vegetables cooked in stock and tenderised so that they may be easily passed through a sieve or mashed into a purée and are then thickened with a white sauce or by the addition of cream.

Proportions: about 1 lb fresh vegetables to $1\frac{1}{2}$ pints stock/milk.

CREAM OF CELERY SOUP

Pressure Cooking Time: 10 minutes

1 large head of celery; 1 small finely chopped onion; 1 pint chicken stock (or stock cube); 1 large tablespoon margarine, 1 tablespoon flour, $\frac{1}{2}$ pint milk; salt and pepper; a few of the young leaves, chopped, for garnish.

Wash celery well, slice it finely (reserve the young green leaves for garnish), put into the cooker with the onion, stock and seasoning, bring to pressure in the usual way, cook for 10 minutes, allow pressure to reduce at room temperature. During the cooking, melt the margarine in another saucepan, add the flour and cook for 2–3 minutes while stirring, without allowing it to colour. Remove from the heat, gradually add the milk, return to a low heat and stir until thickened. Strain the soup, sieve or mash the vegetables, add this purée to the sauce, then beating well, stir in sufficient of the celery stock to give the required consistency to the finished soup. Reheat, taste and correct seasoning, serve piping hot garnished with some of the very finely chopped leaves.

A small teaspoon of cream poured into the centre of each serving at the last moment will make this soup even more delicious.

CREAM OF FRESH PEA

Pressure Cooking Time: 4 minutes

$\frac{3}{4}$ lb fresh shelled peas (or frozen peas which have thawed out); 2 pints white stock; sprigs of mint; salt, pepper; cayenne pepper and cream when serving.

Put the peas (add a few washed pods if fresh peas are used), stock, mint and seasoning into the cooker, bring to pressure in the usual way, cook for 4 minutes, allow pressure to reduce at room temperature. Strain the soup, lift out the pods and mint, sieve or mash the peas into a purée and return to the open cooker. Add sufficient of the stock to give the correct consistency, reboil, taste to correct seasoning and just before serving, piping hot, add the cream and sprinkle lightly with cayenne pepper.

A ham bone cooked with the peas or a little of the stock from a boiled ham added to the purée will give an extra flavour to this soup.

CREAM OF LEEK AND POTATO

Pressure Cooking Time: 10 minutes

2 sliced leeks using the white part only; 1 lb potatoes peeled and quartered; 1 large tablespoon margarine; $1\frac{1}{2}$ pints white stock; salt, pepper; 2 egg yolks thinned with 2 tablespoons milk or cream; a knob of butter.

Melt the margarine in the open cooker and without allowing them to colour, lightly fry the leeks and the potatoes (which should be thoroughly rinsed, after quartering, in cold water). Add the stock and seasoning, bring to pressure in the usual way, cook for 10 minutes and allow the pressure to reduce at room temperature. Mash the vegetables into a smooth purée in the cooker, reheat and taste to correct seasoning but using plenty of pepper. When the soup is really boiling, lift from the heat, stir in the egg yolks and cream and the butter. Serve at once, sprinkled with a little of the very finely chopped green from the leeks.

This soup is difficult to keep hot after the eggs have been added as it must not be allowed to boil again or the eggs will curdle it.

CREAM OF MUSHROOM

Pressure Cooking Time: 4 minutes

¾ lb skinned and finely sliced fresh mushrooms; 1½ pints water; a few bacon rinds if available; ½ teaspoon celery salt; 1 tablespoon margarine, 1 tablespoon flour, ½ pint milk; salt, pepper; cream and butter when serving.

Put the mushrooms, water, bacon rinds, seasoning into the cooker, bring to pressure in the usual way, cook for 4 minutes and allow the pressure to reduce at room temperature. During the cooking, melt the margarine in another saucepan, add the flour and while stirring, cook for 2–3 minutes without allowing it to colour. Away from the heat, gradually add the milk, return to a low heat and stir until thickened. Strain the soup, lift out the bacon rinds, chop the mushrooms finely, add to the sauce, then beating well, stir in sufficient of the stock to give the required consistency. Reheat, taste and correct seasoning, and just before serving, piping hot, add the cream and a knob of butter.

CREAM OF TOMATO

Pressure Cooking Time: 5 minutes

1 lb skinned and sliced tomatoes; 1 sliced onion, carrot; 1 tablespoon butter; 1 pint white stock; 1 heaped teaspoon sugar; salt, pepper; 1 bay leaf; 2 cloves; 1 tablespoon margarine, 1 tablespoon flour, ½ pint milk; chopped parsley; 2 tablespoons cream; fried croûtons (p. 298).

Melt the butter in the open cooker and gently fry the tomatoes and onions without allowing them to colour. Add the stock, sugar, seasoning, cloves and bay leaf, bring to pressure in the usual way, cook for 5 minutes and allow the pressure to reduce at room temperature. During the cooking, melt the butter in another saucepan, add the flour and while stirring, cook for 2–3 minutes without allowing it to colour. Away from the heat, gradually add the milk, return to a low heat and stir until thickened. Strain the soup, lift out the bay leaf and cloves, sieve the vegetables and add this purée to the sauce, then, beating well, add sufficient of the stock to give the required consistency. Reheat, taste and correct seasoning.

In the serving dish, mix well together the chopped parsley and cream, pour on the piping hot soup and serve at once. Hand the croûtons separately.

If you are lucky enough to have your own home-grown vegetables you will be able to make many more of these soups, using the vegetables when they are at their best and most plentiful. For example:

CREAM OF BROAD BEAN

Make as for **Fresh Pea**, cook 5 minutes, serve with croûtons.

CREAM OF CUCUMBER

Make as for **Celery**, using 2 large cucumbers. Wash, cut in half (remove seeds if the cucumbers are getting old), slice finely. Cook 5 minutes. Before serving, add 2 tablespoons very finely diced gherkin but reheat very carefully so that the vinegar will not curdle the soup. Garnish with chopped chives.

CREAM OF ONION

Make as for **Leek and Potato**, using 3 large Spanish onions, cook 7 minutes, garnish with chopped chives.

DRIED VEGETABLE SOUPS

Overnight soaking is not necessary. Wash the dried vegetables, put into a basin, boil half the quantity of the liquid given in the recipe, pour over, cover with a plate and leave for 1 hour.

Proportions: about 4 oz to 1½ pints water or stock.

HARICOT BEAN PURÉE

Pressure Cooking Time: 20 minutes

1 large onion or 3 leeks; 2 sticks of celery; 1 small turnip; ½ lb peeled potatoes; ¼ lb small haricot beans; 2 tablespoons margarine or dripping; 1½ pints stock or water; bouquet garni; ¼ pint milk; salt, pepper.

Cut up the prepared vegetables roughly and put into the cooker with the strained soaked beans (saving the liquid) and margarine. Allow to cook gently for 5 minutes, stirring occasionally. Make the liquid up to 1½ pints, add the bouquet garni and seasoning, bring to pressure on a **medium** heat, cook for 20 minutes, allow the pressure to reduce at room temperature. Remove the bouquet garni, sieve or mash the vegetables into a purée, return to the cooker, add the milk, taste and correct seasoning and serve piping hot. If using large haricots, increase the cooking time to 30 minutes.

LENTIL SOUP

Pressure Cooking Time: 20 minutes

1 large onion; 1 carrot; 2 leeks; 1 ham bone (or small piece of the cheapest bacon joint); 2 sticks celery; 4 oz lentils; $1\frac{1}{2}$ pints water; bouquet garni; 1 tablespoon margarine, 1 tablespoon flour, $\frac{1}{4}$ pint milk for thickening; if available 3 cooked, skinned Frankfurter sausages; fried croûtons when serving (p. 298).

Cut up the prepared vegetables roughly, put in the cooker with the soaked lentils, the liquid made up to the correct quantity, the ham bone, water and bouquet garni, bring to pressure over a **medium** heat, cook for 20 minutes, allow the pressure to reduce at room temperature. During the cooking, melt the margarine in another saucepan, add the flour and cook without allowing to colour. Away from the heat, gradually add the milk, return to a low heat and stir until thickened. Lift out the ham bone, sieve or mash the vegetables into a purée, beat into the sauce and add sufficient of the stock to give the required consistency. Put in the sliced sausages, taste and correct the seasoning and serve piping hot, handing the croûtons separately.

SPLIT PEA SOUP

Pressure Cooking Time: 12 minutes

4 slices of streaky bacon; 2 sliced leeks; 2 chopped sticks of celery; $\frac{1}{4}$ lb split peas; $1\frac{1}{2}$ pints water; 1 bay leaf; salt, pepper; fried croûtons when serving (p. 298).

Cut the bacon into small pieces, put into the open cooker and fry gently so that the fat runs out. Add the leeks and celery and cook for a few minutes without allowing to brown. Add the washed peas, the water, bay leaf and seasoning. Bring to pressure over a **medium** heat, cook for 12 minutes, allow the pressure to reduce at room temperature. Lift out the bay leaf, mash the vegetables into a purée, reheat, taste and correct seasoning, serve piping hot, handing the croûtons separately.

WINTER SOUP

Pressure Cooking Time: 25 minutes

6 oz mixed lentils, beans, peas; 4 oz stewing meat or cheap bacon cut; $1\frac{1}{2}$ pints water; bouquet garni; 2 carrots, 1 onion, 1 leek, 1 stick celery, 2 skinned tomatoes, 4 oz peeled potatoes all finely diced; salt, pepper; chopped parsley for garnish.

Put the soaked vegetables with the liquid made up to the correct quantity, the meat or bacon and the bouquet garni into the cooker.

Bring to pressure over a **medium** heat, cook for 20 minutes, allow the pressure to reduce at room temperature. Lift out the meat, remove the fat and cut the meat into fine dice. Remove any fat from the soup by drawing small pieces of soft paper across the surface. Return the meat to the cooker with the diced fresh vegetables, bring to pressure again, cook for 5 minutes, allow the pressure to reduce at room temperature. Lift out the bouquet garni, reheat, taste and correct seasoning and serve, piping hot, thickly garnished with chopped parsley.

COLD SOUPS

The real secret of making these refreshing soups, just right to start a summer meal or hostess occasion or taken outdoors for picnics, barbecues and so on, lies in their consistency, which must never be stiff or solid. They must, of course, be set but should 'tremble' when shaken and must be more strongly flavoured and seasoned than a hot soup. Their basis must always be a meat, chicken or fish stock made well in advance and chilled so that its 'jell' can be checked.

CONSOMME MADRILENE

¼ pint fresh or tinned tomato juice; 1 teaspoon sugar; a clove of garlic; small sprig of mint; 1–1½ pints rich chicken stock; salt, pepper; dash of Worcester Sauce; red pimento for garnish.

Put the tomato juice, sugar, garlic, mint, seasoning into a saucepan and boil gently for 5 minutes. Strain and add sufficient stock to ensure a 'trembling' set. Add the Worcester Sauce, taste and correct seasoning, reheat and when cool put to chill in the refrigerator. Serve, spooned into individual soup cups, garnished with very fine strips of pimento.

ICED SHRIMP OR PRAWN BISQUE

Pressure Cooking Time: 10 minutes

1 pint cooked shrimps or prawns; 1 slice lemon peel; 1 pint good fish stock; 3 tablespoons crushed cream crackers; ¼ pint cream; 1 yolk egg; pinch of nutmeg; juice of ½ lemon; watercress for garnish.

Put the fish stock, shells of shrimps and lemon peel into the cooker, bring to pressure in the usual way, cook for 10 minutes, allow the pressure to reduce at room temperature. Strain the stock on to the crushed biscuits and allow them to soak. Pound the shrimps, leaving a few for garnish, either in a mortar or liquidiser (a similar result can be obtained, only it takes a little longer, by using a parsley/mint cutter) with the nutmeg and a good squeeze of lemon juice. Gradually stir in to the stock with the biscuits to give a really creamy mixture. Put into a saucepan, cook for 5 minutes over a low heat, stirring all the time and then sieve. In a small basin, beat the egg yolk and cream together, add 2 tablespoons of the hot soup, stir this into the rest of the sieved soup, return to the pan and gently reheat, stirring all the time. Do not allow to reboil or it will curdle. When cool, chill thoroughly in the refrigerator and serve, very cold, garnished with some finely chopped shrimps and watercress.

CRÊME VICHYSSOISE

Pressure Cooking Time: 7 minutes

2 tablespoons butter; 4 sliced leeks; 1 medium onion; 5 potatoes; 2 medium carrots; 1 pint of chicken stock (or a stock cube); $\frac{1}{2}$ pint milk; $\frac{1}{4}$ pint double cream; finely chopped chives; seasoning.

Lift the trivet from the cooker, melt the butter and gently fry the leeks and onions until evenly golden. Add the potatoes, carrots, stock and seasoning, bring to pressure in the usual way, cook for 7 minutes and allow the pressure to reduce at room temperature. Add half the cream to the milk, stirring well, pour into the soup and quickly bring to the boil in the open pan lifting it from the heat at the exact moment when boiling point is reached. Allow to cool slightly, sieve, taste and correct seasoning and put to chill.

Just before serving, stir in the rest of the cream, pour into individual chilled soup cups and sprinkle with the chives.

SECTION II

Vegetables

This is the section dealing with those foods on which the reputation of a pressure cooker—and you, its user—most often rests, as I am sure you will agree.

With vegetables of all kinds there are certain points to know and watch for; then a little trial and error, a little experience of their cooking in and out of season, young and old, fresh or a little tired and you will soon be serving them with all their goodness, colour, flavour—a treat and a revelation each time to you and your family of how vegetables can and should look and taste.

In every way, pressure cooking is **the** way to treat fresh vegetables: to cook in the absence of air, conserves the vitamins; to cook in steam, means little loss of minerals, sugar and soluble proteins; to cook with the small amount of liquid necessary to provide steam, means that no goodness need be wasted as the vegetable water will be used for sauces and gravies or as stock for soups, stews, etc.

When pressure cooking, do not forget that the age, freshness and size of the pieces into which you cut the fresh vegetables will all affect their cookery times, just as they did in an ordinary saucepan. This being so, all the times suggested in the following tables and recipes are intended as a guide, not as hard and fast rules. Indeed, even family tastes may dictate a shorter or longer cooking time; one family may prefer crisp-cooked vegetables, another those which are soft all the way through; one may want a cauliflower served whole, another like it just as well in flowerets. But all these preferences are easily adaptable.

Here are a few general rules for the preparation and pressure cooking of fresh vegetables which will ensure your success in obtaining the best possible results:

Fresh vegetables, except onions, should be carefully washed in plenty of cold water and all have any doubtful parts removed.

Vegetables are best prepared as near cooking time as possible, particularly if they are to be cut up or shredded. If they must be prepared well in advance they will keep best if put directly into plastic bags and then in the refrigerator. Otherwise they should be left in cold water—not put into the cooker itself ready for cooking as this will cause them to discolour and dry out.

The minimum quantity of liquid, $\frac{1}{4}$ pint + $\frac{1}{4}$ pint, should be used except for certain fresh and all dried vegetables in the special recipes as given in the following pages.

All fresh vegetables, unless otherwise stated, should be cooked in steam not in liquid, so the trivet must be used for the larger, easily served vegetables such as potatoes, carrots, while the separators or containers are reserved for the smaller, such as peas, shredded cabbage. Pressure cooked in this way, a selection of different vegetables with different cooking times and different flavours can be cooked together and still be served separately, as they will not move around or mix together during the cooking, nor will their flavours mix as they would if all were being cooked in water instead of steam.

Where fresh vegetables to be cooked together are of different sizes or thicknesses they should be cut down so that all can be given the same pressure cooking time. As green vegetables require the shortest cooking, root vegetables should be cut into halves, quarters or cubes if they are to be cooked with them. A method for doing this is given on p. 49.

Seasoning should be added very sparingly when first pressure cooking fresh vegetables as you may find much less is needed than in an ordinary saucepan because of the higher retention of their own mineral salts when cooked in steam. Salt should always be sprinkled directly on the vegetables as they are being put into the cooker or as they are packed, layer by layer, in the separators or divisions. To ensure even distribution and complete dissolving of the salt grains in the steam, it is better to use the table salt rather than the cooking variety. Spices and herbs are also included before the cooking but pepper is best added just before serving.

The pressure cooker should not be more than two-thirds full when cooking fresh vegetables, so that plenty of room is left for the steam to do its work and so that there will be no chance of the centre vent getting blocked up.

Unless the instructions or recipe state otherwise, pressure should be reduced at once, with cold water, when the cooking time is up.

A time-table for frozen vegetables with suggested cooking instructions is given separately.

Dried Vegetables must be treated quite differently from the fresh ones and instructions, a time-table and recipes for these are also given separately.

Sauces, melted butter, mayonnaise for serving with vegetables are prepared separately and the recipes will be found in Section XVII. Do try and find the pressure cooking time that suits you, your family and the vegetables best—and then stick to it. Over-pressure cooking will do no good at all and can only lead to disappointment all round. Pressure cooking of vegetables, correctly done, means vegetables enjoyed at their natural best, for everyone.

FRESH VEGETABLES

TYPE	PREPARATION AND COOKING	PRESSURE COOKING TIME	METHOD OF SERVING
Artichokes (Jerusalem)	Wash, scrape or peel, cook on trivet. Cut in quarters if large; cut in halves if medium	4–5 minutes	Plain, with melted butter; with a rich, white sauce to which is added lemon juice when boiling; after cooking toss in butter in another pan, serve, pour butter over and sprinkle with golden crumbs
Aubergines (Egg-plant)	Wash, do not peel, cut in $\frac{1}{2}$-inch slices	1–2 minutes	Lift on to absorbent paper. Egg, crumb and fry in hot melted butter
Beetroots	Wash carefully without breaking the skin, cut off tops leaving 1 inch of stem. Cook alone in water without trivet, allow pressure to reduce at room temperature	Small, 1 pint water, 10 minutes Medium, $1\frac{1}{2}$ pints water, 20 minutes Large, old, 2 pints water, 30 minutes	Skin after cooking. Serve hot, sliced or diced, with white sauce. Serve cold, sliced or diced, with dressing of vinegar with a pinch of sugar added
Carrots	Wash, scrape or peel. Slit tops, when young, whole; slice lengthwise for medium and large	Young, whole, 4 minutes Halved, lengthwise, medium, 4 minutes Quartered, lengthwise, large, 4 minutes	With melted butter and garnished with chopped parsley
Carrots and Peas	Wash carrots, peel, cut into really small dice. Cook with shelled peas, sprig of mint, a knob of butter, pinch of sugar in solid container	4 minutes	Strained, with melted butter
Celeriac	Wash, peel thickly, cut in 1-inch strips or dice, and stand, until cooking, in water with a squeeze of lemon juice to keep white	3 minutes	With white sauce, with a little lemon juice added when boiled, poured over celeriac in serving dish and garnished with hard-boiled egg; the white chopped and the yolk sieved

Cucumber	Cucumbers that are too old to eat raw are excellent as a cooked vegetable. Wash, peel if skin is not tender, remove pips, halve lengthwise, cut in slices, quarters or large dice	1–2 minutes	With a white or onion sauce, plenty of pepper and garnished with chopped parsley
Kohl-Rabi	Wash, remove leaves, peel and cut into $\frac{1}{4}$-inch slices or as for potato chips	4 minutes	With cheese or Hollandaise sauce; fried in deep or shallow fat, like potato chips
Leeks	Cut off the tops and roots, slice into the stem from the top to open up and wash thoroughly	4 minutes	With a white or cheese sauce, using some of the cooking liquid, garnished with parsley
Marrow: Courgettes	Wash, top and tail, cook whole	4 minutes	Slice, put in oven-proof dish, pour over melted butter, sprinkle with chives, leave covered in moderate oven until served
Vegetable	Skin, unless very young and tender, cut in thick slices, remove centre core and ends	4 minutes	With white or cheese sauce, garnished with chopped parsley. For **Stuffed Marrow**, see recipe on p. 50.
Mushrooms			See recipes on p. 51.
Onions	Peel off the brown skin, cut off the roots.	Sliced in solid container. 4 minutes	Drain, stir into white sauce, thinned with a little of the cooking liquid
	Wash well, leave skins on	Whole, 6–8 minutes	Lift out carefully, skin, coat with cheese sauce, sprinkle with parsley
	For pre-cooking before roasting. Leave on outer skin	Whole, 4–5 minutes	Remove outer skin. Continue roasting round the joint in hot oven, basting occasionally
Parsnips	Wash, peel, cut in thin lengths or cubes. Put in $\frac{1}{4}$ pint salted water under trivet; other vegetables may then be cooked on trivet or in containers	3–4 minutes	Serve other vegetables, take out trivet, strain off liquid. Put in 2 tablespoons butter, 2 tablespoons sugar and heat in open pan, stirring, until the parsnips are lightly browned.
	Wash, peel, cut as for potato chips	2 minutes	Lift out, drain, dip in batter and deep fry
	Wash, peel, cut in half or leave whole if not too large	8–10 minutes	Lift out, continue roasting round the joint in the oven, basting frequently

FRESH VEGETABLES—*continued*

TYPE	PREPARATION AND COOKING	PRESSURE COOKING TIME	METHOD OF SERVING
Peppers (Pimento): red or green			See recipes, p. 52.
Potatoes: New	Scrub, scrape or cook in skins and peel afterwards	Small, whole, 4–5 minutes Medium, whole, 5–6 minutes Large, quartered or halved, 6–8 minutes	Toss with melted butter, sprinkle with chopped mint; when cold leave whole or slice and fry in shallow fat.
Old	Wash, peel; small, slit through to centre; medium, halved; large, quartered; pre-cooking for frying or roasting	4 minutes 4–6 minutes 4–6 minutes Whole, 4–6 minutes	As boiled or steamed; lift out other vegetables, lift trivet from under potatoes and use to strain off liquid, toss potatoes over low heat until dry, serve sprinkled with chopped parsley
Swedes	Wash, peel thickly cut into $\frac{1}{2}$-inch chunks or slices. Put into $\frac{1}{4}$ pint water in cooker (under trivet if other vegetables are to be cooked at the same time)	4 minutes	Strain off liquid, add butter and plenty of pepper and mash thoroughly. Serve sprinkled with chopped parsley
Tomatoes: For juice	Wash but do not dry. Cut up finely, put in cooker without water or trivet and bring first to boil in the open pan	1 minute	Allow pressure to reduce at room temperature. For cooking: strain only or put through a fine sieve; add 1 teaspoon salt to 2 pints sauce. For drinking: add sugar, Worcester sauce to taste See recipe, p. 53.
Turnips	Wash, peel unless very young and tender	Whole, young, 4 minutes Sliced or diced, 4 minutes	With melted butter mashed as for Swedes; diced with carrots and peas cooked together in perforated container, served hot as Maçedoine or cold as Russian Salad in mayonnaise
Sweet Corn: On cob	Remove husks, brush away 'silk' with nail brush. Cook on trivet	Small, 3 minutes Large, 5 minutes	Serve, thickly coated with melted butter. **Creamed,** see recipe on p. 54

To pressure cook Root and Green Vegetables together in the same time.

Example: **POTATOES, CARROTS AND SHREDDED CABBAGE**

Pressure Cooking Time: 4 minutes

Put into the pressure cooker ½ pint of water, the trivet and on it in two separate piles, potatoes and carrots whole, halved or quartered according to their size and so that they will cook in 4 minutes. Season each layer of vegetables well with table salt as they are being put in. Put the cooker on the heat without the cover and allow the water to come to the boil. In the meantime, pack the shredded cabbage tightly into the perforated containers, salting each layer as it is put in. When the cooker is filled with steam, put the containers in on top of the other vegetables if there is room or if not, at the side, where space has been left on the trivet. Cover, bring to pressure in the usual way and cook for exactly 4 minutes. Reduce the pressure immediately with cold water and serve the vegetables, which will require no straining or draining, according to the methods suggested in the time-tables or recipes in this section.

COURGETTES À LA GRECQUE

Pressure Cooking Time: 10 minutes

6–8 courgettes; 2 tablespoons minced beef, veal or ham, 1 dessertspoon minced onion, 1 teaspoon chopped parsley, 1½ tablespoons rice, seasoning, a little oil and vinegar to mix, for the stuffing; ½ pint water for the cooker; 2 eggs, a little lemon juice for the sauce; chopped parsley and grated cheese for garnish.

Wash the courgettes but do not peel. Cut a small slice off either end of each, loosen the pith with a small knife or a potato peeler and push it out one end. Scrape a little of the pulp away, chop it and mix with the other filling ingredients, adding a little mixed oil and vinegar to give a moist consistency. Stuff the courgettes, leaving room at either end for expansion. Put the water and the trivet into the cooker, then the courgettes and cover with a piece of buttered greaseproof paper. Bring to pressure in the usual way, cook for 10 minutes and allow the pressure to reduce at room temperature. During this cooking, beat the eggs with a squeeze of lemon juice and two teaspoons of cold water in a small bowl until frothy. Serve the courgettes and keep hot. Take a spoonful of the hot stock and add it to the basin, gradually adding five or six more, put into a small saucepan and heat gently, stirring all the time until thick but do not allow to boil or it will curdle. Taste and correct seasoning, pour over the courgettes and sprinkle with the mixed cheese and parsley.

STUFFED MARROW

Pressure Cooking Time: 12 minutes

1 medium marrow; about 6 oz cooked minced meat; 1 medium onion; 2 tomatoes; 1 tablespoon rice; 1 tablespoon butter; mirepoix for braising (p. 300); brown stock or vegetable water; seasoning; a sheet of greased, greaseproof paper.

Peel the marrow, cut a slice from the stalk end, then scoop out the centre pulp with the seeds, using a knife with a long blade or a long-handled spoon. In a frying pan, melt the butter and gently fry the finely chopped onion, the sliced, peeled tomatoes and the washed rice for about 5 minutes. Lift the pan from the heat, add the minced meat and seasonings and mix thoroughly. Fill the mixture into the marrow case, tapping it occasionally to make sure the mixture is evenly packed. Lift the trivet from the cooker, prepare the mirepoix, adding the required amount of liquid, put the marrow on top, replacing the cut-off slice to close the end, cover with the greased paper, bring to pressure in the usual way, cook for 12 minutes and reduce the pressure with cold water. Lift out the marrow, cut into thick slices, lay, overlapping in a deep serving dish and keep hot. Mash or sieve the mirepoix vegetables, taste and correct seasoning and if necessary add a little gravy colouring, reboil with the liquid in the open cooker, then pour round the sliced marrow.

MARROW PIQUANT

Pressure Cooking Time: 4 minutes

1 medium marrow; 1 sliced onion; 1 clove garlic (optional); 2 firm sliced tomatoes; 1 tablespoon butter; seasoning.

Scrub the marrow and slice finely, removing the seeds. Lift out the trivet, melt the butter over a low heat, add marrow and fry gently for a moment or two. Add the onions, chopped garlic if used, tomatoes, seasoning and water. Cover, bring to pressure in the usual way, cook for 4 minutes and reduce pressure at room temperature. Taste and correct seasoning, serve piping hot, garnished with chopped parsley.

STUFFED MUSHROOMS

Pressure Cooking Time: 3 minutes

2 large mushrooms per person; 2 shallots; 2 teaspoons chopped parsley; 1 tablespoon butter; 2 tablespoons fresh breadcrumbs; a little gravy or brown sauce; seasoning; $\frac{1}{2}$ pint water for the cooker.

Have the mushrooms of the same size, peel and cut off the stalks. Chop these with the shallots and parsley and fry gently in the butter, in a small saucepan. Add the breadcrumbs, seasoning and sufficient sauce to make a moist stuffing. Pile this evenly on the mushrooms. Put the the water and trivet in the cooker, then the mushrooms (if they will not all go on the trivet, put in a sheet of greaseproof paper and then a second layer). Bring to pressure in the usual way, cook 3 minutes and reduce pressure immediately. Serve on buttered toast or on triangles of fried bread.

STUFFED ONIONS

Pressure Cooking Time: 3 minutes

4 large Spanish onions; 1 tablespoon butter; 4 oz minced beef or veal, chopped ham or fried bacon; 3 tablespoons fresh breadcrumbs; 1 skinned tomato or teaspoon tomato purée; 1 tablespoon chopped parsley; pinch of nutmeg; salt and pepper; 1 egg; $\frac{1}{2}$ pint water for the cooker; golden breadcrumbs.

Wash the onions, cut off the roots but leave the skin on. Put the water and trivet in the cooker, then the onions, bring to pressure in the usual way, cook for 3 minutes. Allow the pressure to reduce at room temperature. During the cooking, heat the butter in a small pan and gently fry the meat, stirring often to brown evenly. Skin the onions and gently lift out the centres. Chop these and mix with the meat, tomato, seasonings, parsley and egg and fill the stuffing into the onions. Put in an ovenproof casserole, sprinkle with golden breadcrumbs and bake in the centre of a moderate oven, Gas No 4, 350° F, for 30 minutes. These are also delicious if, leaving off the breadcrumbs, a little brown sauce is put into the casserole with the onions and used to baste them well from time to time.

STUFFED GREEN PEPPERS

Pressure Cooking Time: 5 minutes

2 green peppers; $\frac{1}{4}$ lb minced fresh or cooked beef; 1 large cup of cooked rice; 2 tablespoons minced onion; 1 egg; a little tomato soup or purée; seasoning; golden crumbs; butter; $\frac{1}{2}$ pint water for cooker.

Cut the peppers in half and remove the seeds. Mix together the other ingredients, adding plenty of seasoning, sufficient tomato soup or purée to bind the mixture and then pile into the pepper shells. Put the water in the cooker, the trivet and then the stuffed peppers, covering them with a piece of buttered greaseproof paper. Bring to pressure in the usual way, cook for 5 minutes, allow the pressure to reduce at room temperature. Lift the peppers into an ovenproof dish, sprinkle each with golden crumbs, dot with butter and pop under a hot grill for a moment or two.

MASHED POTATOES

Pressure Cooking Time: 4 minutes

When cooking potatoes for mashing, peel and slice them thickly, rinse in plenty of cold water, pile on to the trivet with plenty of salt and cook for 4 minutes. If other vegetables have been cooked at the same time, lift these out and keep them warm. Lift out the potatoes and trivet, pour off the liquid and return the potatoes to the cooker. Over a low heat, keep tossing them until they are quite dry, then mash them very well. In a small saucepan heat 1 tablespoon butter and 1 tablespoon milk per pound of potatoes, add this and beat in until creamy. Taste and correct seasoning using plenty of pepper and a good pinch of nutmeg. Pile, piping hot into the serving dish, forking to a point and sprinkle with chopped parsley.

SCALLOPED POTATOES

Pressure Cooking Time: 5 minutes

1 tablespoon butter or margarine; 1 lb sliced potatoes; 1 tablespoon flour; 3 spring or 1 medium onion, chopped; $\frac{1}{2}$ pint milk and water; seasoning; grated cheese; paprika; butter.

Lift the trivet from the cooker, melt the butter in the open pan, pour in the milk and water and allow to boil. Put in a layer of potatoes, sprinkle with salt, pepper, some onions and a little of the flour and repeat until all ingredients have been added. Bring to pressure in the usual way, cook for 5 minutes and reduce pressure immediately. Lift out into an ovenproof dish, sprinkle thickly with grated cheese and lightly with paprika, dot with butter and brown under a hot grill.

SCOTCH STUFFED POTATOES

Pressure Cooking Time: 10 minutes

1 large potato per person; 1 small smoked haddock (or packet of frozen smoked haddock), 2 tablespoons butter; 3 tablespoons grated cheese; seasoning; a little chopped parsley; ½ pint water for cooker.

Scrub the potatoes, prick well, put the water and the trivet in the cooker, then the potatoes and haddock, bring to pressure in the usual way, cook for 10 minutes and allow the pressure to reduce at room temperature. Cut a slit lengthways in each potato, carefully scoop out the centre and mix this, while still hot with the butter, flaked haddock, seasoning and most of the grated cheese. Fill the mixture back into the potato cases, put on to a baking tray, sprinkle with the rest of the grated cheese and bake for 7–10 minutes until crisp on the middle shelf of an oven heated to Gas No 5, 375° F.

STUFFED TOMATOES

Pressure Cooking Time: 5 minutes

4 large tomatoes; 1 tablespoon butter; 2 tablespoons minced fresh or cooked meat; 2 shallots or 1 small onion; finely chopped parsley, 2 tablespoons white breadcrumbs, 1 egg, a little grated lemon rind, seasoning and a pinch of nutmeg, a dash of Worcester Sauce, for the stuffing: espagnole, madeira, cheese sauce or hot gravy, if served as a supper dish on its own; ½ pint water with lemon juice or vinegar for the cooker.

Wash the tomatoes, cut a small circle from the stalk end and with a tablespoon, carefully remove the centres without piercing the skin. In a separate pan, melt the butter and carefully brown the minced meat and onions. Away from the heat stir in the parsley, breadcrumbs, the tomato pulp, the beaten egg and the seasonings. Stuff the tomatoes with the filling and put each into a buttered cup. Put the water and trivet into the cooker, then the cups covered with a piece of buttered greaseproof paper. Bring to pressure in the usual way, cook for 5 minutes and reduce the pressure with cold water. Lift out the cups, scoop underneath each tomato with a tablespoon so that they can be served the right way up and put back the cut-off slice as a cap. Garnish with sprigs of parsley and serve with a suitable hot sauce or with heated gravy, if any is left over from a joint.

If more than 4 or 5 are to be done at one time, put one lot of cups in the water in the bottom of the cooker, then the piece of greaseproof paper, then the trivet, then another lot of cups and another piece of paper, making 2 layers.

CREAM OF SWEET CORN

Pressure Cooking Time: 3 minutes

3–4 corn cobs; 2 tablespoons butter; 1 tablespoon double cream; seasoning; $\frac{1}{2}$ pint water in cooker.

Remove husks and silk, put water and trivet in the cooker, then the corn, bring to pressure in the usual way, cook for 3 minutes and reduce pressure immediately. Cut the kernels from the cob, scraping every bit off. Melt the butter, add the cream and then the corn, taste and correct seasoning. This may be served as a vegetable, with a poached egg on top or in fillings for stuffed vegetables, etc, in place of rice.

FRESH GREEN VEGETABLES

When vegetables in the following table, whether on their own or with other vegetables or foods are to be pressure cooked, the water which has been put into the cooker must always be allowed to boil so that the pan is filled with steam before such green vegetables are added.

This is the same principle as with an ordinary saucepan; green vegetables started from 'cold' lose their colour and a lot of their goodness; green vegetables started from 'hot' keep their bright green look and more of their vitamins and flavour. Similarly, these vegetables should not be in water when pressure cooked; piled on the trivet or into containers they will lose much less of their minerals and salts.

With fresh, green vegetables timing must be exact; this is 'minute' cooking and 'I'll give them just another minute' will only lead to overcooking and consequent loss of colour, texture and flavour.

TYPE	PREPARATION AND COOKING	PRESSURE COOKING TIME	METHOD OF SERVING
Artichokes (Globe)	Wash, cut stems level, so that the heads can stand upright on trivet	Small, 6 minutes Large, 10 minutes	With browned butter with lemon juice added; with Hollandaise sauce
Asparagus: Whole Stalks	Wash, cut off tough ends (use for soup stock), scrape scales off stalks, tie in bundles of 6–8	According to thickness, 2–4 minutes	With melted butter over tips, Hollandaise or Mousseline sauce
Tips	Wash, cut off green tips, put in perforated or covered solid container with a knob of butter and seasoning	Perforated container, 1–2 minutes Solid container, 3–4 minutes	As garnish just with melted butter; with Hollandaise sauce; cold, combined with a mayonnaise
Beans: Broad	Shell, cook on trivet if alone or in perforated container if with other vegetables	On trivet, 2 minutes In container, 4–5 minutes	With melted butter or Parsley sauce
French or Runner	Wash, remove ends, string and slice. If very young may be cooked whole. Put in a sprig of mint	On trivet, 2–4 minutes In container, 4–5 minutes	With melted butter
Princess	Wash, remove ends, break into 2 or 3 pieces	As above	As above
Broccoli	Wash in salted water. Cut off thick stalks, then snick ends. Cook on trivet or separated from other vegetables underneath by a piece of greaseproof paper	3–4 minutes	With melted butter, either whole or chopped
Brussels Sprouts	Wash in salted water. Remove discoloured old outer leaves. Cut cross in stem	On trivet, 2–3 minutes In perforated container, 3–4 minutes	Whole plain or dotted with knobs of butter

TYPE	PREPARATION AND COOKING	PRESSURE COOKING TIME	METHOD OF SERVING
Cabbage: Green, White Red	Wash in salted water. Remove discoloured, wilted outside leaves. Shred roughly Cut in quarters; cut away some of hard, white core	On trivet. 2–3 minutes In perforated container, tightly packed. 3–4 minutes	With addition of white or black pepper and tossed in melted butter
	Red cabbage should be cooked on its own. Green or white may be separated from other vegetables underneath by a piece of greaseproof paper	On trivet. 4–5 minutes	White and green; dotted with knobs of butter Red. see recipe on p. 60
Cauliflower	Wash in salted water; remove all but young, inner green leaves. Cut away thick stalk. Flowerets: break into small pieces quartered or halved; cut away white core. Separate from other vegetables underneath with a piece of greaseproof paper	On trivet. 2–3 minutes On trivet. 3–4 minutes	With browned breadcrumbs; with a white, parsley or cheese sauce; with grated cheese and chopped parsley
Celery	Scrub in salted water, cut off green leaves, string, cut the outer stems in half, lengthwise, cut in 1–2-inch pieces	In perforated container. 3–4 minutes	With white or parsley sauce; braised as hors d'œuvre with french dressing or Hollandaise sauce
Chicory (Endive)	Wash under gently running cold water, remove any yellowing leaves. Do not cut in any way as this may make it taste bitter when cooked. Lift out trivet, melt 2 oz butter without colouring, put in 2 tablespoons water, 1 teaspoon lemon juice, salt and pepper. Cover with buttered, greaseproof paper	Alone in cooker. 4–6 minutes	Lift on to serving dish, boil liquid in open cooker until well reduced, then pour over chicory. See recipes for serving as supper, vegetarian dish

Peas	Shell, cook with a few washed pods and a sprig of mint. If peas are getting old or it has been a very dry season, cook in solid container as above but with a pinch of sugar also and allow pressure to reduce at room temperature to prevent the peas bursting	In perforated container, 2–4 minutes In solid container, 5 minutes	Tossed in melted butter, sprinkled with finely chopped mint; with diced carrots, turnips, etc, for Maçedoine As above, with vegetables when cold tossed in mayonnaise, as Russian Salad
Spinach	Wash several times in fast running water; remove stalks with the spines of the larger leaves. Cook alone. Do not use trivet. After final rinse, do not drain, pack a layer into cooker, put on high heat and as the water boils pack in further layers, seasoning in between; press down as hard as possible until cooker is two-thirds full	Up to pressure only	Serve well drained, in leaf, with melted butter; chopped with melted butter; sieved with a little nutmeg, melted butter and cream or milk added before reheating
Various:			
Dandelion leaves	Use only young leaves from plants which have not yet flowered	As for **Spinach**	Chop well, toss in melted butter
Kale (Curly)	Wash in plenty of running water	As for **Shredded Cabbage**	As above
Turnip tops	Wash in plenty of running water	As for **Shredded Cabbage**	As above

ASPARAGUS

For the following recipes prepare and cook the bundles of Asparagus as given in the time-table:

Au Gratin: $\frac{1}{4}$ pint cheese sauce; 1 tablespoon grated cheese; knobs of butter.

During the pressure cooking make the sauce, using half quantity of milk only. After reducing pressure, drain the asparagus well, put into a heatproof serving dish and untie the bundles. Add sufficient of the stock to give the sauce a coating consistency, pour over the asparagus, sprinkle with the grated cheese, add small knobs of butter and put under a hot grill until the cheese is melted and the surface an even brown.

Polonnaise: 4 tablespoons melted butter; 1 hard-boiled egg; chopped parsley and chives; golden crumbs.

After reducing pressure, drain the asparagus well, put into a hot serving dish, untie the bundles, coat with the foaming hot melted butter and sprinkle thickly with the mixed chopped hard-boiled egg, parsley, chives and golden crumbs.

Suisse: 2 tablespoons grated Gruyère cheese; a little single cream; chopped parsley.

After reducing pressure, drain the asparagus well, put into a hot serving dish. Melt the Gruyère cheese over a low heat, add sufficient cream to give a coating consistency and pour over the tips. Garnish with finely chopped parsley.

As Salad: 4–6 spears per portion; lemon juice; shredded lettuce; fresh dressing; thin strips of red pepper.

After reducing pressure, drain the asparagus well, untie the bundles and allow to get quite cold. (You may prefer to actually chill it in the refrigerator.) Allow to marinate in a shallow dish with lemon juice for 2–3 hours, carefully turning over once, during this time. Strain well, then serve each portion on finely shredded lettuce, pour over a french dressing and garnish with a thin strip of red pepper across the stalks.

BROAD BEANS PROVENÇALE

Pressure Cooking Time: 3–4 minutes

2 tablespoons butter; 3 tomatoes; 2 tablespoons finely sliced green pepper; $\frac{1}{4}$ pint white stock or water; 1 lb shelled beans; seasoning.

Lift the trivet out of the cooker, melt the butter in the open pan, add the skinned, roughly chopped tomatoes, the finely sliced green pepper and allow to cook gently for a minute or two. Put in the liquid, season well, add the young, shelled beans, cover, bring to pressure in the usual way and cook for 3–4 minutes, according to size. Reduce pressure with cold water, lift the beans into the serving dish and keep warm. Reduce the liquid remaining carefully in the open pan so that it does not burn and until it is thick. Taste and correct seasoning, then pour over the beans.

FRENCH BEANS LYONNAISE

beans, coarsely sliced; 2 onions; 2 tablespoons butter.

Prepare and cook the coarsely sliced beans as given in the time-table (p. 55). During the cooking, fry the finely chopped onions gently in butter in a frying pan until an even golden brown colour. After reducing pressure, add the beans to the onions, tossing all well together and serve piping hot, pouring over any butter that remains.

BROCCOLI

This is delicious if, after cooking and just before serving, piping hot, the spears are thickly sprinkled with grated cheese then hot, foaming butter is poured over.

GREEN OR WHITE SCALLOPED CABBAGE

Pressure Cooking Time: 3 minutes

¼ pint water; 1 onion; 1 cabbage; 1 tablespoon red or green pepper; seasoning; ½ pint white sauce; Worcester Sauce.

Lift the trivet from the cooker, put in the water, the finely chopped onion, the shredded cabbage, the chopped red or green pepper and seasoning. Cook for 3 minutes, reducing pressure with cold water. During the cooking, make a thick white sauce in another pan, using half the quantity of milk and adding one teaspoon Worcester Sauce. Stir in the strained vegetables, using the cooking liquid to thin the sauce, taste and correct the seasoning, using plenty of pepper and reheat quickly before serving piping hot.

RED CABBAGE FLAMANDE

Pressure Cooking Time: 5 minutes

2 slices of streaky bacon; 1 medium onion; 2 tablespoons vinegar; 2 tablespoons water or ham stock; 1 red cabbage; 2 sharp eating apples; 2 cloves; 1 tablespoon butter, 1 tablespoon flour for thickening; 1 tablespoon sugar; seasoning and nutmeg.

Lift the trivet from the cooker, put in the slices of bacon, cut into small pieces and cook over a gentle heat until the fat runs out. Gently fry the chopped onion until soft but not brown, then add the vinegar and water or ham stock, the finely shredded cabbage, the peeled, cored and sliced sharp eating apples and cloves. Bring to pressure in the usual way, cook for 5 minutes, allow the pressure to reduce at room temperature. For the thickening, melt the butter in another pan, add the flour and cook gently without colouring. Strain the liquid into the thickening, allow to boil, stirring all the time, then add the vegetables, together with at least 1 tablespoon of sugar (more may be added to taste) and a good sprinkling of pepper and nutmeg. Taste and correct seasoning and reheat before serving piping hot.

BRAISED CELERY

Pressure Cooking Time: 4 minutes

¼ pint good brown stock; 1 large or 2 small heads of celery; 2 tablespoons tomato purée; pinch of sugar, seasoning; chopped parsley.

Lift the trivet from the cooker, put in the stock (a stock or gravy cube could be used), the prepared celery sticks cut in half and the seasoning, bring to pressure in the usual way and cook for 4 minutes. After reducing pressure, lift the celery into a heatproof dish and put into the oven to keep warm. Boil the stock in the open pan quickly until reduced by half, then stir in the tomato purée, and the sugar, taste and correct seasoning and pour, piping hot, over the celery. Garnish with the chopped parsley.

CAULIFLOWER À LA POLONAISE

Pressure Cooking Time: 6 minutes

1 medium-sized cauliflower; 1 pint water; 1 egg; plenty of salt; 3 tablespoons butter, 3 tablespoons fresh crumbs, 2 tablespoons each finely chopped ham and parsley or chives, a squeeze of lemon juice to taste, for the topping.

Wash the cauliflower well, cutting off all but the four very youngest green leaves and cut a deep cross in the stem. Lift the trivet from the cooker, put in the water, the egg and salt and bring to the boil.

Holding the cauliflower by the stem plunge it for a moment or two in the water, then turn it, stem side down. Bring the cooker to pressure in the usual way, cook for 6 minutes, reduce the pressure immediately, drop the hard-boiled egg into cold water. During this cooking, melt the butter in a frying pan, add the crumbs and cook, stirring all the time until the crumbs are brown and have absorbed the butter. Stir in the ham and parsley and keep hot. Lift out the cauliflower, drain well, put on to the serving dish and keep hot. Shell the egg, chop finely and add to the topping. Reheat, add the lemon juice and plenty of pepper, taste and correct seasoning and spread evenly over the cauliflower.

CAULIFLOWER CHEESE

Pressure Cooking Time: 4 minutes

1 large cauliflower; ½ pint cheese sauce; a little grated cheese; 2 large tomatoes; 12 bacon rolls (p. 297); sprigs of parsley; seasoning; ½ pint water for the cooker.

Wash, trim, divide the cauliflower in two and cut small triangles from the thick stems. Put the water, trivet and cauliflower cut sides down in the cooker, bring to pressure in the usual way, cook for 4 minutes and reduce the pressure with cold water. During this cooking, make the cheese sauce and keep hot; grill the bacon rolls; in four individual buttered ovenproof dishes lay slices of the skinned tomatoes, season well, dot with butter and put under grill. Divide the cauliflower into four portions, put each in its dish and coat with the cheese sauce. Sprinkle with grated cheese and leave under the grill to brown. Garnish with the bacon rolls and sprigs of parsley.

CHICORY AU GRATIN

Pressure Cooking Time: 3 minutes

¼ pint water; 4 heads of chicory; 2 eggs; 2 tablespoons tomato purée; granted cheese; knobs of butter; seasoning.

Prepare the chicory, put the water in the cooker, the eggs and then the chicory, sprinkled with table salt. Bring to pressure in the usual way, cook for 3 minutes, allow pressure to reduce at room temperature, drop the eggs into cold water. Lift the chicory into an ovenproof dish, put a half of hard-boiled egg on each head, pour over the tomato purée thinned with a little of the cooking liquid to a coating consistency, sprinkle thickly with grated cheese, add small dabs of butter and reheat, until golden brown, under a hot grill.

HOT SLAW

Pressure Cooking Time: 3 minutes

1 large white cabbage; $\frac{1}{2}$ pint water; 1 tablespoon of butter; 2 eggs; 1 heaped teaspoon each of salt and sugar; a pinch of pepper; $\frac{1}{2}$ pint milk; 2 tablespoons vinegar; 2 tablespoons sour cream.

Wash and shred the cabbage finely. Put the water in the cooker, bring it to the boil, add in the trivet and the cabbage, bring to pressure in the usual way, cook for 3 minutes and reduce the pressure with cold water. During this cooking, melt the butter in a medium-sized saucepan, add the beaten eggs, the seasonings, the milk and vinegar and cook very gently, stirring all the time until thickened but do not allow to boil or it will curdle. Add the sour cream and beat thoroughly until light and fluffy. Lift out the cabbage, stir it into the sauce, reheat, taste and correct seasoning, and serve piping hot.

PEAS NORMANDIE

Pressure Cooking Time: 3 minutes

1 lb shelled peas; 1 heart of young lettuce; 6 spring onions; 1 tablespoon butter; $\frac{1}{4}$ pint white stock or water; small teaspoon sugar; seasoning; chopped parsley and chives.

Shell the peas, finely shred the lettuce and peel the spring onions. Lift the trivet from the cooker, melt the butter over a low heat, put in the vegetables and toss lightly. Add the white stock or water, the sugar and seasoning, bring to pressure in the usual way and cook for 3–4 minutes. After reducing pressure with cold water, lift the vegetables into the serving dish and keep warm. Boil the remaining liquid in the open pan quickly until reduced by half, use a tablespoon or so just to moisten the vegetables, sprinkle with chopped parsley and chives, and serve piping hot.

FROZEN VEGETABLES

As these will have already had a certain amount of cooking before the deep-freezing process, it is not recommended to use a pressure cooker if this type of vegetable only is to be cooked. Little time would be saved. But if a frozen vegetable is to be served with other fresh or green vegetables, then a very satisfactory result can be obtained if pressure cooked as follows:

Vegetables should not be allowed to defrost before the cooking. Those in a solid block such as Spinach, must, however, be broken up, as otherwise the outer surfaces will cook, while in the centre the vegetables will remain frozen. This is best done with a sharp knife or a small kitchen saw, cutting into cubes. Small vegetables such as peas and beans or those in pieces or spears such as brussels sprouts or broccoli can easily be broken up by knocking several times against a hard surface.

Small green vegetables or those difficult to serve if cooked loose should be put into perforated containers, sprinkled with table salt and be added to the cooker, as with their fresh counterparts, only when the water is boiling and the pan filled with steam.

Root vegetables, still frozen, should be cooked exactly as their fresh counterparts.

If frozen vegetables have been allowed to defrost, that is, have stood for at least an hour in the kitchen temperature, they will require only half the time given in the time-table below. Always reduce pressure immediately with cold water.

When serving, follow the suggestions given in the previous tables for fresh vegetables.

TYPE	PREPARATION AND COOKING	PRESSURE COOKING TIME
Asparagus	Separate stalks or tips	In solid container, 4 minutes
Beans:		
Broad	Tap to break up	In perforated container, 4 minutes
French	Tap to break up	In perforated container, 4 minutes
French (whole)	Tap to break up	In perforated container, 4 minutes
Broccoli	Tap to break up	In perforated container, 4 minutes
Brussels Sprouts	Tap to break up	In perforated container, 4 minutes
Carrots	Tap to break up	On trivet, 4 minutes
Mixed Vegetables	Tap to break up	In perforated container, 4 minutes
Peas	Tap to break up	In perforated container, 4 minutes
Spinach	Cut block into cubes	In perforated container, 4 minutes
Sweet Corn	Allow to defrost	Alone on trivet up to pressure only

DRIED VEGETABLES

Pressure cooking will save hours in the preparation of dried vegetables and is particularly useful if one has not got a good memory as it is not necessary to soak them overnight. They should however, be washed, picked over and pre-soaked before pressure cooking. Put them when prepared into a basin, add sufficient boiling water to just cover them, put a plate on top and leave for 1 hour.

As dried vegetables require to take up a lot of water during the cooking, the trivet is not required and 2 pints of water or stock should be allowed for each pound. This can be the soaking water made up to the correct amount.

The liquid in the cooker should always be boiling before the soaked vegetables are put in.

Soda should not be added as this will discolour the inside of the cooker.

After adding the vegetables, together with any seasoning, herbs, etc, bring to the boil on a high heat in the open pan and skim well. Lower heat until the liquid is gently boiling but not rising up in the pan, then bring to pressure in the usual way, but without altering the heat. This will take a little longer than normal but it is necessary, to ensure that the vegetables do not boil into the cover and perhaps block the centre vent causing the safety plug to come into action. Pressure should be reduced at room temperature.

TYPE	PRESSURE COOKING TIME
Haricot Beans (small)	20 minutes
Haricot or Butter Beans (large)	30 minutes
Lentils	15 minutes
Peas (split)	15 minutes
Peas (whole)	20 minutes

BAKED BEANS

Pressure Cooking Time: 20 minutes

½ lb small haricot beans; 3 or 4 slices streaky bacon; 1 small chopped onion; 2 tablespoons brown sugar; 1 teaspoon dry mustard; 1 small tin of tomato juice; 2 tablespoons tomato purée or sauce; 1 pint water; seasoning; flour for thickening.

Wash and pre-soak the beans as instructed. Lift the trivet from the cooker, put in the chopped bacon and allow to heat gently in the open pan until the fat runs out. Fry the onions until golden brown, then add the sugar, mustard, tomato juice, the purée or sauce dissolved in the water, the beans and the seasoning. Bring to pressure as instructed, cook for 20 minutes and allow the pressure to reduce at room temperature. Strain off the liquid, put the beans into an ovenproof dish and put uncovered into the top of a hot oven, Gas No 6 or 400° F for 15 minutes. Add a little of the liquid to one to two tablespoons of flour and when well blended pour into the rest of the liquid, return to the heat and stir until boiling and cook for a minute or two. Taste to correct the seasoning, pour over the beans, cover and keep hot until served.

SPLIT PEA PURÉE

Pressure Cooking Time: 20 minutes

4 oz yellow split peas; 1½ pints water or ham stock; butter; black pepper and a little salt.

Wash and presoak the peas as instructed. Lift the trivet from the cooker, put in the water or stock and the peas tied firmly in a pudding cloth. Bring to pressure in the usual way, cook for 20 minutes and reduce pressure at room temperature. Lift out the cloth, open and turn the peas into a warmed bowl. Beat thoroughly with a good knob of butter, the pepper and the salt until light and fluffy. Keep hot until ready to be served.

This is a delicious accompaniment to boiled bacon or ham, or boiled brisket of beef or silverside and can be put with these joints into the cooking water.

PEASE PUDDING

Pressure Cooking Time: 12 minutes

½ lb split green peas soaked according to the instructions; 1 pint ham or bacon stock; 1 large or 2 small eggs; a large knob of butter; seasoning.

Lift the trivet from the cooker, put in the stock (a ham or bacon bone could be added with 1 pint of water if no stock is available, and removed when the cooking time is up) and the soaked peas. Bring to the boil in the open cooker stirring and skimming as necessary. Lower the heat until the peas are just simmering, put on the lid, bring to pressure without altering the heat and cook for 8 minutes. Allow the pressure to reduce at room temperature.

Mash the peas well with a fork or potato masher, then stir in the well-beaten egg, add butter, taste and correct seasoning if necessary. Put in a greased bowl or solid container and cover with greaseproof paper. For the second cooking, the Peace Pudding can be cooked on its own for 4 minutes or, as given on p. 64, with a selection of other vegetables to be served at the same time.

SALAD BRETONNE

Pressure Cooking Time: 20 minutes

½ lb small haricot beans; 2 tablespoons vinegar; 1 tablespoon fresh olive oil; 1 teaspoon lemon juice; 2 medium onions; slices of cooked ham, liver or salami sausage or cold fried beef or pork sausages; 2 tablespoons chopped parsley; lettuce leaves.

Prepare, pre-soak and cook haricot beans as instructed. Allow the pressure to reduce at room temperature and then strain. Mix together the oil, vinegar and lemon juice and while still warm stir into the beans, mixing all well together. Allow to get quite cold then stir in the raw, finely diced onions and the cold meat cut into neat squares. Line the salad bowl with the washed and dried lettuce leaves, pile in the haricot bean mixture and sprinkle with chopped parsley.

This makes a delicious light summer supper, served with heated French bread and accompanied by a dry, white wine such as a Graves.

DEHYDRATED VEGETABLES

Pressure Cooking Time: 4 minutes

These can be pressure cooked most successfully, though it is not recommended if they are to be cooked on their own, as there would be little saving of time.

As a green vegetable being cooked with others for the same meal, use a solid container, adding half the amount of water given on the packet (this is because they will be cooked more quickly and there will be no loss of liquid by evaporation). Season well, add a sprig of mint with peas and pressure cook in the usual way for 4 minutes. Peas only should have the pressure reduced at room temperature to prevent them bursting. For other vegetables, reduce pressure immediately with cold water. Strain and serve tossed in butter or as in recipes given.

TINNED VEGETABLES

As tinned vegetables are already cooked and require no more than reheating, it is not recommended to do this in the pressure cooker for any green vegetables such as peas and beans, which would quickly become overcooked. Root vegetables, however, such as carrots, potatoes, can be turned out of the tin and be heated through by just bringing the cooker to pressure, lifting it from the heat and reducing pressure immediately.

If tinned vegetables are to be added to stews, braises, etc, open the tin and use the liquid as stock for the stew, putting in the vegetables as above, just before the pressure cooking time would be up.

For campers, caravanners and on boats, it may be found more convenient to reheat the vegetables in the tins. This is quite safe but, if there is other food in the cooker at the same time, remove the paper and give the tin a good wash before putting it in.

SECTION III

Fish

It is well known that fish is an excellent food, tasty and delicious as well as a source of many of the essentials of a well-balanced diet. It has become, however, quite an expensive item in the household budget so it is even more important that it should be carefully and economically prepared and served.

Pressure cooking is an ideal method of doing this as, requiring only the minimum of liquid to provide the steam, all the goodness can be retained, the cooking stock need never be wasted and the fish holding together better in steam than in liquid is easier to serve attractively.

Again, although the saving of time may not be so great as with those foods which require much longer cooking by ordinary methods, you will notice at once the much improved flavour and will be glad not to have quite so much of the cooking smell through the house, as usually happens when preparing fish dishes.

For pressure cooking, small fish may be cooked whole; larger fish be filleted or cut into steaks. Allow approximately 1 lb of filleted fish for three people. Care should be taken when buying fish to make sure that it is fresh with the flesh firm and not flabby and the eyes bright. If you ask the fishmonger to remove the heads or tails or to fillet the fish for you, be sure he gives you all the bits and pieces as these you will use either before or during the cooking to make a good fish stock. Fresh fish should be washed in a little salted water during preparation and is best cooked on the day it is purchased. If it is to be kept, it should be unwrapped, rinsed in salted water and put in a cool place or the refrigerator between two plates or dishes, in an unsealed plastic bag or loosely 'parcelled' in foil.

Pressure cooked, fish can be steamed or poached, using the trivet, casseroled directly in the liquid or be pan-fried first before pressure cooking.

If fish stock is not available, it can be made with most recipes, at the same time as the fish is cooked; it must then be strained before adding to the accompanying sauce.

Certain recipes, to give the correct result, must be made with a specially prepared liquor known as Court Bouillon. The recipe, quick and easy to prepare, is given on p. 71.

Frozen fish may be substituted for fresh in many of the following recipes. Do not defrost, give the same pressure cooking time but use only half the given quantity of liquid to allow for the juices that will come from the fish as it thaws out.

To ensure a perfect fish dish, the accompaniments must be well chosen: vegetables and garnishes of contrasting colour to give attractiveness and a well-made sauce with a sharp or piquant flavour.

For those special evenings, when wine is to be served, a Chablis or dry Sauterne would be a good choice.

The following recipes are to serve four people. Use **High** (15 lb) pressure.

TYPE	PREPARATION AND COOKING	PRESSURE COOKING TIME	METHOD OF SERVING
Brill **Cod** **Haddock** **Hake** **Halibut** **Plaice** **Rock Salmon** **Sole** **Turbot**	Put the prepared fish on the buttered trivet or on a piece of buttered greaseproof paper if being cooked with other vegetables or other foods. Use $\frac{1}{2}$ pint water or stock or $\frac{1}{4}$ pint water and $\frac{1}{4}$ pint wine 1. Sprinkle with lemon juice and seasoning. Cover with paper 2. Lay thick slices of peeled tomatoes on the fish, sprinkle with finely chopped onions and seasoning. Cover with buttered paper	1–1$\frac{1}{2}$-inch steaks, 4–6 minutes Tail, middle cut or whole, weighing 1–1$\frac{1}{2}$ lb, 5–6 minutes per pound	Reduce pressure immediately. Lift out carefully and skin and bone when possible 1. Serve with a coating sauce such as Anchovy, Cheese, Hard-boiled egg or Parsley using fish stock and milk. Garnish with lemon and parsley 2. Serve with a separate sauce such as Caper, Hard-boiled egg. Hollandaise, Mouselline or Tartare. Can be dotted with butter and quickly browned under a hot grill
Salmon and Salmon-Trout	To serve hot or cold: sprinkle with plenty of lemon juice, salt and pepper. Cook on buttered trivet covered completely with a well-buttered piece of greaseproof paper	1–1$\frac{1}{2}$-inch steaks, 6–8 minutes Tail or middle cut weighing up to 3 lb, 6 minutes per pound	**Hot:** with Anchovy or Hollandaise sauce **Cold:** unwrap and cover again to keep moist. Serve with Mayonnaise, Tartare or Vinaigrette sauce or coated with Chaudfroid and accompanied by a crisp green or mixed salad
Herrings **Mackerel** **Muilet** **Whiting**	1. Cooked whole, with or without heads. Scaled when necessary. Brown the fish all over first in hot butter in the cooker then lift out. Put in $\frac{1}{2}$ pint hot water, stock or $\frac{1}{4}$ pint water, $\frac{1}{4}$ pint wine, then the trivet and the fish well seasoned, covered with buttered paper	Whole, according to size, 5–8 minutes	Lift into overproof dish, sprinkle with golden crumbs, dot with butter and leave to further brown under a hot grill while cooking vegetables and making suitable sauce such as Mustard. Hollandaise. Caper, using the fish stock. Garnish with chopped parsley
	2. Scale, cut off heads, cut down soft side, open and lay flat, skin side uppermost and pressing all the way down backbone to loosen it. Turn over and lift out backbone. Wash well. Sprinkle with lemon juice and seasoning. Spread with a mixture of herbs, made mustard, chutney or a thick layer of thinly sliced mushrooms. Cook flat or folded, on the buttered trivet covered with buttered paper	Whole, according to size, 5–8 minutes Boned, according to thickness, 4–5 minutes	Serve with suitable coating sauce, garnish with lemon and parsley or coat thickly with chopped almonds and parsley stirred into melted butter and brown quickly under hot grill
	3. Using fish whole or boned, fill three-quarter-full with suitable stuffing and secure by sewing with coarse thread, small skewers or parcelling securely in buttered paper. Cook on trivet, covered with buttered paper	Stuffed, according to size. 10–12 minutes	Lift out, brush with melted butter, sprinkle with golden crumbs and brown under hot grill. Garnish with parsley and lemon quarters

COURT-BOUILLON

1 wineglass of a white wine; $\frac{1}{4}$ pint water; 1 small onion; a clove of garlic; a bay leaf; salt and pepper including black pepper if available; a strip of lemon peel.

Bring all the ingredients slowly to the boil in a small saucepan, simmer gently in the open pan for 10 minutes, cover and allow to cool.

Court-bouillon is used when cold and strained, or not, according to the recipe.

COD CREOLE

Pressure Cooking Time: 5 minutes

1 lb of fresh or frozen cod in the piece or steaks; $\frac{1}{4}$ pint water or fish stock; 1 teaspoon lemon juice or vinegar; seasoning; good pinch of mixed herbs; 2 oz butter; 4 medium skinned tomatoes; 4 medium onions; thin slices of green pepper for garnish if available or chopped parsley.

Heat the oven at No 4, 350° F, and set the shelf, second runner from the top. Lift the trivet from the cooker, put in the liquid, lemon juice, a little salt, the mixed herbs and the fish covered with a piece of buttered paper. Bring to pressure in the usual way, cook for 5 minutes, allow the pressure to reduce at room temperature, lift out the fish and allow to drain. During the cooking, heat the butter in a frying pan; gently cook the thinly sliced tomatoes and lift into an ovenproof dish and keep hot in the oven. Fry the very thinly sliced onions carefully so that all are an even, golden brown and have absorbed the butter. Flake the fish, seasoning lightly with pepper and pile on to the tomatoes. Cover completely with the onions, then the strips of green pepper and bake in the oven for 10 minutes. During this time, the accompanying vegetables can be pressure cooked. If the pepper strips have not been used, sprinkle the fish with parsley just before serving.

FISH AU GRATIN WITH STUFFED TOMATOES

Pressure Cooking Time: 5 minutes

1 steak of fresh or frozen fish such as Cod, Haddock, Halibut per person; lemon juice; 1 stuffed tomato per person, see recipe on p. 53, substituting 2 oz grated cheese for the meat; 1 tablespoon butter, 1 tablespoon flour, 2 oz grated cheese, $\frac{1}{4}$ pint milk for sauce; seasoning; golden crumbs, dots of butter for browning; chopped parsley; $\frac{1}{2}$ pint fish stock for the cooker (or water with some sliced carrots, onion, leek, a few peppercorns, mixed herbs and a thin slice of lemon peel).

Lift the trivet from the cooker, put in the stock or water with stock ingredients, the four cups with the stuffed tomatoes covered with a piece of greaseproof paper and the trivet well-buttered. On this put the steaks of fish, well-seasoned and sprinkled with lemon juice and with a piece of buttered paper laid on top. Bring to pressure in the usual way, cook 6 minutes, allow the pressure to reduce at room temperature. During the cooking, melt the margarine in another saucepan, add the flour and cook without allowing to colour. Away from the heat, gradually add the milk, the grated cheese, return to a low heat and stir until thickened. Slip the fish off the trivet on to an ovenproof serving dish, leaving a space between each steak for the tomatoes. Lift out the cups and keep warm. Add sufficient of the strained liquid from the cooker to give the sauce a coating consistency, pour this over the fish and sprinkle thickly with the mixed grated cheese and golden crumbs. Brown quickly under a hot grill and add the stuffed tomatoes, sprinkling each with chopped parsley.

STUFFED HADDOCK WITH VEGETABLES

Pressure Cooking Time: 10 minutes

1 fresh haddock 1–1½ lb in weight; seasoning and lemon juice; stuffing (recipe, p. 299); potatoes; carrots; melted butter; golden crumbs; sprigs of parsley; ½ pint water for cooker; ½ pint of suitable sauce such as tomato, cheese, caper.

Wash, trim the fish and remove backbone if liked; sprinkle the inside with seasoning and lemon juice, then stuff three-quarters full, closing the fish with small skewers or folding into a parcel of buttered greaseproof paper. Put the water into the cooker, add the fish trimmings, the trivet, the potatoes and carrots well salted, then a piece of greased greaseproof paper and the fish. Bring to pressure in the usual way, cook for 10 minutes and allow the pressure to reduce at room temperature. During the cooking, make the sauce using half the milk or liquid only. Lift the fish on to an ovenproof serving dish, brush with melted butter, sprinkle with golden crumbs and brown quickly under a hot grill. Serve the potatoes and carrots sprinkled with chopped parsley. Add sufficient of the strained stock to the sauce to give a thick, pouring consistency, reheat, taste and correct seasoning. Garnish the fish with sprigs of parsley and hand the sauce separately.

A little extra, piping hot melted butter may be served with this dish, instead of the sauce.

HALIBUT AU GRATIN

Pressure Cooking Time: 6–8 minutes

1–1½ lb halibut in the piece or in steaks; seasoning and lemon juice; ½ pint fish stock; 1 finely chopped onion; 1 tablespoon butter, 1 tablespoon flour, 2 tablespoons tomato purée or paste for sauce; chopped parsley; a little white wine (optional); golden crumbs; knobs of butter.

Lift the trivet from the cooker, put in the fish stock, the onion, the buttered trivet and the fish sprinkled with seasoning and lemon juice and covered with a piece of buttered paper. Bring to pressure in the usual way, cook according to size and weight, reduce pressure with cold water.

During the cooking, melt the butter in a small saucepan, add the flour and cook without browning for a moment or two. Lift the fish into a buttered ovenproof dish. Gradually add the fish stock to the thickening, stir in the tomato purée and the chopped parsley and the wine if used. Coat the fish with the sauce, sprinkle with golden crumbs, dot with butter and brown quickly under a hot grill.

STUFFED PLAICE AND VEGETABLES

Pressure Cooking Time: 4 minutes

4 large fillets of fish; lemon juice; shrimp paste; potatoes; carrots; fresh or frozen peas; a small packet of frozen shrimps; 1 tablespoon butter, 1 tablespoon flour, ¼ pint milk, ¼ pint fish stock, a drop or two of cochineal for sauce; butter; lemon butterflies (p. 299), chopped and sprigs of parsley for garnish; ½ pint water for the cooker; 4 large bewhiskered prawns if obtainable.

Wash the fish, skin the fillets, sprinkle with lemon juice and seasoning on the skinned side, then spread thickly with shrimp paste and roll up. Prepare the potatoes and carrots (new ones will make this a delicious summer evening dish) to a size to cook in 4 minutes. Put the water into the cooker, the trivet and the potatoes and carrots well salted, in two piles. Parcel the rolled fillets up lightly in a buttered piece of greaseproof paper and put to one side, resting on the vegetables. Put the cooker on the heat and when the pan is filled with steam put in the salted frozen peas packed in a perforated container. Bring to pressure in the usual way, cook for 4 minutes and reduce the pressure with cold water. During the cooking, melt the butter in a small saucepan, add the flour and cook for a minute or two without discolouring. Away from the heat add the milk and the chopped shrimps; return to the heat and cook, while stirring, until thick. Lift out the peas, toss with a little butter and keep hot. Lift the fish on to a round serving dish, arranging the fillets in a circle, and keep hot. Serve the potatoes and carrots garnished with the parsley. Lift the trivet out and use sufficient of the fish stock to give the sauce a coating consistency. Add enough colouring to give the sauce a pinkish tinge. Taste and correct seasoning, then pour over the fish. Take a spoonful of peas and fill into the centre serving the rest with the other vegetables. Garnish each fillet with a lemon butterfly and a sprig of parsley.

If you talk to your fishmonger nicely when you buy the plaice he will give you four large whiskery prawns and these should be put between the fillets just before serving so that their whiskers meet in the centre above the peas to make this dish as attractive as it is delicious.

SOLE MONTREUIL

Pressure Cooking Time: 4 minutes

1 large or 2 small fillets of fresh or frozen sole per person; seasoning and lemon juice; 1 tablespoon melted butter; just less than $\frac{1}{2}$ pint milk, small piece of carrot and turnip, 1 small onion halved and stuck with 3 or 4 cloves; 1 lb potatoes; frozen or fresh peas; 1 tablespoon margarine, 1 tablespoon flour, 1 tablespoon cream for Bechamel sauce (p. 292); grated cheese; knobs of butter.

Wash and skin the fillets, sprinkle the skinned side with seasoning and lemon juice and roll up. (To help the fillets stay rolled, it is a good idea to secure each with a cocktail stick, removing this after the fillets have been put on the serving dish.) Rinse the sliced potatoes in plenty of cold water. Prepare the carrot, turnip and onion. Lift the trivet from the cooker, melt the margarine, add the milk, the vegetables, the trivet and the well-salted potatoes piled on one side. Put the cooker on the heat and when the pan is filled with steam put in the container with the salted peas, then a double thickness of buttered greaseproof paper and the rolled fillets. Bring to pressure in the usual way, cook for 4 minutes and reduce the pressure with cold water.

During the cooking, melt the margarine in a small saucepan, add the flour and cook for a minute or two but without colouring.

Lift the fillets on to an oval dish, laying these in a line down the centre. Lift out the potatoes and overlap them to form a border round the fish. Toss the peas with a little butter and keep warm. Lift out the trivet, add sufficient of the stock to the thickening to give a coating consistency to the sauce, taste to correct the seasoning and lastly add the cream. Coat the fish carefully, sprinkle thickly with grated cheese, dot with butter and put under a very hot grill until golden brown. When ready to serve, pile the peas at each end of the dish as garnish.

TURBOT IN WINE SAUCE

Pressure Cooking Time: 6–8 minutes

1–1½ lb of turbot in the piece or steaks; 2 tablespoons butter; ¼ pint white wine; ¼ pint water; 2 diced shallots or 1 medium onion; 2 oz finely sliced button mushrooms; good pinch of mixed herbs; seasoning; 1 tablespoon butter; squeeze of lemon juice; sprigs of parsley for garnish.

Lift the trivet from the cooker, put in the butter and when heated lightly brown the turbot on both sides, lift out. Put in the wine, water, shallots, herbs, seasoning and then the fish, covered with the sliced mushrooms. Bring to pressure in the usual way, cook according to size and weight, reduce the pressure with cold water. Carefully lift the fish out on to a serving dish and keep warm. Lift out the trivet, boil the remaining stock vigorously until reduced by half. In another small saucepan, melt the butter, then add the strained stock and boil until thick; lastly add a dash of lemon juice. Garnish the fish and hand the sauce separately.

POACHED SALMON WITH NEW POTATOES

Pressure Cooking Time: 6 minutes

New potatoes; 1 steak of salmon per person; seasoning; lemon juice; Hollandaise sauce (p. 293); knobs of butter; ½ pint water for cooker; cucumber slices and chopped mint for garnish; fresh green peas cooked separately.

Put into the cooker the water, the containers with small, even-sized new potatoes well salted, covered with a piece of buttered grease-proof paper, the trivet, the salmon steaks well-seasoned and sprinkled with lemon juice and covered with a piece of buttered greaseproof paper. Bring to pressure in the usual way, cook for 6 minutes, reduce pressure with cold water.

During the cooking, make the Hollandaise sauce and, in a separate saucepan, cook the fresh green peas, toss with knobs of butter and sprinkle with the finely chopped mint. Serve the salmon on to a dish large enough to arrange the steaks in a circle with each piece pointing to the centre. Garnish each slice with a line of cucumber slices to give a wheel effect and pile the strained peas, tossed in butter, in the centre and at the edge of the dish between the salmon steaks. Hand the Hollandaise sauce separately.

TROUT AU BLEU

Pressure Cooking Time: 5 minutes

This dish must be cooked with a court-bouillon prepared in advance.

Court-bouillon (p. 71); 1 trout per person; melted maître d'hôtel butter.

Wash and clean the trout but leave the heads on. Lift the trivet from the cooker, put in the cold, strained court-bouillon and the trout and cover with a piece of greaseproof paper. Bring to pressure in the usual way, cook 5 minutes, reduce the pressure with cold water. Carefully lift out the fish on to the serving dish laying them alternately head to tail. Serve at once, handing round the melted maître d'hôtel butter, piping hot, in a sauce boat.

Trout cooked this way are delicious served cold, with mayonnaise. They should be left to get cold in the court-bouillon after the pressure has been reduced, and allowed to drain well before serving.

DEVILLED HERRINGS

Pressure Cooking Time: 6–8 minutes

$\frac{1}{2}$ pint court-bouillon (p. 71); (or $\frac{1}{4}$ pint water, $\frac{1}{4}$ pint vinegar with a sliced onion, slice of lemon peel, bouquet garni (p. 297), 2 cloves and seasoning); 4 herrings; some made English or French mustard; 1 teaspoon curry powder; seasoning; 2 tablespoons butter; chutney to serve separately.

Wash the cleaned herrings well and season them inside with salt, pepper and a little lemon juice. Make two or three diagonal cuts down the back of each, then spread with the made mustard mixed with the curry powder. Lift the trivet from the cooker, put in the strained court-bouillon and the herrings and cover with a piece of buttered greaseproof paper. Bring to pressure in the usual way, cook for 6–8 minutes according to size, reduce the pressure with cold water. Lift the fish on to an ovenproof serving dish, brush with melted butter and keep hot under a heated grill. In a small saucepan, melt the butter and gradually add the strained court-bouillon, whisking all the time until the sauce thickens. Serve separately or poured piping hot, over the herrings and hand round the chutney as an accompaniment.

SOUSED HERRINGS OR MACKEREL

Pressure Cooking Time: 6–8 minutes

4 herrings or mackerel; $\frac{1}{4}$ pint vinegar; $\frac{1}{4}$ pint water; 1 sliced onion; 6 peppercorns; 4 cloves; bay leaf; a slice of lemon peel; a clove of garlic if available; seasoning; chopped capers, chives or parsley as garnish.

Wash the fish, trim and scale and cut off heads. Lift the trivet out of the cooker, put in the liquid and the fish lying alternately head to tail. Sprinkle with the rest of the ingredients, cover with a double thickness of greaseproof paper. Bring to pressure in the usual way, cook for 6 to 8 minutes according to size. Reduce pressure with cold water if serving hot. Lift out the fish on to the serving dish and keep hot. Boil the liquid rapidly in the cooker until reduced by half, then strain, piping hot, over the fish. Garnish with the capers, parsley or chives.

To serve cold: allow the pressure to reduce at room temperature, leaving the fish in the cooker until quite cold, then lift out and drain (the cooker trivet on a large plate is just right for this purpose). Boil the liquid rapidly in the cooker until reduced by half, allow to cool again then strain over the fish which may be left whole or carefully boned and divided into 'fillets'. Serve with very finely sliced raw onion rings and chopped parsley.

SPICED MACKEREL

Pressure Cooking Time: 6 minutes

4 small mackerel; 4 good tablespoons of finely chopped parsley; 2 tablespoons of chopped fennel leaves (if these are obtainable it will make all the difference to this dish) or 3 or 4 crushed caraway seeds, 2 tablespoons of chopped capers, 2 tablespoons of melted butter, 1 teaspoon of grated lemon peel, a pinch of cayenne and black pepper, salt, for the filling; 4 pieces of buttered greaseproof paper large enough to parcel up each fish completely; $\frac{1}{2}$ pint water for the cooker.

Split the mackerel, clean and wash well. Mix all the ingredients for the filling well together, binding them with the melted butter. Put a quarter of this into each fish, then wrap it in the buttered paper making a secure parcel so that none of the butter or juices will run out. Put the water and the trivet in the cooker and then the parcelled fish. Bring to pressure in the usual way, cook for 6 minutes and reduce the pressure with cold water. Lift each parcel out separately and open it out, upside down, on the hot serving dish so that all the juices pour over the fish.

This is an economical, appetising and nutritious supper dish and does not require an accompanying sauce; serve with thick slices of hot French bread, recipe on p. 298.

SALMON LOAF

Pressure Cooking Time: 12 minutes

1 medium-sized (approx. 8 oz) tin of salmon; 2 large tablespoons white breadcrumbs; 2 tablespoons melted margarine; 2 teaspoons chopped parsley; pinch of nutmeg; 2 tablespoons chopped chutney (optional); 1 teaspoon finely chopped onion or chives; seasoning; 2 eggs; $\frac{1}{2}$ pint water with lemon juice or vinegar for the cooker; golden crumbs; cucumber or gherkin slices for garnishing.

Flake the salmon, put into a basin with the other ingredients and plenty of seasoning; bind with the beaten eggs, mixing all well together. Put the mixture into a well-buttered bowl or seamless loaf tin and cover with a double thickness of greased, greaseproof paper. Put the water, the trivet and the loaf into the cooker, bring to pressure in the usual way, cook for 12 minutes and allow the pressure to reduce at room temperature. During the cooking, heat the oven to Gas No 5, 375° F, and have the shelf in the middle of the oven. Leave the loaf standing for 5 minutes, then turn out on to the serving dish, sprinkle evenly with the golden crumbs and put into the oven for 10 minutes or so. During this time, the accompanying vegetables can be pressure cooked. Serve the loaf with overlapping slices of cucumber or gherkin along the top.

SCALLOPS PARISIENNE

Pressure Cooking Time: 5 minutes

4 large or 5 small scallops; $\frac{1}{2}$ lb peeled, sliced potatoes; 1 egg; $\frac{1}{4}$ pint milk; 2 oz finely sliced mushrooms; seasoning; 1 tablespoon butter, 1 tablespoon flour, a spoonful of cream if available, for sauce; 1 tablespoon butter, a little milk for mashed potatoes; grated cheese; $\frac{1}{2}$ pint water for the cooker; sprigs of parsley for garnish.

Wash the scallops well and put them into a round dish or bowl that will fit into the cooker, with the milk, the mushrooms and the seasoning. Lift the trivet from the cooker, put in the water, then the bowl covered with a piece of greaseproof paper and, at the side, the egg. Put in the trivet on top and then the well-salted potatoes. Bring to pressure in the usual way, cook for 5 minutes and allow the pressure to reduce at room temperature. Lift out the potatoes with the trivet and the bowl, and drop the egg into cold water. Strain the water from the cooker, put back the potatoes over a low heat, toss until dry then mash well with the butter, milk and plenty of seasoning. Strain the liquor from the bowl and use to make a white sauce with the butter and flour.

Slice the scallops and stir into the sauce with the mushrooms and chopped hard-boiled egg, reheat thoroughly and add cream. Dress into scallop shells or individual dishes, pipe or fork a border of mashed potato round each, sprinkle thickly with grated cheese, dot with butter and put under a hot grill until golden brown. Garnish with a sprig of parsley.

Many other fish such as salmon and lobster, tinned or fresh, turbot, haddock and cod, fresh or frozen but used when thawed, may be served in the same way, making delicious supper dishes or, in small portions, as a 'starter' for a dinner party. (When served in scallop shells these are called coquilles.)

AMERICAN FISH PIE

Pressure Cooking Time: 4 minutes

$\frac{1}{2}$ lb of any white fresh or frozen fish; seasoning and lemon juice; 1 lb of peeled sliced potatoes; $\frac{1}{4}$ pint of anchovy or hard-boiled egg sauce; 1 beaten egg, a little milk; parsley sprigs and slices of peeled tomatoes and lemon for garnish; $\frac{1}{2}$ pint water for the cooker; 3 tablespoons golden crumbs; 1 tablespoon melted butter.

Preheat the oven to Gas No 5, 375° F, and put a shelf on the middle runner. Lift the trivet from the cooker, put in the water, the trivet, the sliced potatoes (which should have been put through plenty of cold water), then the fish on a piece of greased greaseproof paper. Bring to pressure in the usual way, cook for 4 minutes and reduce the pressure with cold water. Lift out the fish, the potatoes and the trivet; pour out the stock and keep on one side, rinse the cooker. Put the potatoes back into the cooker, season well, mash thoroughly, then reheat adding nearly all the egg and a little milk and beating until creamy and white.

Grease a shallow tin or plate well. Mix the golden crumbs with the melted butter and press into the tin to make an even lining. Then spread with the mashed potato, brush over with the rest of the egg, bake until firm and crisp—about 30 minutes. Make the sauce, using a little of the fish stock as well as the milk, flake the fish, add it and keep piping hot. Gently lift the case on to the serving dish, fill with the hot fish mixture and garnish with the slices of tomato, lemon and parsley sprigs.

FISH CAKES

Pressure Cooking Time: 5 minutes

$\frac{1}{4}$ lb of any white fish, $\frac{1}{4}$ lb potatoes for 8 fish cakes; 1 tablespoon melted butter; a little anchovy essence, chopped parsley or chives as alternative flavourings; egg and golden crumbs for coating; fried sprigs of parsley (p. 298); $\frac{1}{2}$ pint parsley sauce (p. 291).

Prepare and cook the fish and potatoes as in the previous recipe. When cool, mix the flaked fish, mashed potatoes, melted butter, flavouring and seasonings well together and form into cakes patting them well to make them firm so that they will hold together. Have ready a tablespoon of seasoned flour on one piece of greaseproof paper, a flat plate with the beaten egg and another piece of paper with the golden crumbs. Toss each cake in the flour, pass it through the egg and coat thoroughly with the golden crumbs lightly tossing from one hand to the other to shake off any loose crumbs. Fry in hot fat, lift on to kitchen paper to drain. Garnish with fried parsley and hand the parsley sauce separately.

KEDGEREE

Pressure Cooking Time: 5 minutes

$\frac{1}{2}$ lb smoked haddock; 1 cup (about 6 oz) long rice; 1 egg for hard-boiling; 2 tablespoons margarine or butter; pepper; $\frac{1}{2}$ pint water for the cooker with lemon juice or vinegar; chopped parsley for garnish.

Lift the trivet from the cooker, put in the water, the egg and a solid container filled with the washed rice and one and a half cups of salted water and covered with greased, greaseproof paper. Place the trivet on top with the haddock dotted with butter and also covered with greaseproof paper. Bring to pressure in the usual way, cook for 5 minutes, allow the pressure to reduce at room temperature. Lift out the fish, the trivet, drop the egg into cold water; turn the rice into another saucepan and shake gently over a low heat until quite dry but do not allow it to catch. Add the margarine and as it melts stir it into the rice, then put in the flaked fish, correct seasoning and keep hot. Chop the white of egg and put the yolk through a sieve. Pile the kedgeree high on a hot dish and sprinkle with the egg and chopped parsley.

LOBSTER

Pressure Cooking Time: 10 minutes

1 live lobster that will fit into the pressure cooker; at least 2 pints of boiling water.

Lift the trivet from the cooker, put in the water and bring it to the boil. When boiling rapidly, plunge the lobster in, bring to pressure in the usual way, cook for 10 minutes and reduce pressure with cold water. Plunge the lobster into cold water and when cool, dress ready for serving either cold with salad or for your chosen dish.

LOBSTER THERMIDOR

1 cooked lobster for 2 portions; $\frac{1}{2}$ pint of cheese sauce made with $\frac{1}{4}$ pint court-bouillon (p. 71) and a $\frac{1}{4}$ pint milk; 2 tablespoons freshly chopped parsley; made mustard; grated cheese.

Cut the lobster in half lengthwise, remove all the meat and break into small pieces. Add the parsley to the hot cheese sauce and then use just sufficient of the sauce to bind the meat together. Spread the empty shells with mustard, fill with the lobster mixture, coat with the rest of the sauce, sprinkle with grated cheese and put under a hot grill until golden brown.

SECTION IV

Meat, Poultry and Game

For those who have to prepare the meals, meat dishes are probably the most important part of the daily cooking as they provide the family with the bulk of the protein, body-building elements which are a must in everyone's diet. If we could afford it, it would be nice to live all the time on roast meat, juicy steaks, fresh young chickens, but most household budgets cannot run to this and besides, 'variety is the spice of life' and never more so than when it is applied to cookery and it is here that your pressure cooker is going to be invaluable. The cheaper cuts and joints can be made into an endless selection of dishes and remember that these cuts are often more flavourful and nutritious than many of the more expensive ones. Busy housewives with families or the career-housewife may be tempted to spend more than the household budget can really stand because of the time required in ordinary cooking to tenderise these economical meats and the less tender chickens, but now you and your family are going to be able to enjoy a full quota of this essential food at a price you can afford; pot roasts, braises, stews in a wide selection of appetising dishes full of flavour and goodness, fork-tender with rich gravy and with a saving of cooking time and cooking fuel which means that your pressure cooker is going to pay for itself over and over again in the years ahead.

Before going on to the time-tables and recipes, here are just a few general points to note with regard to meat pressure cookery, particularly if you are going to adapt a favourite recipe from ordinary cooking methods and times:

Smaller cuts, such as chops, fillets and meat for stewing and braising should have as much fat as possible trimmed off before cooking.

Tougher and cheaper cuts which normally take 3 to 4 hours will require approximately one-seventh of the usual time.

Pot-roasts, boiling joints, chickens normally timed 20 to 30 minutes per pound + 20 minutes over will require no more than 10 to 12 minutes per pound.

If frozen meats are used, be sure to allow them to thaw completely and then treat them as the fresh meats in the following recipes.

It is important not to overcook meats in the pressure cooker. Each additional minute at pressure is equal to about 10 minutes in the ordinary way and will not always mean that the meat will be better cooked. The protein fibres in fact, can reach a point in all cooking where continued exposure to heat makes for a hard, stringy result instead of the done-to-a-turn, easily eaten and digested texture which we all look for in a meat dish.

As pressure cooking times are so short, meat cookery can be done with a minimum of liquid which means that none of the meat juices are wasted. Whether from a pot-roast, casserole, braise or stew the gravy will be rich and concentrated and, to ensure the correct consistency, it is best to thicken after the cooking either by the addition of thickening agents or reducing the liquor by boiling rapidly in the open pan.

The most usual thickening agent is flour and the average proportion would be 1 tablespoon to each pint of liquid. The new super-sifted flours are very easy to blend with water, stock, a little of the cooled cooking liquid or milk but for others, the easiest way is to keep a small screw-top jar or covered plastic cup for the purpose, putting a little of the liquid in the jar first, measuring in the flour, screwing on the top and then shaking vigorously.

When cut-up meats are to be floured before cooking, a good tip is to do this in a paper bag. Put in a couple of tablespoons of flour, a shake of salt and pepper, then the meat a little at a time and toss well. Any flour left over will go towards the thickening to be added at the end of the cooking.

Pressure cooked meat recipes must always include a liquid which, when boiled, will turn into the steam necessary to build up pressure. This may be stock or dissolved stock cubes, bought or home-made soups, thin gravy and sauces or cider, beer or any variety of wines.

As the sample recipes given show, the meat may be cooked in just sufficient liquid for the portions to be served as for stews, with a minimum quantity of liquid under the trivet as for pot-roasts or with the cooker half full of liquid as when boiling hams or for Silverside of Beef.

When stewing, braising, casseroling, the root vegetables used for flavouring can be given the same pressure cooking time as the meat but accompanying vegetables, such as potatoes and all varieties of green vegetables, should be added towards the end of the cooking time for the meat so that all will be ready to serve together. Whether this can all be done together will depend on whether there is enough space in the cooker so that it is not over-filled and whether getting the vegetables in and out is a reasonably easy proposition. If it is not, then there is little loss of time and hardly any extra work in giving the meat its full time and cooking the accompanying vegetables separately while the meat is kept hot.

To retain as much as possible of the meat juices, flavour and goodness, many of the following recipes recommend that the seasoned or floured meat be browned first in hot fat. This is known as searing and may be done lightly as with veal, to no more than seal the outside surface of the meat or continue until the meat is well-browned and, when onions included in the recipe are fried too, to give the finished dish the rich brown colour which will make it so appetising when brought to table. This preliminary browning is always done in the open cooker, without the trivet and any surplus fat is afterwards drained off.

The liquid required for the pressure cooking should be added hot or if cold, the cooker should be allowed to cool before it is put in otherwise too much may be lost in steam as the cold liquid is poured into the hot pan and then there will not be enough left to last the cooking time. This can mean that the cooker will boil dry, spoiling the food and perhaps distorting the cooker base.

It is never a good idea to try and cook too large a joint or chicken in your pressure cooker. Better and more accurate results are obtained if the weight is kept below 3 lb in the larger cookers with proportionally smaller joints according to the cooker size, as this allows plenty of room for the steam to circulate to the centre of the joint to ensure even cooking right through.

A variation in cooking times is given in most of the recipes and a little experience will soon enable you to judge what is necessary to obtain the degree of 'doneness' that you and your family prefer. It will be obvious that the quality of the meat, its weight, size, thickness and the proportions of lean, fat and bone are all factors to be considered when gauging the pressure cooking time. As a general rule for cut-up meats, a coarser meat will take longer to tenderise than a finer one; the larger the amount of fat and the smaller the proportion of bone in a joint, the more minutes per pound will be required.

The suggested quantities given in the following recipes are for an average family of four. If more or less is to be cooked remember that when the meat is cut up into cubes, even-sized pieces or joints or is minced, the pressure cooking time will remain the same; with joints which are timed by the pound the adjustment will be for longer or shorter pressure cooking according to the weight of the piece.

A summary time-table for meats can be found on p. 304 where you can check the cooking times, at a glance, should you be trying out a recipe of your own. Use **High** (15 lb) pressure.

BEEF

POT-ROAST

POT-ROASTED

Suitable joints: rump, topside, brisket, rolled rib.

Pressure Cooking Time: 12–15 minutes per pound

A suitable joint weighing not more than 3 lb; a little fat for browning; seasoning; hot water, stock, thin gravy or dissolved stock cube; 1–1½ tablespoons flour in a little liquid for thickening.

Trim the meat, removing any surplus fat, wipe with a damp cloth, tie or skewer firmly into shape, weigh and decide the cooking time. Lift the trivet from the cooker, heat the fat in the open pan and carefully brown the meat all over. Do not use a fork when turning the joint and be sure not to over-brown; letting the outside get too hard will mean that the steam cannot penetrate and the centre may remain underdone. Lift out the meat and dust it all over with plenty of salt and pepper. Strain the fat from the cooker, put in the hot liquid (or if cold, allow the cooker to cool) and stir well to lift from the bottom any 'browness' from the frying, as this will give colour to the gravy. The amount of liquid added will depend on the cooking time but must not be less than ½ pint. This amount will be sufficient for 1 lb of meat at 12 to 15 minutes per pound; an extra ¼ pint will then be required if the joint weighs up to 2 lb and a further ¼ pint if up to 3 lb. It will not matter if this comes above the trivet; the preliminary browning will have 'sealed' the meat so that it does not absorb the liquid.

Put in the trivet and joint, bring to pressure in the usual way, cook for the required time and reduce the pressure with cold water. Lift out the joint and keep hot. Remove the trivet, add the thickening, return the pan to the stove, stir until boiling, taste to correct the seasoning and cook for 2 to 3 minutes.

A little gravy browning should be added if necessary.

If it is practical and there is sufficient room around and above the joint, accompanying vegetables such as potatoes and carrots or green vegetables can be added 4 to 5 minutes before the cooking time of the meat is up. Lift the cooker from the heat, reduce the pressure with cold water, put in the vegetables, bring the cooker to pressure again in the usual way and continue the cooking. In this way, the meat will have had its full time, the vegetables their correct time and all will be ready to serve together. The liquid too will make a delicious gravy as it will combine both the meat and vegetable juices.

Extra flavour and colour can be added by browning a sliced onion in the fat after the meat has been lifted out and leaving it in the liquid under the trivet during the cooking, straining it out or leaving it, to serve in the gravy. Pot-roasted meat makes a delicious cold joint with salad and is an excellent method of quickly preparing meat for sandwiches, rolls, etc, for picnics and outdoor occasions.

BEEF À LA MODE

Pressure Cooking Time: 12–15 minutes per pound

A suitable joint such as topside or round weighing not more than 3 lb; a marinade made from $\frac{1}{4}$ pint of red wine, 2 tablespoons vinegar, 1 tablespoon olive oil, a crushed clove of garlic, a medium sliced onion, a few peppercorns, a bay leaf, a pinch of thyme or mixed herbs, salt and pepper; 2 tablespoons butter or some fatty rinds of bacon; enough young carrots and small onions to form a 'bed' on which to stand the joint; not less than $\frac{1}{2}$ pint liquid for the cooker.

Mix together the ingredients for the marinade and put into as small and deep a dish as will take the joint. Trim, wipe and weigh the meat and put to marinate the evening before the dish is to be cooked, covering with a clean tea-towel. The next morning, turn the joint over in the marinade. When ready to start cooking lift out the meat and dry it well, then brown with the onions as given in the preceding recipe, drain off the fat, strain the liquid from the marinade and put into the cooled cooker with the carrots and onions. Make up the liquid with equal quantities of water and vinegar until it just shows through the top of the vegetables, then stand in the meat. Bring to pressure in the usual way, cook for the required time and reduce the pressure with cold water. Lift out the meat and keep hot. The vegetables lifted from the liquid can be served around the meat or separately. Boil the liquid in the open pan until reduced by half, taking care that it does not burn, taste to correct seasoning and hand round separately.

It is sometimes easier to carve this joint before taking it to table. Lay the slices overlapping on the serving dish, then pour the sauce over them.

STUFFED BEEF

Pressure Cooking Time: 15 minutes per pound

A piece of round or topside weighing not more than 3 lb, and shaped into a long roll; 3 medium onions, 3 slices of streaky bacon, 2 tablespoons of freshly chopped parsley, a good pinch of mixed meat herbs, 1 beaten egg, for the stuffing; seasoning; liquid to just cover the trivet but not less than $\frac{1}{2}$ pint.

Trim and wipe the meat and make deep cuts along its length about $\frac{1}{2}$ inch apart and three-quarters of the way through. In a frying pan, gently heat the chopped bacon so that the fat runs out and it is crisp, then fry the chopped onions until golden brown. Mix with the rest of the ingredients, add sufficient egg to bind the mixture, fill this stuffing into the cuts, tie the meat securely as if it were a parcel and weigh it. Continue as given for the Pot-roast but lifting the joint when cooked, on to an ovenproof dish, basting with a little hot fat as for a roast joint and putting it on the second shelf of an oven heated to Gas No 5, 375° F, while the accompanying vegetables are being cooked.

BOILED

BOILED BEEF WITH DUMPLINGS

Pressure Cooking Time: 15 minutes per pound

Joint of salted silverside weighing not more than 3 lb; water for the cooking; medium carrots and onions; bouquet garni; $\frac{1}{2}$ lb self-raising flour + $\frac{1}{2}$ teaspoon baking powder, $\frac{1}{2}$ teaspoon salt, 3 oz shredded suet, cold water to mix, for dumplings.

Trim, wipe and weigh the meat, put into the cooker without the trivet. Cover with water, bring to the boil, lift out and throw this water away. (This is instead of leaving to soak overnight.) Put the joint back and add sufficient water to half fill the cooker. Bring to pressure in the usual way, cook for all but 5 minutes of the cooking time, reduce the pressure with cold water. During the cooking, prepare the carrots which should be neatly trimmed and shaped to an even size, and the onions. Add these to the cooker, bring to pressure again, cook for a further 5 minutes, reduce pressure with cold water. During this cooking make the dumplings by sieving the flour, baking powder and salt, mixing in the suet and forming into an elastic dough with cold water. With well-floured hands, make this into eight even-sized dumplings. Return the cooker to the heat and when the liquid is again boiling drop in the dumplings, just lay the lid on top or cover with a plate and boil gently for 10 minutes.

Serve at once, lifting the meat, vegetables and dumplings on to a large serving dish. Pour a little of the liquor over and hand more separately.

A parsley or mustard sauce can be served with this dish made with three-quarters of the milk and a quarter of the cooking liquid from which the fat should first be removed by drawing pieces of absorbent paper across the surface.

As a change from dumplings, the Split Pea Purée makes an excellent accompaniment for Boiled Beef.

BOILED BEEF WITH VEGETABLES

Pressure Cooking Time: 12 minutes per pound

Joint of fresh brisket weighing not more than 3 lb; water for the cooking; medium potatoes, onions and carrots, a quartered medium cabbage, for serving; $\frac{1}{2}$ pint of mustard or onion sauce (see note below).

Trim, wipe and weigh the meat, prepare vegetables leaving the onions whole and cutting the carrots and potatoes to a size to cook in 5 minutes. Lift out the trivet, put in the joint and sufficient water to half fill the cooker, adding plenty of salt. Bring to pressure in the usual way, cook for all but 5 minutes of the required time, reduce the pressure with cold water. Take out $\frac{1}{4}$ pint of the liquid and return the pan to the heat, reboil, then put in the potatoes, onions, carrots and the quartered cabbage. Bring to pressure again, cook for a further 5 minutes and reduce the pressure with cold water. During this cooking make the mustard sauce using half milk and half cooking liquid. Taste and correct the seasoning and keep hot. Serve the meat, either in the joint or as overlapping slices, arrange vegetables around and pour a little of the cooking liquid over. Hand the sauce separately.

If onion sauce is preferred, put two large onions trimmed and well-washed but with the skins still on, in with the meat. Lift these out after the first cooking, skin, chop and add to the sauce made with half milk and half cooking liquid.

BRAISED

This is a method of cooking meat so that the food is not actually in the liquid but resting on a bed of vegetables, known as mirepoix (p. 300). It is suitable for the cheaper pieces of beef, such as buttock, skirt or chuck steak, usually cut ready into individual portions; for a joint such as topside, for liver and kidneys.

BRAISED STEAK

Pressure Cooking Time: 10 minutes

4 pieces of chuck or other braising steak; 1 tablespoon of dripping; 1 slice of streaky bacon, 1 large onion, carrot and turnip, 1 stick of celery, bouquet garni, seasoning, for mirepoix; potatoes, carrots or separate vegetables if wanted; stock for the cooker; chopped parsley for garnish; sauce to choice.

Trim, wipe meat and toss in seasoned flour, shaking well to remove any surplus. Slice the onion and roughly cut the other vegetables; prepare the potatoes and carrots for serving separately, leaving whole unless very large, when cut in half. Lift out the trivet and in the open cooker heat the dripping, fry the meat quickly until well browned on both sides and lift out. Put in the bacon and onions, fry in the same way; lift the cooker from the heat, add a $\frac{1}{4}$ pint hot stock (if added cold, allow the cooker to cool) and stir until there are no 'browny' bits left sticking to the base of the pan; put in the rest of the vegetables and add more stock just to show through them. Put back the meat and then if cooking separate vegetables, the trivet, and the potatoes and carrots in separate piles. Bring to pressure in the usual way, cook for 10 minutes and reduce the pressure with cold water.

Lift out the vegetables, sprinkle with parsley; lift out the trivet, serve the steak and keep hot. The mirepoix vegetables, after removing the bacon and bouquet garni, may be thoroughly mashed in the cooker, tasted and seasoning corrected and a little browning be added if necessary and then served as an accompanying sauce.

Otherwise, use the strained stock to make a Brown Gravy Sauce (p. 292).

BEEF BOURGUIGNON

Pressure Cooking Time: 10 minutes

4 portions of braising beef; $\frac{1}{2}$ pint red wine (or $\frac{1}{4}$ pint wine, $\frac{1}{4}$ pint brown stock); bacon fat; 3 sliced onions; a crushed clove of garlic; bouquet garni; $\frac{1}{4}$ lb (or a small tin) of button mushrooms; seasoning; chopped parsley.

Trim, wipe the meat and toss in seasoned flour. Lift the trivet from the cooker, put in some pieces of bacon fat and heat until the fat runs out. Quickly brown the meat on both sides, lift out and brown the sliced onions until dark but not burnt. Lift the cooker from the heat, add the hot water (or if cold allow the cooker to cool) and stir well to lift any 'brown' bits from the bottom. Put in the meat, add the wine, return the cooker to the heat and when boiling put in the crushed garlic, the bouquet garni and seasoning. Bring to pressure in the usual way, cook for 10 minutes and reduce the pressure with cold water. During the cooking, slice the prepared mushrooms very finely and fry lightly in a little butter. Remove the bouquet garni, serve the meat and onions into a casserole dish, cover with a layer of mushrooms and keep hot. Thicken the sauce with a little blended flour or reduce it by boiling rapidly, without burning, in the open pan. Taste and correct seasoning and pour into the casserole. Garnish with the chopped parsley.

BEEF OLIVES

Pressure Cooking Time: 15 minutes

1–1¼ lb rump or good lean stewing steak cut about ¼ inch thick; stuffing made from 1 tablespoon of breadcrumbs, 1 level tablespoon suet, 1 teaspoon chopped parsley, a pinch of mixed herbs, seasoning and a little egg or milk to bind or 4 tablespoons of made-up packet stuffing; 1 tablespoon dripping; mirepoix (see recipe, p. 300); stock for the cooker; ½ pint Brown Gravy or Tomato Sauce (p. 292).

Wipe, trim meat and cut into long strips about 3 inches wide. Sprinkle each with a little salt and pepper, spread with the made stuffing not taking it too close to the edges. Roll and secure tightly by tying each with a piece of cotton or using half a cocktail stick. Continue the cooking and serving as for Braised Steak, p. 90. With this dish, it would be better to cook the accompanying vegetables separately while keeping the Beef Olives hot and during this cooking, the sauce could be finished off in another pan.

For a really different flavour to this dish, instead of using stuffing as above, roll each strip of beef around a thin slice of streaky bacon and a halved, stoned, cooked prune.

BEEF ROLL WITH VEGETABLES

Pressure Cooking Time: 20 minutes and 5 minutes

1½ lb. fresh or cooked minced beef, 6 oz sausage meat, 3 tablespoons fresh white breadcrumbs, 2 medium onions, a good shake of Worcester Sauce, 1 tablespoon chopped parsley, pinch of mixed herbs, 1 egg, a little brown stock or meat extract for the roll; a little milk and golden breadcrumbs; 2 tablespoons dripping; ½ pint brown stock for the cooker; flour for thickening and a little gravy colouring; potatoes, carrots, green vegetables to choice.

Mix all the ingredients together in a large bowl, binding with the beaten egg and sufficient stock to give a firm, solid texture. Moisten the outside by brushing over with milk and rolling in golden breadcrumbs. Lift the trivet from the cooker, heat the fat and very carefully brown the roll on all sides. Lift out and tie loosely in a double thickness of greaseproof paper. Add the boiling stock (if cold, allow cooker to cool) stir well to remove any brown bits from the bottom, put back the trivet and the parcelled roll, bring to pressure in the usual way, cook for 20 minutes and allow the pressure to reduce at room temperature. During the cooking, preheat the oven to Gas No 5, 375 ° F and set a shelf towards the top. Prepare the accompanying vegetables. Lift out the roll, unwrap, put on a baking sheet and into oven. Now cook the vegetables and serve. Lift out the trivet, add the thickening and colouring, reboil, taste and correct seasoning and pour the sauce over the roll or hand separately.

BRAISED OXTAIL

Pressure Cooking Time: 40 minutes

1 oxtail; 2–3 large onions; 2 tablespoons dripping or other fat; 2–3 large carrots; bouquet garni; seasoning; 1 pint brown stock or water; 2 heaped tablespoons flour with a little cold water for blending; 1 small glass dry red wine or port (optional); 1 dessertspoon redcurrant jelly.

Wipe the joints, trim off any surplus fat and season with salt and pepper. Lift the trivet from the cooker, melt the fat and when hot fry the sliced onions until golden brown, lift out, then brown the ox-tail joints evenly all over. Strain off any fat left, put in the hot liquid (if added cold, allow the cooker to cool), the onions, the carrots cut into slices or lengths and the bouquet garni. Bring to pressure in the usual way, cook for 40 minutes and reduce the pressure with cold water. Lift the joints on to a serving dish, strain the stock, put the vegetables and the meat in a low oven to keep hot. Return the stock to the cooker, add the blended flour and stirring all the time cook for 2 to 3 minutes. Add the wine and the redcurrant jelly, taste and correct seasoning, pour the sauce over the meat and garnish with the carrots.

As Oxtail can be rather fatty, it may be found better to prepare and pressure cook it the previous day. The meat and vegetables should be lifted from the strained stock which should be stored in a deep bowl and all the fat be removed from it before the second cooking. Return the meat and stock to the cooker, bring to pressure and allow to reduce at room temperature. Continue as above.

For an extra nourishing meal, small haricot beans can be served with Oxtail. After 20 minutes cooking, reduce the pressure with cold water, add 4 oz of prepared beans and a further $\frac{1}{2}$ pint of water or stock and pressure cook for the last 20 minutes. Continue as before.

BRAISED TONGUE

Pressure Cooking Time: 15 minutes per pound if fresh;
20 minutes per pound if smoked

1 ox-tongue; 1 onion stuck with 2 cloves; 1 carrot; 2 sticks of celery; 1 small turnip; a bay leaf; sprig of parsley; a few peppercorns; water according to cooking time; seasoning; gravy or Madeira Sauce (p. 292).

Soak the tongue for 2 hours in cold water. Weigh and decide on cooking time (it will be easier to handle if loosely tied in a piece of butter muslin). Lift the trivet from the cooker, put in the tongue, add sufficient water to cover, bring to the boil in the open pan and throw the water away. Put back the tongue, all the ingredients including salt if the tongue is fresh, and the water. Bring to pressure in the usual way, cook for the required time and allow the pressure to reduce at room temperature. During the cooking, prepare a thick gravy or Madeira Sauce which can later be thinned with some of the cooking liquid. Lift out the tongue, carefully remove the skin and all the bones and cut into thick slices overlapping these on an oval serving dish and put in oven. Strain the stock and add sufficient to the sauce to give a rich, coating consistency. Taste and correct seasoning, pour over the tongue and serve piping hot.

A delicious accompaniment for this dish would be a quartered green cabbage and some whole young carrots pressure cooked for 5 minutes without the trivet and in $\frac{1}{2}$ pint of the cooking stock; this could be done while boning and skinning the tongue and finishing off the sauce. These, well-strained, should then garnish the dish.

For a Smoked Tongue, soak overnight in cold water. Add two tablespoons of vinegar but no salt to the cooking water and after pressure has been reduced, boil the liquid rapidly in the open pan for 2 to 3 minutes. Use a little of this concentrated stock to thin down some horseradish sauce, bring to the boil, stir in a tablespoon of cream and hand round separately.

STEWED

It is usual to allow 6 oz raw meat per person and 1 pint sauce or gravy per lb.

BEEF STEW WITH VEGETABLES

Pressure Cooking Time: 15–20 minutes

$1\frac{1}{2}$ lb stewing steak such as skirt, shin, flank, chuck; a selection of seasonable vegetables including onions, carrots, a little turnip, swede, parsnip, some sticks of celery, etc; dripping or fat for frying; bouquet garni or a good pinch of meat herbs; 1 pint of hot stock or water; seasoning.

Wipe meat, trim off fat, cut into 1-inch cubes and toss in seasoned flour, shaking well to remove any surplus; prepare the vegetables and cut into neat 1-inch cubes or pieces. Lift the trivet from the cooker, heat about two tablespoons of fat and when hot fry the onions until a good brown colour but not burnt. Lift out, then fry the meat keeping it moving to brown evenly all over. Lift the cooker from the heat, take out the meat and add the hot liquid (if cold, allow the cooker to cool), stir well until there are no 'browny' bits left on the bottom of the pan, put in the onions, meat, all the other vegetables, the bouquet garni and seasoning. Bring to pressure in the usual way, cook for the required time and reduce the pressure with cold water. During the cooking time, prepare the thickening and add this to the cooker returning to the heat and stirring until boiling, then cooking for a further 2 to 3 minutes. Remove the bouquet garni, taste and correct seasoning and serve piping hot.

If the meat and onions have been well-browned this stew should be a good colour, but browning can be added with the thickening if it is necessary or if it is preferred to cook the stew without browning the meat and onions first.

BEEF STROGONOFF

Pressure Cooking Time: 8 minutes

1 lb good chuck or rump steak; 2 tablespoons butter; 1 small onion, finely chopped; $\frac{1}{2}$ lb fresh button mushrooms; seasoning; $\frac{1}{4}$ pint good brown stock; a sprig of marjoram or half a bay leaf; seasoning; 2 tablespoons of cream (soured cream is excellent, if obtainable); hot potato crisps as accompaniment; chopped parsley as garnish.

Wipe, trim the steak and cut across the grain into lengths which should be the width of a thick shoe-lace. Wash the mushrooms and slice finely lengthwise without removing the stalks. Lift the trivet from the cooker, heat the butter, brown the meat and onion quickly and evenly. Lift the cooker from the heat, add the hot liquid (or if added cold, allow the cooker to cool), the seasonings and the mushrooms, stirring well. Bring to pressure in the usual way, cook for 8 minutes and allow the pressure to reduce at room temperature. During the cooking, preheat the oven at Gas No 3, 325° F, and put the crisps in to warm at the bottom. Serve the meat and vegetables into an ovenproof dish and keep hot. Boil the liquid rapidly in the open pan until reduced and thickening, taste and correct seasoning, add cream and immediately pour over the meat. Serve garnished with chopped parsley and hand the potato crisps separately.

When serving this dish for a special occasion, the meat may first be left to marinate as for Beef à la Mode (p. 87), the strained liquid being used for the cooking.

CURRIES

Everyone has their own ideas, it seems, on how to make a good curry and certainly there are many varieties of this dish, depending on the country and even region of its origin. Here is given a standard recipe, one which can of course be altered and varied; added to perhaps if there is a particular flavour or ingredient which is a family favourite or changed if all the ingredients suggested are not available. Again, the 'hotness' of the curry is a matter for the individual and careful attention should be given to tasting to correct for this, during the cooking and before serving.

BASIC SAUCE FOR CURRIES

This quantity will be sufficient for 1 lb of fresh meat, a jointed chicken, etc.

2 tablespoons of coconut and ¾ pint good white stock: 2 tablespoons butter: 1 medium onion: 1 small crisp apple: 1 dessertspoon each flour, curry powder: 1 tablespoon mango chutney: 1 teaspoon lemon juice: 1 teaspoon red jelly or jam: seasoning.

FRESH BEEF CURRY

Pressure Cooking Time: 15–20 minutes

1 lb steak; 1 teacup savoury rice and 1 teacup of hot, salted water.

Put the coconut in a small basin, pour over the boiling stock, cover and leave to infuse for at least half an hour. Wipe, trim the meat and cut into 1-inch cubes. Chop the onion and apple finely. When the coconut is ready, strain off the stock. Lift the trivet from the cooker, heat the butter, lightly fry the meat and lift out. Put in the onion and apple and fry gently but without browning for about 10 minutes. Add the flour and curry powder and fry again for a few minutes. Away from the heat, add the chutney and stock, stirring to make sure no bits have been left on the bottom of the pan. Return to the heat and when boiling, add the meat, bring to pressure in the usual way, cook for 10 minutes and reduce the pressure with cold water. Stir the curry and if getting too thick add a little more hot stock. Put in the trivet and a solid container with the rice and water covered with a piece of greaseproof paper. Bring to pressure again, cook for the last 5 minutes and allow the pressure to reduce at room temperature. During this cooking, preheat the oven to Gas No 4, 350° F, and put into the bottom the ovenproof dish on which you will serve the rice. Have ready a kettle of boiling water. Lift out the rice, tip it into a colander, pour over the boiling water and shake to separate the grains. Pile into the serving dish, turn off the oven, and leave the rice on the centre shelf to dry off. Lift out the trivet, stir the curry, add the strained lemon juice and jelly, reboil, taste and correct seasoning and serve piping hot, handing the rice separately.

If a curry is to be made with cooked meat, make the sauce and put in the rice as above, bring to pressure in the usual way, cook for 5 minutes and reduce the pressure at room temperature. Lift out the rice, stir the sauce, add more stock if necessary. Put in the diced, cooked meat, bring to pressure again, remove from the heat and allow the pressure to reduce at room temperature. During this time, finish the rice as in previous recipe, then add the last of the ingredients to the curry before serving.

Other suitable foods for currying are fresh lamb—cooked as for beef—prawns, hard-boiled eggs, cooked or tinned cocktail sausages, bananas halved lengthways, reheated in the Curry Sauce.

GOURMET MEAT LOAF

Pressure Cooking Time: 25 minutes

$\frac{1}{2}$ lb each of fresh, finely minced beef, veal and pork; 4 tablespoons fresh white crumbs; 1 medium onion; 2 tablespoons butter; 2 tablespoons milk; 2 tablespoons red wine; 1 crushed clove of garlic (optional); salt and pepper; pinch of mixed spice; $\frac{1}{2}$ teaspoon each of crushed mace, thyme and bay leaves; 1 large egg; 2 tablespoons dripping or fat; 1 pint hot water for cooker; $\frac{1}{2}$ pint rich brown gravy or tomato sauce as accompaniment (p. 292).

Wipe and trim all fat from the meat and mince finely. Prepare the breadcrumbs, dice the onion finely. Melt the butter in a small saucepan and simmer the onion until transparent but do not allow to colour. Add the milk and breadcrumbs, cook for a moment or two, then add the wine. Combine with the meats, seasonings, herbs and beaten egg, then shape into a thick roll that will fit into the cooker, with floured hands. Lift the trivet from the cooker, heat the fat, carefully brown the loaf all over, lift out and tie in a triple thickness of greaseproof paper which should be pleated once to allow for expansion. Drain out the fat, put in the water, the trivet and the loaf. Bring to pressure in the usual way, cook for 25 minutes and reduce the pressure with cold water. If accompanying vegetables are to be pressure cooked pre-heat the oven to Gas No 3, 325° F, lift the loaf on to a greased baking sheet and keep hot. Use $\frac{1}{2}$ pint of the cooking water for the vegetables and add this stock to the gravy or tomato sauce before pouring round the loaf on the serving dish.

This Gourmet Loaf is excellent cold. Roll in golden crumbs while still hot, chill, then serve, sliced, garnished with sliced tomatoes and cucumber and quartered hard-boiled eggs. A potato salad with chopped chives added will make a delicious accompaniment.

LANCASHIRE HOT POT

Pressure Cooking Time: 12 minutes

1 lb of good, lean stewing steak; $1\frac{3}{4}$ lb potatoes; $\frac{3}{4}$ lb large onions; seasoning; 2 tablespoons dripping or fat; $\frac{1}{2}$ pint good brown or vegetable stock with a little browning added for colour; chopped parsley for garnishing.

Wipe, trim the meat, season and cut into neat pieces about $\frac{1}{2}$ inch square; slice the prepared onions and potatoes thickly. Lift the trivet from the cooker, heat the fat and quickly brown the meat evenly all over. Lift out and strain away the fat. Put in the hot liquid (if added cold allow the cooker to cool), then the meat, onions and potatoes in layers, well seasoned and with potatoes as the last layer. Bring to pressure in the usual way, cook for 12 minutes and allow the pressure to reduce at room temperature. During the cooking, preheat the grill and prepare a little blended flour for thickening then carefully transfer the Hot Pot to an ovenproof casserole or dish keeping the potato layer at the top. Add the thickening to the stock in the cooker, boil well to cook and pour down the side of the dish. Dot the top with knobs of butter and leave under the grill until golden brown. Garnish with chopped parsley.

To make a delicious change of flavour to this appetising and nourishing dish, white stock, vegetable or plain water to which tomato juice or purée is added can be used instead; a bay leaf should be put in the middle layer and lifted out during the transfer to the serving dish.

SAVOURY MEAT BALLS WITH SPAGHETTI

Pressure Cooking Time: 16 minutes

$\frac{3}{4}$ lb minced lean beef; 4 tablespoons rice; 1 medium onion; 1 egg; seasoning; 1 tablespoon chopped parsley; 1 pint liquid made up from tomato purée or soup and water; 1 tablespoon Worcester Sauce; 1 bay leaf; 6 oz spaghetti; $\frac{1}{4}$ pint boiling water, if necessary.

Mix together the beef, finely chopped onion, half the washed rice, the parsley and seasoning, bind with the beaten egg and form into eight balls, shaping carefully with well-floured hands. Lastly press each ball firmly into the rest of the rice to give a 'prickly' appearance. Lift the trivet from the cooker, put in the liquid, sauce and bay leaf and bring to the boil in the open pan. Drop in the meat balls, bring to pressure in the usual way, cook for 10 minutes, reduce the pressure with cold water.

During the cooking time, preheat the oven to Gas No 2, 300° F, and prepare the spaghetti. Lift the meat balls on to a large deep serving dish and keep hot. Add the water to the sauce in the cooker, stir well, bring to the boil, add the spaghetti. Bring to pressure in the usual way, cook for 6 minutes, reduce pressure with cold water. With a straining spoon or tongs, lift out the spaghetti and serve around the meat balls. Reboil the sauce, taste and correct seasoning and pour into the dish. If tomato purée has been used, a teaspoon of sugar may be added to the sauce before serving. As an additional flavour, 2 tablespoons of diced apple may be added with the tomato liquid.

SAVOURY MINCE

Pressure Cooking Time: 7 minutes

1 lb fresh minced beef; 2 tablespoons dripping or fat; 1 large onion; 1 large carrot; 2 medium tomatoes; seasoning; $\frac{1}{2}$ pint thin gravy or stock; flour for thickening; gravy colouring if necessary; 2 slices of toast and chopped parsley for garnish.

Season the meat well with salt and pepper. Slice the onion, dice the carrot finely, skin and slice tomatoes. Lift the trivet from the cooker, heat the fat and brown the meat evenly stirring frequently. Lift out, fry the vegetables, take these out and strain off the fat. Put in the liquid, return to heat and boil, stirring to remove any brown bits from the bottom of the pan. Put back the meat and vegetables, bring to pressure in the usual way, cook for 7 minutes and reduce the pressure with cold water. During this cooking, make the toast. Add the blended flour and colouring to the mince, stir until boiling and allow to cook for 2 to 3 minutes. Put into the serving dish and garnish with the triangles of toast and chopped parsley.

If fresh vegetables are not available or you are in even more of a hurry than usual, a packet of frozen mixed vegetables would do instead. If used unfrozen, only $\frac{1}{4}$ pint of liquid will be needed as they will supply the extra as they thaw out.

SWISS STEAK

Pressure Cooking Time: 15 minutes

4 portions of rump or good, lean stewing steak about 1 inch thick; 2 tablespoons dripping or fat; 1 diced onion; 2 large, firm tomatoes; $\frac{1}{4}$ pint tomato juice or 2 tablespoons tomato purée dissolved in $\frac{1}{4}$ pint water; potatoes, carrots (frozen or fresh peas, in perforated container if space allows), to serve separately; chopped parsley for garnish.

Wipe, trim the meat and toss in seasoned flour, shaking well to remove any surplus. Skin the tomatoes, cut into rough pieces, mix with the diced onion and season well. Lift the trivet from the cooker, heat the fat and fry the meat quickly until golden brown all over. Take the cooker from the heat, lift out the meat, add the hot liquid (if cold, allow the cooker to cool) and stir well until any brown bits have been lifted off the bottom of the cooker. Put in the meat, then on each piece pile some of the onion and tomato mixture. Bring to pressure in the usual way, cook for 10 minutes and reduce the pressure with cold water. During the cooking, prepare the potatoes and carrots to cook in 4 minutes. Cover the meat well with a piece of buttered greaseproof paper, put in the trivet, the salted potatoes and carrots, and if peas are to be added, allow the pan to fill with steam before putting them in. Bring to pressure again and cook for the last 5 minutes. Serve the vegetables and keep hot. Lift the meat into a deep serving dish and keep hot. Reduce the liquid in the cooker by boiling rapidly in the open pan, taste and correct seasoning, then pour round the meat, garnishing with a few of the peas or some chopped parsley.

TRIPE AND ONIONS

Pressure Cooking Time: 15 minutes

$1\frac{1}{2}$–2 lb blanched tripe, as prepared by the butcher; 4–5 medium onions; seasoning; water; 1 tablespoon flour; $\frac{1}{4}$ pint milk; fried croûtons (p. 298) and chopped parsley for garnish.

Cut the tripe in $1\frac{1}{2}$-inch pieces. Lift the trivet from the cooker, put in the tripe and sufficient water to cover. Bring just to the boil in the open cooker and throw the water away. Add the onions, left whole, the seasoning and sufficient cold water just to cover. Bring to pressure in the usual way, cook for 15 minutes and allow the pressure to reduce at room temperature. Strain off the liquid. Blend the flour with a little of the milk and a tablespoon of hot stock, add to the cooker with the rest of the milk, then return to the heat and stirring all the time, bring to the boil and allow to cook for 2–3 minutes. Taste and correct seasoning and, if necessary, add more stock to give a pouring consistency. Serve piping hot, garnished with fried croûtons dipped in chopped parsley.

As variation, sliced carrots and mushroom stalks with a flavouring of crushed garlic may be added when this dish is called **Tripe à la Bourgeoise**.

VEAL

POT-ROASTED

STUFFED SHOULDER OF VEAL

Pressure Cooking Time: 12–14 minutes per pound

A boned shoulder of veal, weighing not more than 3 lb; a diced rasher of bacon, a tablespoon chopped parsley, 1 finely chopped onion, 4 tablespoons of fresh breadcrumbs, grated rind of $\frac{1}{2}$ lemon and 1 egg for the stuffing; 3 tablespoons of dripping, bacon or other fat; seasoning; white stock or a chicken cube dissolved in water for the cooking; 1 level tablespoon of flour blended with milk for thickening; gravy colouring.

Wipe, trim the meat, then lay flat with the boned surface upwards. Mix all the ingredients for the stuffing and bind together with the beaten egg. Spread evenly over the joint but not taking it too close to the outer edges. Roll the joint, tie securely with thin string or hold in position with short skewers and weigh. Rub the outside of the meat with salt and pepper and roll in flour. Lift the trivet from the cooker, heat the fat and carefully brown the joint all over. Lift out, drain away the fat, add the required amount of hot liquid (if added cold, allow the cooker to cool), return to the heat and bring to the boil stirring all the time, making sure that all the 'brown' bits are lifted from the bottom of the cooker. Put back the trivet and the meat, bring to pressure in the usual way, cook for the required time and reduce the pressure with cold water. Lift out the meat and keep hot. Lift out the trivet, reduce the liquid a little in the cooker by boiling rapidly in the open pan, lift from the heat and when cooled slightly add the thickening and colouring, reboil, taste to correct seasoning and hand separately.

VEAL NIÇOISE

Pressure Cooking Time: 12 minutes per pound

A piece of roasting veal such as fillet, loin, shoulder weighing not more than 3 lb; 2 tablespoons olive oil or dripping; 2 lb skinned tomatoes; 1 lb of small onions; a clove of garlic; a sprig or two of thyme, rosemary or other suitable herbs as available; seasoning; white stock or water as required.

Wipe and trim the meat, weigh, then rub all over with the garlic, salt and pepper. Lift the trivet from the cooker, heat the fat and brown the meat carefully all over. Lift out, drain away the fat, put in the required amount of liquid, the trivet and the meat, bring to pressure in the usual way, cook for all but 4 minutes of the cooking time and reduce the pressure with cold water. Lift out the meat and the trivet and strain out all but enough liquid to just cover the bottom of the cooker. Put in the whole onions, the seasonings, then the meat on top and the whole tomatoes around the joint. Bring to pressure again, cook for 4 minutes and allow the pressure to reduce at room temperature.

Lift out the meat, put the onions on to the serving dish with the meat on top and the tomatoes around, reboil the liquid, taste and correct the seasoning and either pour around the meat or hand separately.

This sauce should not be too thick, but it can be reduced by boiling rapidly in the open cooker or by cooking together 1 tablespoon of butter and 1 tablespoon of flour in a small saucepan without allowing to colour and then adding the liquid gradually for the required consistency and cooking for 2 to 3 minutes.

BOILED

KNUCKLE OF VEAL WITH RICE

Pressure Cooking Time: 10 minutes per pound

1 knuckle of veal, not more than 3 lb; 1 carrot; 1 turnip; 1 onion stuck with 4 cloves; bouquet garni; seasoning; water for the cooking; 4 oz rice; 1 pint of parsley sauce (p. 291); lemon quarters and bacon rolls (p. 297) for garnish.

Wipe, trim and weigh the meat. Peel and cut carrot and turnip into rough cubes; peel onion and stick with cloves. Lift the trivet from the cooker, put in the meat, vegetables, seasonings and enough water nearly to cover but not to fill the base more than half full. Bring to the boil in the open pan and skim well. Bring to pressure in the usual way, cook for all but 5 minutes of the required time, reduce the pressure with cold water. Lift out the vegetables, return the pan to the heat, bring to the boil, throw in the washed rice, bring to pressure and cook for the last 5 minutes. Allow the pressure to reduce at room temperature. During this cooking, make the parsley sauce but using only half the quantity of milk. Make the bacon rolls and leave under a low grill or in the warming oven. Lift the meat on to the serving dish, strain the rice (saving the stock) and put round the joint as a border. Keep hot. Use sufficient of the stock to give the sauce a thick, pouring consistency; taste and correct seasoning and hand separately. Garnish the rice with the bacon rolls and lemon quarters.

STUFFED VEAL ROLLS

Pressure Cooking Time: 12 minutes

1 lb lean veal cut into thin slices; $\frac{1}{4}$ lb sliced bacon; lemon juice and seasoning; 2 tablespoons butter; 1 medium sliced onion; a thin slice of lemon peel; bouquet garni; $\frac{1}{4}$ pint water, small glass of white wine or $\frac{1}{2}$ pint white stock; sprigs of parsley for garnish.

Wipe and trim the meat and cut into strips approximately 5 inches by 2 inches. Stretch each slice of bacon by drawing the back of a cook's knife along its length. Sprinkle the veal strips with lemon juice and seasoning, lay a piece of bacon on each, roll up and fix with a half cocktail stick or by tying with cotton, then toss in seasoned flour. Lift the trivet from the cooker, heat the butter, gently brown the rolls and onion and lift out. Add the hot liquid (if cold, allow the cooker to cool), return to the heat and stir, making sure that any 'brown' bits from the frying have been lifted from the bottom. Put back the rolls and onion; add the seasonings, bring to pressure in the usual way, cook for 12 minutes and reduce the pressure with cold water. Lift the rolls on to the serving dish, take out the sticks or remove the cotton and keep hot. Reduce the liquid by boiling rapidly in the open pan, taste and correct seasoning and strain over the veal rolls. Garnish with sprigs of parsley.

A variation of the sauce can be made by adding tomato purée to taste.

STEWED

VEAL BLANQUETTE

Pressure Cooking Time: 12 minutes

1 lb veal pieces; 1 small onion; a slice of lemon peel; seasoning; $\frac{1}{2}$ pint white sauce (p. 291); 2 tablespoons cream; 1 yolk of egg; $\frac{1}{2}$ pint white stock or water; chopped parsley, lemon quarters and bacon rolls (p. 297) for garnish.

Wipe and trim the meat and toss in plenty of salt and pepper. Lift the trivet from the cooker, put in the meat and sliced onion, add the liquid and seasonings, bring to pressure in the usual way, cook for 12 minutes and reduce the pressure with cold water. During the cooking, make a white sauce using only half the quantity of milk. Lift the meat into a deep serving dish, strain the stock and add sufficient to the sauce to give a rich, coating consistency. Reheat, taste and correct seasoning, add cream and egg and cook for a minute or two but without allowing it to boil or it will curdle. Pour over the veal and garnish with chopped parsley, bacon rolls and lemon quarters.

VEAL FRICASSE

Pressure Cooking Time: 12 minutes

1 lb veal pieces; 2 tablespoons butter; 4 baby carrots; 8 spring onions; 2 young turnips; 12 new potatoes; 1 teaspoon sugar; bouquet garni; seasoning; $\frac{1}{2}$ pint white stock or water; $\frac{1}{2}$ pint white sauce (p. 291); 2 tablespoons cream; chopped parsley for garnish.

Wipe and trim the meat and toss in plenty of salt and pepper. In a frying pan, heat the butter, lightly cook the meat, without browning, until sealed and lift out. Take the trivet from the cooker, put in the stock, the meat and seasonings, bring to pressure in the usual way, cook for 8 minutes and reduce the pressure with cold water. During the cooking, add the sugar to the butter, put in the peeled whole carrots, onions and potatoes and the turnips cut into neat pieces. Cook gently, shaking the pan often, so that the vegetables are softened and take on a glazed, light brown look. Add these to the cooker, bring to pressure again, cook for a further 4 minutes and reduce the pressure with cold water. During this cooking, make the sauce using only half the quantity of milk. Lift the meat and vegetables into a deep serving dish and keep hot. Use sufficient of the stock to give a rich, pouring consistency; reboil, taste and correct seasoning, add cream, pour over the meat and garnish with chopped parsley.

CALF'S HEAD

Pressure Cooking Time: 35 minutes

$\frac{1}{2}$ calf's head; small piece of collar or flank boiling bacon; a small carrot, onion, turnip, a squeeze of lemon juice; bay leaf; 1 pint of parsley sauce (p. 291); 1 pint of boiling water; seasoning; lemon quarters.

Wash the head, remove the brain and tongue, put the head into the cooker without the trivet, add sufficient water to cover and blanch by bringing to the boil in the open pan, then lift out the head and throw the water away. Put in the 1 pint of boiling water, the head, the piece of bacon and seasonings, bring to pressure in the usual way, cook for 25 minutes and reduce the pressure with cold water. During this cooking tie the brain and tongue in a piece of muslin, then add, together with the vegetables, into the cooker. (Before doing this, you may find it necessary to skim the surface of the liquid.) Bring to pressure again, cook for a further 10 minutes and reduce the pressure with cold water. During this cooking, make the parsley sauce, using only half the quantity of milk. The meat from the head may now be removed from the bones but carefully, so as to reassemble in the original shape or may be cut into small pieces. Put on to serving dish and keep hot. Lift out the brain and the piece of bacon, strain the stock and use sufficient to give the sauce a rich, coating consistency. Add the lemon juice, bring to the boil, taste and correct seasoning and pour over the meat. Garnish with the chopped brain and tongue, the bacon cut in slices and quarters of lemon.

CALF'S LIVER VILLAGEOIS

Pressure Cooking Time: 7 minutes

About $\frac{3}{4}$ lb of liver in as large pieces as possible; slices of lean bacon; $\frac{3}{4}$ lb baby carrots; $\frac{1}{4}$ pint of water or stock and $\frac{1}{4}$ pint white wine; a mirepoix (p. 300) seasoning; a knob of butter.

Wipe the liver, season well and make a number of small cuts in rows, in each piece. Cut the bacon slices into thin strips lengthways and put one into each cut in the liver. Lift the trivet from the cooker, prepare the mirepoix, adding liquid to come just to the top. Put in the liver, the trivet and the carrots, bring to pressure in the usual way, cook for 7 minutes and reduce the pressure with cold water. Lift out the carrots, the trivet and put the liver in the centre of a deep serving dish. Keep hot with the carrots. Strain off the liquid into a small saucepan, remove the fat by drawing pieces of soft paper across the surface, then boil rapidly until the sauce is reduced by half. Put in the knob of butter, pour over the liver, garnish with the carrots and serve piping hot.

SWEETBREADS

No matter in what recipe they are to be used, sweetbreads must always be precooked; they are then ready to be stewed, braised, fried and so on.

To precook

Wash the sweetbreads, put in a saucepan with sufficient water to cover and bring slowly to the boil. Plunge at once into cold salted water, adding a squeeze of lemon juice. Trim carefully, removing all the tubes and membranes. Press between two plates until cool. The sweetbreads are now ready to be used as required.

CREAMED SWEETBREADS

Pressure Cooking Time: 6 minutes

2 prepared sweetbreads; $\frac{1}{4}$ pint white stock; a small onion; 2 or 3 small carrots; a piece of lemon rind; a few peppercorns and a blade of mace; seasonings; 1 pint of white sauce (p. 291); 2 tablespoons cream; a squeeze of lemon juice; 2 tablespoons chopped cooked ham, 4 triangles of fried bread and lemon butterflies (p. 299) as garnish.

Lift the trivet from the cooker, put in the stock, sliced sweetbreads, the vegetables and seasonings, bring to pressure in the usual waay, cook for 6 minutes and allow the pressure to reduce at room temperature. During this cooking make the sauce, using only half the quantity of milk; fry the bread and cut into triangles. Lift the sweetbreads into a deep serving dish and pile chopped ham at each end. Keep hot. Strain the stock and add sufficient to the sauce to give a thick, coating consistency. Reheat, add the lemon juice and cream, taste and correct seasoning and coat the sweetbreads only with the sauce. Garnish with the fried bread and lemon butterflies.

BRAISED SWEETBREADS

Pressure Cooking Time: 8 minutes

2 prepared sweetbreads; 4 medium onions; 2 tablespoons butter; 2 oz mushrooms; $\frac{1}{2}$ pint brown stock (or dissolved meat cube); seasonings; 4 slices of bread; flour for thickening; a little sherry or red wine (optional); chopped parsley for garnish.

Cut each sweetbread into eight pieces and roll in seasoned flour; slice the onions and mushrooms finely. Lift the trivet from the cooker, heat the butter and fry the onions and mushrooms golden brown. Lift out, fry the pieces of sweetbread until evenly brown and lift out; add the stock, stir well to remove any 'brown' pieces from the bottom of the cooker, put back the vegetables, the sweetbreads, add the seasoning, bring to pressure in the usual way, cook for 8 minutes and allow the pressure to reduce at room temperature. During this cooking, prepare the thickening; fry the bread and lay the slices ready in the serving dish. Lift out and serve the sweetbreads and vegetables and keep hot. Thicken the sauce, add the wine, reheat, taste and correct seasoning and pour into the dish. Garnish thickly with chopped parsley.

LAMB AND MUTTON

POT-ROASTED

ROLLED, STUFFED BREAST OF LAMB

Pressure Cooking Time: 10–12 minutes per pound

A boned breast of lamb, approx. 2 lb; 1 finely diced onion; 4 tablespoons fresh breadcrumbs, 4 tablespoons finely chopped celery, a pinch of sage, 1 teaspoon chopped parsley, seasoning, 1 beaten egg for the stuffing (or made-up packet stuffing); 2 tablespoons dripping or fat; stock or thin gravy; flour for thickening; gravy colouring.

Unroll the meat, wipe, season the cut surface well with salt and pepper. Mix the stuffing ingredients together and bind firmly with sufficient beaten egg. Spread this over the meat, roll the joint again and close securely with small skewers or tie with string and weigh. Lift the trivet from the cooker, melt the fat and fry the meat all over until really brown. Lift out, add the required amount of liquid according to the cooking time, but not less than $\frac{1}{2}$ pint. Put in the trivet and the meat, bring to pressure in the usual way, cook for the required time and reduce the pressure with cold water. Lift out the meat and keep hot. Add the thickening and colouring to the stock, reheat, taste and correct seasoning and hand separately.

If your butcher gave you the breast bones, these should be put into the cooker with the liquid to enrich the stock and be lifted out before adding the thickening.

BOILED

LEG OF MUTTON WITH CAPER SAUCE

Pressure Cooking Time: 15–18 minutes per pound

1 leg of mutton weighing not more than 3 lb; medium carrots, medium onions; sprigs of thyme and parsley; 2 bay leaves; a crushed clove of garlic (optional); seasoning; $\frac{1}{2}$ pint caper sauce (p. 291); water for cooking.

Wipe, trim and weigh the meat, peel the vegetables and leave whole. Lift the trivet from the cooker, put in the joint, vegetables and seasonings and sufficient water to half fill the cooker. Bring to pressure in the usual way, cook for the required time and reduce the pressure with cold water. During the cooking, make the caper sauce using only half the quantity of milk. Lift the meat on to the serving dish, garnish with the vegetables lifted out carefully with a straining spoon. Strain the stock and use sufficient to give the sauce a pouring consistency. Reheat, taste and correct seasoning and hand separately.

BRAISED

BRAISED LAMB CHOPS WITH VEGETABLES

Pressure Cooking Time: 10 minutes

Lamb chops per person; 2 tablespoons dripping; mirepoix (p. 300); seasoning; accompanying vegetables, potatoes, carrots, green vegetable to choice; brown stock; a little gravy colouring if necessary; chopped parsley for garnish.

Wipe and trim the chops and season well with salt and pepper. Prepare the vegetables, having the potatoes, carrots, etc., of a size to cook in 7 minutes. Lift the trivet from the cooker, melt the fat over a low heat, quickly brown the chops on both sides and lift out. Prepare the mirepoix, adding sufficient stock to come just to the top and put back the chops. Put in the trivet and the vegetables piled on each side, bring to pressure in the usual way, cook for 3 minutes and reduce the pressure with cold water. During this cooking, prepare and pack the green vegetable into a perforated container. Return the open pan to the heat and when filled with steam put in the container, bring to pressure again, cook for a further 4 minutes and reduce the pressure with cold water. Lift out and serve the vegetables. Take out the trivet, serve the chops into a deep dish and keep hot. Remove the bouquet garni and mash the vegetables very thoroughly or better still, put through a sieve. Return to the pan, add colouring if necessary, reheat, taste and correct seasoning and pour over the chops, garnishing thickly with chopped parsley.

LAMB CUTLETS—COUNTRY STYLE

Pressure Cooking Time: 7 minutes
Oven Time: 15 minutes

8 small lamb cutlets; 2 tablespoons butter or other fat; 6 small onions; a crushed clove of garlic (or garlic flavouring); bouquet garni; $\frac{1}{2}$ pint white stock; $\frac{3}{4}$ lb medium potatoes; seasoning; a little nutmeg; chopped parsley for garnish.

Wipe and trim cutlets; peel and slice onions, peel potatoes. Lift the trivet from the cooker, melt the butter over a low heat and quickly fry the cutlets on both sides and then the onions, until golden brown. Add the stock, garlic and bouquet garni, the trivet and the salted potatoes in a perforated container. Bring to pressure in the usual way, cook for 7 minutes, reduce the pressure with cold water. During this cooking, preheat the oven to Gas No 4, 350° F, setting a shelf towards the top. Lift out the potatoes and trivet, serve the cutlets and onions into a shallow casserole, boil the stock rapidly in the open pan until reduced by half; lift out the bouquet garni, taste and correct seasoning and pour over the meat. Slice the potatoes and lay in the casserole as a top layer, seasoning well with plenty of salt, pepper and a sprinkle of nutmeg. Put as high in the oven as possible and bake until the potatoes are browned—about 15 minutes. Garnish with chopped parsley.

While the casserole is baking, use the pressure cooker for the accompanying vegetables; young carrots, fresh peas or beans sprinkled with finely chopped mint would be a good choice.

KIDNEYS LIEGEOISE (IN WINE SAUCE)

Pressure Cooking Time: 7 minutes

6 ($1\frac{1}{4}$ lb) lamb's kidneys; 4 thin slices of streaky bacon; 1 tablespoon butter; $\frac{1}{4}$ lb button mushrooms; $\frac{1}{3}$ pint red wine (inexpensive vin rosé recommended); 1 tablespoon butter, 1 tablespoon flour for sauce; seasoning; chopped parsley for garnish.

Wipe kidneys, skin and with scissors cut along the rounded edge. Lay flat and again with the scissors trim away the tubes and membranes, then cut in quarters and season well. Make twelve bacon rolls (p. 297) and put on two short skewers. Skin the mushrooms, or if very young, wash well and dry. Cut into slices lengthways. Lift the trivet from the cooker, fry the bacon rolls until golden brown, lift out and take off skewers. If there is not enough fat in the cooker, add the butter and when hot, lightly brown the kidneys. Lift the cooker from the heat and when cooled, add the wine, stir well then put in the bacon rolls and mushrooms. Cover, bring to pressure in the usual way, cook for 7 minutes and reduce the pressure with cold water. During this cooking, melt the butter in a medium-sized saucepan, add the flour and cook slowly until turning a golden brown. Strain the liquid from the cooker and add sufficient to the sauce to give a rich, coating consistency. Return the cooker, stir while reheating, taste and correct seasoning and serve piping hot garnished with parsley.

This recipe can be made with brown stock, a dissolved stock cube or thin gravy if preferred.

BRAISED STUFFED HEARTS

Pressure Cooking Time: 30 minutes

4 sheep's hearts; stuffing (p. 299/300); or ready-made; 2 tablespoons dripping or fat; 1 onion; 1 carrot; 1 turnip; $\frac{1}{2}$ pint brown stock; flour for thickening; seasoning.

Wash the hearts thoroughly, remove all fat and tubes and slice halfway down to make a pocket. Season inside with salt and pepper, three-quarter fill with the stuffing, then secure loosely either sewing up or lacing with thin string round small skewers or using cocktail sticks. Toss in seasoned flour. Lift the trivet from the cooker, heat the fat and brown the hearts all over. Lift out, then lightly fry the vegetables. Pour in the hot stock (if cold, allow cooker to cool), add seasoning, put back the hearts, bring to pressure in the usual way, cook for 30 minutes and reduce the pressure with cold water. Lift the hearts on to a hot serving dish and keep hot. Mash the vegetables well into the gravy, add blended flour and colouring if necessary, bring to the boil, taste and correct seasoning and pour over the hearts.

A dash of sherry added to the strained, thickened sauce just before serving makes this dish extra special.

STEWED

SUMMER LAMB STEW

Pressure Cooking Time: 12 minutes

1 lb middle neck or breast of lamb; 3 tablespoons of butter; ½ bay leaf; 2 onions; 1 lb new potatoes; 2 or 3 baby turnips; 8 young carrots; 1 lb of shelled peas; 1 teaspoon fresh chopped mint; seasoning; ½ pint brown stock; a little flour for thickening.

Wipe, trim the meat, cut from the bone and into 1-inch squares and toss well in salt and pepper. Slice the onions. Lift the trivet from the cooker, melt the butter over a low heat and gently cook the meat and onions until golden brown. Add the hot stock (or if cold, allow the cooker to cool), the bones and seasonings, bring to pressure in the usual way, cook for 7 minutes and reduce the pressure with cold water. During this cooking, peel the potatoes, carrots and turnips which must be really small and left whole but to ensure they will be cooked, just make a slit to the centre in each. Add these and the peas to the cooker, bring to pressure again, cook for the last 5 minutes, reduce the pressure with cold water. Very gently, lift out the bones, then add sufficient blended flour to give a rich, creamy sauce, taste to correct the seasoning, cook for 2 to 3 minutes and serve piping hot.

HARICOT MUTTON

Pressure Cooking Time: 10 minutes and 20–25 minutes

4 oz haricot beans; 1 small sliced onion; ½ pint water; seasoning for precooking.

1 small best end of neck of mutton or small leg of lamb (about 1½ lb); 1 onion; 2 tablespoons dripping or fat; 1 carrot; 1 turnip; bouquet garni; ¾ pint brown stock; blended flour for thickening; slices of grilled tomato for garnish.

Prepare the beans (p. 64) and pressure cook for 10 minutes, allowing the pressure to reduce at room temperature. Strain and throw away the water. During this cooking, wipe and trim the meat and season well. Peel and slice the vegetables. Put the fat into the cooker and when hot fry the meat and lift out and then the onion, pour in the boiling stock, add the vegetables, seasonings and the beans, stir well, put back the meat, bring to pressure in the usual way, cook for 20 to 25 minutes and reduce the pressure with cold water. During this cooking, peel and slice the tomatoes, dot with butter, season and grill lightly. Lift the meat on to the serving dish and keep hot. Strain the vegetables into a deep dish, add the blended flour to the stock, reboil, taste and correct seasoning, pour over the vegetables and garnish with the sliced tomatoes.

IRISH STEW

Pressure Cooking Time: 12 minutes

1 lb of best end or middle cut of neck chops; 2 lb large potatoes; 4 large onions; 4 small carrots (to give colour if liked); seasoning; $\frac{1}{4}$ pint hot water; chopped parsley or chives for garnish.

Wipe and trim off surplus fat from chops and sprinkle well with salt and pepper; peel the potatoes and onions and cut into really thick slices (peel but leave the carrots whole). Lift the trivet from the cooker, put in the hot water and the chops, then a layer of onions and lastly the potatoes (and carrots). Bring to pressure in the usual way, cook for 12 minutes, reduce the pressure with cold water. Lift the potatoes on to a hot serving dish, forming them into an overlapping border, serve the chops and onions into the centre and pour the liquor over. Set a carrot at each corner and garnish thickly with parsley.

NAVARIN OF LAMB

Pressure Cooking Time: 10 minutes

$1\frac{1}{2}$ lb best end of neck or cutlets or lamb pieces; 3 medium onions; 2 oz button mushrooms (or a small tin); a few strips of green pepper or a small packet of frozen peas; 2 tablespoons of dripping or fat; seasoning; 1 tablespoon of mint sauce or jelly; 1 small tin of tomato soup; $\frac{3}{4}$–1 lb small or new potatoes for serving separately; a little chopped mint; chopped parsley for garnish.

Cut the meat into 1-inch cubes and toss in salt and pepper; peel and slice the onions and mushrooms. Lift the trivet from the cooker, melt the fat over a low heat and gently cook the onions but without allowing them to brown. Add the mushrooms, the meat, the peppers or peas, the mint sauce or jelly and the tomato soup, bring to the boil, stirring well. Put in the trivet and the potatoes, sprinkled with mint in a perforated container. Bring to pressure in the usual way, cook for 10 minutes and reduce the pressure with cold water. Serve the potatoes, lift out the trivet, taste to correct seasoning, reheat and serve piping hot, garnished with parsley.

SAVOURY LIVER WITH VEGETABLES

Pressure Cooking Time: 4 minutes

12 oz liver; 1 tablespoon butter; 2 rashers of streaky bacon; 3 medium onions; $\frac{1}{4}$ pint water and 2 tablespoons vinegar; 1 clove; sprig of parsley; seasoning; small or quartered medium potatoes and frozen or dehydrated peas, with a sprig of mint, to serve as separate vegetables; chopped parsley for garnish.

Wash the liver, dry, cut in $\frac{1}{2}$-inch strips and toss in seasoned flour. Slice the onions, chop the bacon, prepare the potatoes and put in a perforated container and the peas in a solid container adding the necessary amount of water if using the dehydrated kind. Lift the trivet from the cooker, heat the fat, fry the bacon and onions until golden brown and lift out. Strain off the fat, put in the hot liquid, the bacon and onions, the seasonings and the strips of liver on top. Add the trivet and the salted potatoes, put the cooker on the heat and when the pan is filled with steam, add the peas. Bring to pressure in the usual way, cook for 4 minutes and reduce the pressure at room temperature. Serve the potatoes and the strained peas and lift the liver on to a serving dish. If the gravy is a little too thin, thicken with blended flour and milk or reduce by boiling in the open pan. Taste and correct seasoning, pour over the liver and garnish with chopped parsley.

PORK

BOILED

PICKLED PORK WITH HARICOTS

Pressure Cooking Time: 15 minutes per pound

A piece of pickled pork weighing not more than 3 lb; 2 medium-sized onions; 12 peppercorns, 4 cloves and a pinch of sage or mixed herbs tied in muslin; sufficient water to cover; 4 oz of small haricot beans; seasoning; $\frac{1}{2}$ pint thick brown gravy (p. 292).

Weigh the joint and soak in cold water for 1 hour, prepare the beans as given on p. 64 and then tie them loosely in a piece of muslin. Lift the trivet from the cooker, put in the pork, the sliced onions and seasonings and sufficient water to cover or not more than to half fill the base of the cooker. Bring to pressure in the usual way, cook for all but 20 minutes, reduce the pressure with cold water. Put the open pan back on the heat, bring to the boil, drop in the beans, bring to pressure again, cook for a further 20 minutes and allow the pressure to reduce at room temperature. Serve the pork surrounded by the drained beans on a deep serving dish; strain the stock, add sufficient to make the brown gravy and pour this, piping hot, over the beans.

It may be found easier to carve this joint before taking it to table. Lay the slices overlapping on the serving dish surrounded by the beans and pour the gravy over.

PIGS' TROTTERS WITH VEGETABLES

Pressure Cooking Time: 30 minutes

If the pigs' trotters have been salted they should be soaked overnight in cold water.

4 pigs' trotters; seasoning; a pinch of allspice; $\frac{1}{4}$ pint vinegar; $\frac{1}{4}$ pint water; bouquet garni; 4 small onions, carrots, turnips; sufficient potatoes for 4; 1 tablespoon butter, 1 tablespoon flour for thickening; fried parsley (p. 298) for garnish.

Scrub the pigs' trotters well, drain and dry, season with salt and pepper. Lift the trivet from the cooker, put in the liquid, the seasonings and the trotters, bring to pressure in the usual way, cook for 25 minutes, reduce the pressure with cold water. During this cooking, prepare the vegetables, leaving the young carrots, onions, turnips whole and cutting the potatoes to a size to cook in 5 minutes. Add the vegetables in to the stock, put in the trivet and then the potatoes, bring to pressure again, cook for the remaining minutes, reduce the pressure with cold water. During this cooking, prepare and fry the parsley. Serve the potatoes, lift out the trivet, dish the trotters surrounded with the vegetables and garnished with parsley and keep hot. Remove the fat from the stock by drawing pieces of absorbent paper across the surface. In a separate saucepan, melt the butter, add the flour and cook without browning for a moment or two. Away from the heat, add the stock gradually, stirring well, reheat, taste and correct seasoning and cook for 2 to 3 minutes. Hand separately.

As a delicacy, pigs' trotters can be served grilled. Pressure cook for 25 minutes only, adding the carrots, turnips and onions into the stock at the beginning of the cooking. Lift out the trotters, drain, halve, dip in melted butter and then breadcrumbs and brown under the grill, turning them from time to time. Garnish with fried parsley and serve with a mustard sauce, using half milk and half-strained stock.

BRAISED

BRAISED PORK CHOPS

Pressure Cooking Time: 10–12 minutes

4 pork chops about $\frac{3}{4}$ inch thick; 1 large eating apple; 2 tablespoons butter; a mirepoix (p. 300); stock; seasoning; a little gravy colouring; a small packet of frozen or dehydrated peas for garnish.

Wipe, trim off excess fat from the chops and season well. Peel, core the apple and cut into four thick slices. Lift the trivet from the cooker, melt the butter over a low heat, brown the chops on both sides and lift out. Quickly fry the apple rings, lift out and put one on each chop. Prepare the mirepoix, adding sufficient stock to come just to the top and put back the chops. Bring to pressure in the usual way, cook for the required time, reduce the pressure with cold water. During this cooking, prepare the peas in another saucepan. Lift the chops carefully on to a serving dish and keep hot. Thoroughly mash the vegetables into the gravy, reheat, taste and correct seasoning, add a little browning to give a rich colour and pour round the chops. Fill the peas into the centre of the apple rings as garnish. Alternatively the stock can be strained, thickened with blended flour and colouring be added. Serve as above.

PIQUANT PORK CUTLETS

Pressure Cooking Time: 8 minutes

4 thin cutlets of pork; 1 tablespoon dripping; $\frac{1}{4}$ pint dry cider; $\frac{1}{4}$ pint water; seasoning; a crushed clove of garlic (optional); 2 or 3 cloves; a little flour for thickening.

Wipe the cutlets, trim off excess fat, season well with salt and if available, black pepper. Lift the trivet from the cooker, heat the fat, brown the chops on both sides, lift out and drain off the fat. Allow the cooker to cool, add the cider, water, cutlets and seasonings, bring to pressure in the usual way, cook for 8 minutes, reduce the pressure with cold water. Lift the cutlets on to the serving dish and keep hot. Remove the cloves, add the blended flour to the sauce, reheat, taste to correct seasoning, cook for 2 to 3 minutes, pour over the fillets.

PORK FILLETS IN CREAM SAUCE

Pressure Cooking Time: 8–10 minutes

4 pork fillets $\frac{1}{2}$–$\frac{3}{4}$ inch thick; 2 tablespoons butter; 1 small onion; $\frac{1}{2}$ lb button mushrooms; $\frac{1}{4}$ pint stock or water; $\frac{1}{4}$ pint sour cream (p. 300) seasoning; chopped parsley or chives for garnish.

Wipe and trim the fillets, peel and dice the onion finely, wash and dry the mushrooms (peel only if necessary) and slice finely, stalk and all. Lift the trivet from the cooker, heat the butter and lightly fry the onion and the fillets on both sides. Pour in the liquid, bring to pressure in the usual way, cook for 6 minutes, reduce the pressure with cold water. Pile the mushrooms on the chops, bring to pressure again, cook 2 minutes, reduce the pressure with cold water. Carefully lift the chops on to a serving dish and keep hot. Add cream, re-heat sauce without allowing it to boil, whisk well and pour over the chops. Garnish with parsley or chives.

STUFFED PORK CHOPS

Pressure Cooking Time: 12–15 minutes

4 thick loin chops; a little made mustard; stuffing made from 3 tablespoons of fresh breadcrumbs, 1 medium onion, 1 teaspoon chopped parsley, pinch of mixed herbs with sage, seasoning, 1 tablespoon butter, sufficient milk or beaten egg to bind; 8 small onions; 2 tablespoons dripping or bacon fat; $\frac{1}{2}$ pint brown stock or water; sufficient potatoes for 4; seasoning; flour for thickening; a little gravy colouring if necessary.

Wipe the chops, trim off excess fat and cut a slit in each to make a pocket. In a separate pan, melt the butter and cook the onions gently until transparent, add the breadcrumbs, seasoning and herbs and continue cooking until all the fat has been absorbed. Add sufficient liquid to bind and fill into the chops, securing with small skewers or cocktail sticks. Sprinkle the chops well with salt and pepper and spread thinly with mustard. Lift the trivet from the cooker, heat the fat, brown the chops well on both sides and lift out. Brown the onions left whole until golden, lift out. Add the hot liquid (if cold, allow the cooker to cool), the trivet and the chops. Bring to pressure in the usual way, cook for all but 4 minutes of the cooking time, reduce the pressure with cold water. During this cooking, peel the potatoes and cut to cook in 4 minutes. Put the onions round the chops, then the potatoes on top in a perforated container. Bring to pressure again, cook for 4 minutes, reduce the pressure with cold water. Serve the potatoes; lift out the chops on to a serving dish garnished with the onions and keep hot. Lift out the trivet, add the blended flour, reheat, taste and correct seasoning, add colouring if necessary, cook for 2 to 3 minutes and hand separately.

A delicious accompaniment for this dish would be spinach; a packet of the frozen variety could be cooked and served with butter or a little cream stirred in, during the pressure cooking.

HAM

When pressure cooking ham or bacon joints, the method of preparation will depend on whether it is fresh (green) or smoked and on the type of joint, whether it is of a lean, expensive cut such as gammon, hock or back or an inexpensive more fatty cut such as streaky, collar or flank. The joint should not weigh more than 3 to 3½ lb for the largest cookers.

BOILED

Pressure Cooking Time: 12 minutes per pound

Fresh ham and bacon joints should be put into the open cooker without the trivet and covered with water, be brought to the boil and the water thrown away.

Smoked joints should be soaked for at least 2 hours and then be treated as above, before pressure cooking.

Lean joints, to keep their moisture, should be cooked without the trivet and with sufficient water to cover if possible but not to fill the cooker more than half full.

Fatty joints are best cooked on the trivet with just enough water to last the cooking time, but never less than half a pint.

Prepacked, boned ham should be cooked according to the instructions but allowing just the 12 minutes per pound for pressure cooking.

A selection of vegetables such as onions, carrots and celery may be added to taste, to the cooking liquid or a choice of herbs, such as a bouquet garni. If a sweet flavour is preferred, the liquid used may be diluted peach, pineapple or orange juice.

Pressure should be allowed to reduce at room temperature. If the ham or bacon is to be served cold, then the joint should be left in the cooker until quite cold before being lifted out.

TO SERVE HOT

Lift out the joint, untie the string and remove the skin by slipping a prong of a fork under it at one side and rolling the fork over and over, bringing the skin with it. Have some golden crumbs ready on a piece of greaseproof paper and coat the fat side of the joint with them, pressing the paper firmly to make sure that the crumbs really adhere. Put the joint on the serving dish into the oven, to keep hot. Add about two tablespoons only of the stock to make a $\frac{1}{2}$ pint of parsley sauce (p. 291) and hand separately or simply serve a little of the plain, strained stock from which the fat should be removed by drawing pieces of absorbent paper across the surface before pouring, piping hot, into the sauce boat.

TO SERVE COLD

When the joint and liquid are cold, skim off any fat, lift out the joint and dress as above. Serve with a green or mixed salad and new or jacket potatoes.

Ham cut from the cold joint may be used for many dishes such as **Chicory Bruxellois** (p. 142) or diced, alone or with chicken, mushrooms, etc, as fillings for pastry dishes such as the **Vol-au-Vents,** chopped as garnish as for **Cauliflower Polonaise** (p. 60) or for **Ham Maillot** (p. 142) as a supper dish.

BAKED

PLAIN BAKED

Pressure cook according to the directions given but allow only 10 minutes per pound. During the cooking, preheat the oven to Gas No 5, 400° F, lift out the ham, remove the skin, put into a roasting tin and bake in the centre of the oven until the fat is golden brown, about 15 to 20 minutes.

SWEET BAKED

When the skin has been removed, lightly spread with ready-made mustard, rub brown sugar into the fatty side and stick with cloves at inch intervals. Bake as above, until glazed and crisp.

SWEET BAKED—AMERICAN STYLE 1

Prepare for oven as above but arrange the cloves in the shape of diamonds. Have ready in the roasting tin the juice from a small tin of pineapple chunks and baste the joint before putting it in the oven and once or twice more during the baking. Before serving, place a small cube of pineapple on a halved cocktail stick, in the centre of each diamond.

SWEET BAKED—AMERICAN STYLE 2

Prepare for the oven as **Sweet Baked**, have ready in the roasting tin the juice from a small tin of halved apricots or peaches, baste the ham well with this and put the fruit round it. Baste at least twice more and serve with the fruit on the dish, as garnish.

BRAISED

BRAISED HAM WITH ONIONS

Pressure Cooking Time: 12 minutes per pound

A piece of ham or bacon weighing not more than 3–3½ lb; 2 tablespoons of dripping or fat; bouquet garni; ½–¾ pint water; 12–15 pickled onions; a little melted butter for glazing.

Weigh the joint, preboil as given in the instructions on p. 116, then carefully cut off the skin with a sharp knife and score the fat across in 1-inch squares. Lift the trivet from the cooker, heat the fat, thoroughly brown the skinned side of the joint, lift out and drain off the fat. Put in the required amount of hot water (if cold, allow the cooker to cool), the trivet, the joint, bring to pressure in the usual way, cook for the required time, reduce the pressure with cold water. During this cooking, preheat the grill (if the joint will fit under it) or the oven to Gas No 5, 375° F. In a small saucepan, melt a little butter without allowing it to brown and toss the drained and dried onions so that they are completely coated. Lift out the joint, put an onion on a cocktail stick in each of the scored sections and put under the grill or in the oven until browned.

This can be served with a brown gravy or parsley, mustard or madeira sauce (pp. 291 and 292), using a little of the cooking liquid to obtain the correct consistency.

HAM SLICES—HAWAII STYLE

Pressure Cooking Time: 10 minutes

1-inch thick slice of lean uncooked ham; 2 tablespoons butter; salt, pepper, made mustard; 2 or 3 cloves; 1 small tin of pineapple slices; sufficient medium potatoes for 4; large packet of frozen peas; ½ pint parsley sauce (p. 292).

Trim all fat from the ham and cut into four portions; peel the potatoes; strain the pineapple slices, keeping the juice. Lift the trivet from the cooker, heat the butter and brown the pieces of ham on both sides. Lift the pan from the heat, take out the ham, spread thinly with the mustard and sprinkle lightly with pepper. Put the pineapple juice made up to $\frac{1}{4}$ pint in the cooker, then the ham with a pineapple slice on each portion, the trivet and the salted potatoes piled to one side. Bring to pressure in the usual way, cook for 6 minutes, reduce the pressure with cold water.

During this cooking, put the peas in a perforated container and make the parsley sauce using only half quantity of milk. Put the open cooker back on the heat, allow the liquid to boil and the pan to fill with steam, put in the peas, bring to pressure again, cook for a further 4 minutes and reduce the pressure with cold water. Lift out the peas, serve the potatoes, take out the trivet. Put the ham with pineapple on the serving dish and keep hot with the vegetables. Add sufficient of the stock to the sauce to give a coating consistency, reheat, taste and correct seasoning and pour round the ham. Garnish with the peas, putting a few in the centre of each pineapple slice and the rest in a pile at each end of the dish.

SWEET–SOUR HAM BALLS

Pressure Cooking Time: 8 minutes

1 lb minced lean, raw ham, 4 oz fresh breadcrumbs, 1 egg, pinch of mixed herbs, seasoning, sufficient milk to mix; 2 tablespoons dripping or fat; 4 oz brown sugar, 1 teaspoon dry mustard, $\frac{1}{4}$ pint water and vinegar mixed, for sauce; $\frac{1}{2}$ pint water with a little vinegar or lemon juice added for the cooker.

Mix together the finely minced ham, breadcrumbs and seasonings; stir in the beaten egg and sufficient milk to bind into a firm mixture, form into eight balls and roll in seasoned flour. In a frying pan, heat the dripping and carefully brown balls all over then lift into a heat-proof dish or bowl which will fit easily into the pressure cooker. Add the sugar and mustard to the remaining fat in the pan and heat gently until it dissolves. Stir in the liquid and, when boiling, pour over the balls and cover with a double sheet of greaseproof paper. Put the water, trivet and then the covered dish in the cooker, bring to pressure in the usual way, cook for 8 minutes and allow the pressure to reduce at room temperature. A container of rice could be cooked with this dish if there is sufficient room in the cooker. Put the covered meat dish directly on the bottom of the cooker in the water and use the trivet on top for the container with rice to stand on.

Serve the rice as a border, with the ham balls in the centre and the sauce poured over.

TIMBALES OF HAM AND EGG

Pressure Cooking Time: 5 minutes

1 egg per person; 4 tablespoons finely chopped cooked ham; a tablespoon of butter mixed with a little powdered mustard; salt and pepper; 6 oz rice; $\frac{1}{2}$ pint water with a little lemon juice or vinegar for the cooker; $\frac{1}{2}$ pint of white sauce (p. 291) with tomato purée for flavouring; 4 sprigs of parsley.

Take four ordinary teacups, grease them very well with the butter and mustard mixture then coat thickly with the chopped ham pressing it well against the bottom and half-way up the sides. Break an egg into each cup and dust with salt and pepper. Put the water into the cooker, then the cups covered right over with a double sheet of greaseproof paper, the trivet and the rice which should be prepared and finished off as given on p. 150. During this cooking, make the tomato sauce and keep hot. Make a thick round of rice on the serving dish, loosen round the top of each egg, unmould it on to the rice and pour the tomato sauce round. Top with parsley sprigs. Alternatively the eggs could be served on rounds of buttered toast each with a slice of grilled tomato on it and with cheese sauce poured round.

MEAT SUET PUDDINGS AND PIES

STEAK AND KIDNEY PUDDING

Method 1: with raw meat

Steaming Time: 15 minutes
Pressure Cooking Time: 55 minutes

A china, oven-glass, metal or boilable plastic bowl can be used. The covering should be double greaseproof paper, foil or a pudding cloth.

1 lb stewing steak; 2 kidneys; $\frac{1}{4}$ pint brown stock or water; 2 heaped tablespoons seasoned flour for the filling; 8 oz self-raising flour, 4 oz shredded suet, salt, a little water to mix, for the pastry; $1\frac{1}{2}$ pints boiling water with a little vinegar or lemon juice for the cooker.

Wipe the meat, remove excess fat, cut in 1-inch strips; skin the kidney, halve, remove all tubes and membranes and cut in small pieces. Toss all in seasoned flour, then roll up each strip of steak with a piece of kidney inside. To make the pastry, mix together the dry ingredients and mix to an elastic, not wet, dough with cold water. Roll out two-thirds into a circle and line the basin, pressing the pastry firmly against the sides and base. Put in the meat, half the liquid, moisten the edges of the lining with cold water, cover with the one-third pastry left, rolled into a circle to form a lid and pinch the edges together all round. Tie down with a double thickness of greased greaseproof paper and put on the trivet in the boiling water in the cooker. (If you have difficulty putting the basin in the cooker or lifting it out, leave a long end of string after tying the knot securing the covering and take it across to the other side to form a handle.) Put on the lid, wait until the steam escapes from the open vent, lower the heat and steam very gently, like an ordinary steamed pudding, for 15 minutes. Raise the heat, bring to pressure in the usual way and cook for 55 minutes. Allow the pressure to reduce at room temperature. Take off the covering, cut a hole in the centre of the crust and fill the pudding with a little more boiled stock. Serve in the basin wrapped around with a white napkin.

If the same quantity is divided into four individual Steak and Kidney Puddings, using small aluminium or boilable plastic bowls, they will require 10 minutes' steaming, 35 minutes' pressure cooking with 1 pint water for the cooker and the pressure reduced at room temperature.

STEAK AND KIDNEY PUDDING

Method 2: with pre-cooked meat

Steaming Time: 15 minutes
Pressure Cooking Time: 25 minutes

Ingredients prepared as in previous recipe.

Lift out the trivet from the cooker, put in $\frac{1}{2}$ pint of stock or water and the meat, stir well, bring to pressure in the usual way, cook for 10 minutes and lift the cooker into a deep bowl of cold water to reduce the pressure and cool the meat. During this cooking, make the suet crust, line the basin and roll out the pastry cap as in the previous recipe. Lift the meat into the lined basin with a straining spoon, adding half the gravy. Continue the cooking and serving of the pudding as in the previous recipe.

If the same quantity of meat is precooked as in the pudding recipe and the instructions followed but making four individual Steak and Kidney Puddings they will require 10 minutes' steaming and 15 minutes' pressure cooking, with 1 pint water in the cooker and allowing the pressure to reduce at room temperature.

MEAT SUET ROLL

Steaming Time: 10 minutes
Pressure Cooking Time: 35 minutes

1 lb stewing steak; 1 sheep's kidney (optional); 1 small onion; 1 tablespoon chopped parsley; a little flour and seasoning; 6 oz sieved self-raising flour, pinch of salt, 3 oz shredded suet, cold water to mix, for the pastry; 1 pint boiling water for the cooker; rich, brown gravy (p. 292).

Cut the meat into small squares or, if cooking kidney, into thin strips, removing most of the fat. Wash the kidney in salted water, skin, cut in half, remove all the tubes with pointed scissors and cut into small pieces. Toss the squares of meat in seasoned flour or put a piece of kidney on each strip, roll up and dust with seasoned flour and mix in a bowl with the chopped onion and parsley. Make the suet crust by mixing together the dry ingredients and adding sufficient cold water to give an elastic, not too moist, dough. On a floured surface, roll out the paste into a long strip a little narrower than the base of the cooker, spread evenly with the meat mixture, moisten the edges with cold water and roll up like a Swiss Roll pinching the ends and long edge well together. Wrap in a double sheet of greased, greaseproof paper and tie the ends loosely with string. Have ready in the cooker the boiling water and the trivet. Put in the roll, cover the cooker and when the steam escapes through the vent, lower the heat and steam very gently for 10 minutes like an ordinary steamed pudding. This is to make the suet crust nice and light. Then, turn up the heat, bring to pressure in the usual way, cook for 35 minutes and allow the pressure to reduce at room temperature. Serve whole or sliced, covered with a little good brown gravy and with the rest handed separately.

SEA PIE

Steaming Time: 5 minutes
Pressure Cooking Time: 15 minutes

1 lb chuck or good stewing steak; 2 dessertspoons seasoned flour; 1 medium onion and turnip; 2 medium carrots; 2 sticks celery; $\frac{1}{2}$ pint brown stock or dissolved beef cube; bouquet garni; 6 oz sieved self-raising flour, pinch of salt, 3 oz shredded suet, cold water to mix, for the pastry; circle of doubled greased greaseproof paper the size of the cooker base; sprig of parsley for garnish.

Trim the fat off the meat, cut into 1-inch cubes and toss in seasoned flour shaking off any surplus. Peel the vegetables and cut into squares or slices. Make the suet crust by mixing together the dry ingredients and adding sufficient cold water to give a stiff dough. On a floured surface roll the paste into a circle just smaller than the cooker base. Lift the trivet from the cooker, put in the hot stock, the vegetables, meat and seasonings, bring to the boil stirring well and leave simmering on a gentle heat. Dust the top of the pastry circle lightly with flour, fold in half and then in quarters, lay on top of the meat and quickly open out flat again. Cover with the circle of paper, put the lid on the cooker and when the steam escapes through the vent, lower the heat and steam very gently for 5 minutes like an ordinary steamed pudding. This is to make the suet crust nice and light. Then, turn up the heat, bring to pressure in the usual way, cook for 15 minutes and allow the pressure to reduce at room temperature. Lift off the paper, cut the crust into four and lift on to a hot dish. Reheat the meat, stirring well, taste and correct the seasoning and put into a hot, deep serving dish, laying the suet crust back on top. Garnish with a sprig of parsley in the centre.

MEAT PASTY

Pressure Cooking Time: 5 minutes
Baking Time: 25 minutes

$\frac{3}{4}$ lb fresh minced beef; 2 medium onions; 1 oz dripping or fat; 1 tablespoon of sweet chutney; a dash of Worcester Sauce or tomato sauce or purée to taste; $\frac{1}{4}$ pint brown stock, gravy or water with gravy colouring added; seasoning

12 oz shortcrust pastry (ready-made or frozen would be suitable); a little beaten egg or milk to glaze.

Prepare and pressure cook the meat and other ingredients as given for Savoury Mince. Reduce the pressure by standing the cooker in a deep bowl of cold water and leave until the meat is cold. During this cooking, preheat the oven to Gas No 6, 400° F, and set the shelf in the centre of the oven. Make the pastry, divide in two and line a pie plate with half. Damp the edges, put on the strained cooked ingredients, cover with the second circle and press the edges together. Trim the edges, flake with a sharp knife and make a cross in the centre. Brush with beaten egg, decorate with diamonds cut from the trimmings and bake until well-risen and golden brown. Just before serving, reboil the gravy, taste and correct seasoning and fill into the pastry or, if there is no room, hand separately.

PORK AND LIVER PIE

Pressure Cooking Time: 6 minutes
Baking Time: 25 minutes

¾ lb lean pork; ¼ lb pig's liver; 1 dessertspoon flour; 1 large onion; 2 oz mushrooms; 1 oz cooking fat; ¼ pint apple juice, cider or small can of shandy; ¼ pint water; 1 tablespoon brown sugar; seasoning; 2 teaspoons meat herbs or bouquet garni; an 8 oz packet of ready made puff pastry; blended flour for thickening; a little beaten egg.

Wipe the meats, cut into 1-inch pieces, toss in seasoned flour; slice the peeled onions and mushrooms. Blend the sugar with the liquids and stir until the sugar is dissolved. Lift the trivet from the cooker, heat the fat and lightly fry the meats. Add the liquid and stir very well, then put in the vegetables, herbs and seasoning. Bring to pressure in the usual way, cook for 6 minutes, then stand the cooker in a deep bowl of cold water to reduce the pressure and cool the meat. During this cooking, preheat the oven to Gas No 8, 450° F, and set a shelf in the middle. Roll out the pastry to the size of the pie-dish being used. Lift the meat and vegetables with a straining spoon into the dish and, if necessary, add a little blended flour to the gravy, taste to correct seasoning and pour over the meat. Cover with the pastry, trim, then flake the edges with the blade of a sharp knife, cut a cross in the centre and decorate with small circles or diamonds of pastry cut from the trimmings. Cook for 15 minutes, then lower the heat to Gas No 5, 375° F, and continue baking until well browned and risen.

RABBIT PIE

Pressure Cooking Time: 10 minutes
Oven Time: 30 minutes

1 rabbit jointed into 8 pieces; 4 slices of streaky bacon; 1 egg; a slice of lemon rind; a pinch of meat or mixed herbs; seasoning; sliced onions if liked; ½ pint of white stock (or made with a stock cube) or water; 6 oz flaky pastry (or short) for the pie crust (can be bought ready made), a little beaten egg for glazing.

Wipe the rabbit, joint neatly and season well. Make eight bacon rolls, put on two short skewers; wrap the egg in aluminium foil. Lift the trivet from the cooker, lightly brown the bacon rolls in their own fat, take off the skewers and leave in the cooker. Add the hot liquid and the other ingredients, bring to pressure in the usual way, cook for 10 minutes and reduce the pressure in cold water, leaving it until the meat is cold. Lift out the egg, unwrap and drop in cold water. During this cooking, preheat the oven to Gas No 5, 375° F, for shortcrust or

Gas No 6, 400° F, for flaky pastry. Make the pastry, line the edge of the pie-dish and damp with cold water. Put in the meat, the other ingredients, the sliced hard-boiled egg and about one-third of the stock. Cover with the pastry, press down round the edges, trim and flake with a sharp knife. Brush with egg, cut a cross in the centre and decorate with pastry diamonds cut from the trimmings. Bake on the middle shelf of the oven until brown and well-risen. Just before serving, boil the rest of the stock until reduced by half, taste and correct seasoning and fill up the pie through the hole in the centre.

STEAK AND KIDNEY PIE

Pressure Cooking Time: 10 minutes
Baking Time: 30 minutes

Make this with bought shortcrust pastry for a really Hurry-Along dinner.

1 lb beef steak; $\frac{1}{4}$ lb kidney; seasoned flour; bouquet garni; $\frac{1}{2}$ pint stock or water; 6 oz shortcrust or flaky pastry; a little beaten egg or milk.

Wipe the steak, wash, halve, skin and remove the tubes from the kidney; cut into neat pieces and toss in seasoned flour. Lift the trivet from the cooker, put in the hot liquid and the meat, bring to pressure in the usual way, cook for 10 minutes, then stand the cooker in a deep bowl of cold water to reduce the pressure and cool the meat. During this cooking, preheat the oven to Gas No 6, 400° F, and set a shelf in the middle. Make the pastry, or use the bought pastry, and roll it to a slightly larger size than the pie-dish it is to cover. Lift the meat into the dish, add about two tablespoons of the stock, sprinkle with a little more seasoned flour and stir well. Cut thin strips of pastry to edge the dish, damp with a little cold water, then put on the pastry cover. Press down around the edges, trim, flake them with a sharp knife, cut a cross in the middle for ventilation; brush with the egg or milk and decorate the centre with pastry leaves in the form of four diamonds marked down and across like veins. Stand on a baking tray and bake until golden brown and well-risen. About 5 minutes before serving, heat the rest of the stock, put into a jug and carefully fill up the pie through the hole in the centre.

CHICKEN AND HAM VOL-AU-VENTS

6 tablespoons diced chicken; 3 tablespoons diced ham; 4 medium vol-au-vent cases (these can be bought, fresh baked or frozen); 1 small tin of button mushrooms; ½ pint white sauce; crisp lettuce leaves and sprigs of parsley as garnish.

Reheat the vol-au-vent cases at the top of an oven preheated to Gas No 8, 450° F, for 8 to 10 minutes. Make the white sauce, add the chopped chicken and ham, the drained, sliced mushrooms and reheat until piping hot. Fill into the cases, put on their lids and a sprig of parsley and serve with the lettuce leaves as decoration.

POULTRY AND GAME

	PREPARATION AND COOKING	PRESSURE COOKING TIME	METHOD OF SERVING
Chicken			
Poussin (very young)	Halved	7 minutes	Braised or fricasséd
	Jointed	4 minutes	In a cream sauce
Roasting (2½–3 lb)	Roasted whole, plain or stuffed	5 minutes per pound	Browned off in hot oven
	If frozen, completely thawed	5 minutes per pound	Coq au vin
	Jointed	5 minutes	Suprême
Boiling (3½–4 lb)	Whole	10 minutes per pound	With boiled rice
	Halved or jointed	20 minutes	Casseroled or braised
	Jointed	10 minutes	As blanquette
Frozen Pieces	Completely thawed, skinned	5 minutes	As for fresh pieces
Duckling	Whole, marinated	12–15 minutes per pound	Braised
	Jointed	12 minutes	Bigarade—with oranges
Hare	Jointed	35–40 minutes	Jugged
Rabbit	Jointed	12–15 minutes	Stewed, fricasséd, blanquette
	Precooked for a pie	10 minutes	With shortcrust pastry
Partridge and Pheasant	Whole	7–10 minutes	Braised with cabbage
	Halved or jointed	5–7 minutes	Braised or casseroled

When considering chicken, other poultry and game for pressure cooking it is important to decide on the recipe you intend to follow and to choose, according to size, age and condition, which will give the best results. Some recipes will not be successful if an old, tough boiling fowl is used, while with others where a young one or a roaster is recommended too long a cooking time could spoil the flavour, tenderness and texture. Where the chicken or fowl is to be left whole, the cooking time is given per pound so that the weight must be known and, if the bird is stuffed, it should be the weight of the stuffed bird. When jointed, a choice of times is given and a little experience will soon allow you to decide whether this needs to be the shorter or the longer—but try not to give more than is necessary as poultry has a delicate flavour and texture which can easily be lost by overcooking. Where pieces are to be coated with a sauce it is usually preferable to skin them. If whole frozen poultry are used for roasting or boiling they must be allowed to completely thaw before cooking—and don't forget to lift out the giblets which are usually packed inside! Frozen pieces too must be thawed before use.

ROAST STUFFED CHICKEN

Pressure Cooking Time: 5 minutes per pound

1 roasting chicken 3–4 lb in weight; 1 tablespoon breadcrumbs, ½ oz shredded suet, a pinch of mixed herbs, a little grated lemon rind, 1 table spoon chopped parsley, the giblets, seasoning, a little milk or egg for the stuffing; 2 or 3 slices of thin, streaky bacon; 2 tablespoons dripping; at least ½ pint water for the cooker; flour for thickening. Bacon rolls (p. 297) and bread sauce (p. 295) as accompaniments, sprigs of watercress for garnish.

Put the giblets to soak in salted water for at least half an hour, then rinse thoroughly. Wipe the chicken well, inside and out, dust with salt and pepper. Finely dice the liver (be sure and remove the gall bladder carefully), heart and kidneys, and add to the other ingredients for the stuffing, binding with a little milk or egg. Stuff the chicken closing the opening by sewing with string or with small skewers and weigh. Lift the trivet from the cooker, heat the fat and brown the chicken well all over. Lift out and drain off the fat into a roasting tin. Put the water and the rest of the giblets, the feet, etc, into the cooker, then the trivet and the chicken. Lay the bacon across the breast and cover the whole chicken tightly with a piece of greaseproof paper. Bring to pressure in the usual way, cook for the required time and reduce the pressure with cold water. During this cooking, preheat the oven to Gas No 5, 375° F, and set a shelf towards the top. Make the bread sauce and keep hot. Just before the cooking time is up, put the roasting tin in the oven to heat the fat. Lift out the chicken, take the bacon off, dust the breast with seasoned flour, put into the hot fat, baste the whole chicken thoroughly and leave in the oven for 15 minutes, basting once again. Cut the bacon slices in two, roll up, put on skewers and lay across the roasting tin to brown with the chicken. Dish the chicken, garnished with the bacon rolls and a bunch of watercress. Strain the stock and make the gravy in the roasting tin, handing separately with the bread sauce.

BOILED CHICKEN WITH RICE

Pressure Cooking Time: 10 minutes per pound

1 boiling fowl about 3½–4 lb; lemon juice and strips of lemon rind; a knob of butter; seasoning; 1 pint of water; 1 large carrot; 1 onion stuck with 2 cloves; 2 sticks of celery, 1 leek, as available; bouquet garni, a few extra peppercorns; 1 cup savoury rice; flour for thickening; chopped parsley for garnish; 1 egg, 4 tablespoons of cream for cream sauce, if preferred.

Wipe the chicken, weigh it, season with salt and pepper, rub over with lemon juice; put a knob of butter and a strip of lemon inside. Slice the carrot, celery and leeks and prepare the onion. Lift the trivet from the cooker, put in the water and chicken, bring to the boil in the open pan and skim well. Add the vegetables, seasonings and herbs, bring to pressure in the usual way, cook for all but 5 minutes of the cooking time and reduce the pressure with cold water. Lift out the chicken, strain the stock, make up to 1½ pints if necessary with more water, put back in the cooker, bring to the boil, throw in the rice, add the chicken, bring to pressure again and cook for the last 5 minutes. Allow the pressure to reduce at room temperature. Lift out the chicken and serve whole or preferably, cut into portions, skin, put in the serving dish and keep hot. Strain the rice and serve as a border round the dish, sprinkled with parsley. The stock may be thickened with blended flour, tasted to correct the seasoning, reboiled and cooked for 2 to 3 minutes and handed separately.

If a cream sauce is preferred, beat the egg with the cream and a squeeze of strained lemon juice in a small bowl, add 1 tablespoon of hot stock then a further ½ pint of the boiling stock, stirring all the time. Put into a small saucepan, reheat very carefully and without reboiling or the sauce will curdle, and when thickened, pour over the chicken and sprinkle thickly with parsley.

COQ AU VIN

Pressure Cooking Time: 25 minutes

1 plump chicken (about 3 lb); 3 tablespoons butter; 4 oz slice bacon or uncooked ham; seasoning and lemon juice; bouquet garni; 1 small glass of brandy; ¼ pint red wine such as Maçon or Beaujolais; 4 oz baby onions; 4 oz button mushrooms; 1 tablespoon butter; 1 tablespoon of sugar and 1 more tablespoon of red wine; a crushed clove of garlic or a squeeze of prepared garlic juice.

Wipe the chicken, which should be trussed securely and season, inside and out with salt, pepper and lemon juice; wash the giblets thoroughly in salted water; cut the piece of bacon into large cubes;

take the trivet from the cooker, heat the butter, brown the bacon and lift out. Fry the chicken all over, doing this on a medium heat only and turning the chicken carefully and frequently so that it is an even golden brown. In a small saucepan warm the brandy, pour into the cooker and set it alight with a match. When the flames have died down, pour in the red wine, add the giblets, cover the chicken with a piece of buttered paper, bring to pressure in the usual way, cook for 20 minutes and reduce the pressure with cold water. During this cooking, melt the butter in a small saucepan, lightly cook the mushrooms for a minute or two and lift out. Add the sugar to the butter that remains, put in the whole onions and cook until lightly brown. Put back the mushrooms and stir in the red wine and garlic. Put the trivet on top of the chicken and then the mushrooms and onions in a small bowl or solid container covered with a piece of greaseproof paper. Bring to pressure again, cook for 5 minutes and allow the pressure to reduce at room temperature. Lift out the container and keep hot. Lift out the trivet, the giblets and then the chicken; carve this into portions, lay in the serving dish and surround with the bacon lifted out with a straining spoon. Boil the sauce rapidly in the open pan until thickened to a coating consistency, taste and correct seasoning, pour over the chicken and arrange the mushrooms and onions on top.

BRAISED CHICKEN WITH VEGETABLES

Pressure Cooking Time: 5–8 minutes

Boiling fowl, jointed or portions of frozen chicken; $\frac{1}{2}$ lb chipolata sausages; a mirepoix (p. 300); seasoned flour; 2 tablespoons dripping or fat (bacon rinds if available); sufficient potatoes, carrots and a green vegetable for 4; flour for thickening; gravy colouring if necessary; a little sherry or Madeira to add to the sauce if liked.

If using frozen chicken, allow to thaw completely. Skin the chicken pieces and toss in seasoned flour. Prepare the mirepoix ingredients, the potatoes, carrots or other chosen vegetables. Lift the trivet from the cooker, put in the bacon from the mirepoix and the fat, heat, then brown the sausages quickly in the very hot fat. Lift out, brown the chicken pieces and lift them out. Finish making the mirepoix, adding just enough liquid to show through the surface. Put back the chicken pieces, the sausages, covered with a piece of greaseproof paper, the trivet and the potatoes and carrots in separate piles. Put the cooker on the heat, bring to the boil, add the green vegetable in a perforated container (in the smaller cookers there may not be room for this), bring to pressure in the usual way, cook for 5 minutes if frozen chicken, 8 minutes if fresh and reduce the pressure with cold water. Serve the vegetables separately and lift the chicken and sausages into the serving dish and keep all hot. Strain the stock, thicken and colour, return to the heat, reboil, taste and correct seasoning, cook for 2 to 3 minutes, add the wine and pour over the chicken.

Alternatively, the mirepoix vegetables, after the bouquet garni has been lifted out, may be well mashed or put through a liquidiser and sufficient stock be added to give the gravy the required consistency.

CHICKEN À LA CRÊME

Pressure Cooking Time: 4 minutes

2 young chickens or poussins (weight about $1\frac{1}{2}$ lb); 2 tablespoons butter; 1 medium finely diced onion; $\frac{1}{4}$ pint hot chicken stock or water; $\frac{1}{4}$ pint double cream; hard-boiled egg and chopped parsley for garnish.

From each chicken cut away the breast from each side in one complete piece taking as much meat from the wing as possible, and skin them. Season well with salt and pepper. Lift the trivet from the cooker, heat the butter and cook the onion for a minute or two but without browning; put in the hot liquid (if added cold, allow the cooker to cool) and the chicken breasts, bring to pressure in the usual way, cook for 4 minutes and reduce the pressure with cold water. Pour in the cream, return to the heat and boil rapidly until the sauce thickens but be sure it does not burn. Turn the chicken pieces over once, in the sauce, taste and correct seasoning. Lift the pieces on to the serving dish, laying them down the centre and standing up against each other. Coat with the sauce then garnish alternately with lines of chopped egg and parsley.

The legs, wings and carcases left can be used for the **Chicken Casserole** (p. 134) or **Chicken Curry** (p. 133) recipes.

CHICKEN BLANQUETTE

Pressure Cooking Time: 7–10 minutes

4 portions of boiling fowl or frozen pieces; 1 large onion; 1 crushed clove of garlic or squeeze of garlic juice (optional); 2 or 3 sticks of celery; bouquet garni; seasoning; $\frac{1}{4}$ pint water; 1 tablespoon butter, 1 tablespoon flour, $\frac{1}{4}$ pint milk for sauce; chopped parsley and fried bread for garnish.

Wipe the chicken joints, trim off the fat, skin and toss in seasoning. Quarter the onion and slice the celery. Lift the trivet from the cooker, put in the water, chicken, vegetables, seasoning and herbs, bring to pressure in the usual way, cook for 7 minutes if frozen chicken, 10 minutes if fresh and reduce the pressure with cold water. During this cooking, fry two slices of bread without crusts and cut into triangles. Make the sauce. Lift the chicken on to a deep serving dish, and keep hot. Strain the stock and add sufficient to the sauce to give a coating consistency. Reheat, taste and correct seasoning. Dip half of each triangle of bread into the sauce and then into the chopped parsley. Pour the sauce over the chicken and garnish with the prepared fried bread.

To enrich this recipe, two tablespoons of cream with a yolk of egg may be added to the sauce and cooked for 2 to 3 minutes but without boiling again or the sauce will curdle.

CHICKEN À LA KING

Pressure Cooking Time: 10 minutes per pound and 5 minutes

1 boiling fowl weighing up to 3½ lb; ½ pint water; a few mixed vegetables including carrot, onion, celery, 2 cloves, a bay leaf, seasoning, for the stock; 1 cup rice cooked and served according to instructions on p. 96; 1 small packet of frozen peas; 2 tablespoons butter, 2 tablespoons flour, ¾ pint of the chicken stock, ¼ pint single cream, 2 oz button mushrooms or small tin; 4 tablespoons of diced green peppers; seasoning, for the sauce.

Wipe the chicken and weigh. Lift the trivet from the cooker, put in the chicken, vegetables, water and seasonings, bring to pressure, cook for the required time and reduce the pressure with cold water. Lift out the chicken, strain and keep the stock. Put ½ pint water in the cooker with a little lemon juice and vinegar, the rice in a solid container, the trivet and the frozen peas, and sliced mushrooms if fresh, in another container. Bring to pressure, cook for 5 minutes and allow the pressure to reduce at room temperature. During this cooking, skin the chicken, remove the meat and cut into medium-sized strips. Make the sauce by melting the butter, blend in the flour and cook without colouring for a minute or two. Add the chicken stock gradually and cook until thickened, stirring constantly. Lift out the rice and finish ready for serving. Put the sliced mushrooms, the diced peppers, the strained peas, the chicken pieces into the sauce, check the consistency and seasoning and lastly add the cream. Reheat but do not allow to boil. Serve in a deep dish and hand the rice separately.

CHICKEN MARENGO

Using a young chicken, jointed into portions or chicken pieces instead of the veal follow the instructions, for **Veal Marengo** on p. 228. Pressure cook for 7 minutes. Serve with a garnish of fried croûtons.

CHICKEN SUPRÊME

Pressure Cooking Time: 5 minutes

4 pieces, fresh or frozen, of chicken wing with breast; 4 slices uncooked ham about $\frac{1}{4}$ inch thick; $\frac{1}{4}$ pint double cream; seasoned flour; 2 tablespoons butter; 4 oz of button mushrooms; $\frac{1}{2}$ pint chicken stock (a stock cube can be used); pepper; 2 tablespoons butter, 2 tablespoons flour, seasoning, sprigs of parsley for garnish.

$\frac{1}{4}$ pint chicken stock, $\frac{1}{4}$ pint milk, rest of cream, 1 yolk of egg, seasoning, for sauce.

If using frozen pieces allow to thaw completely. Carefully lift the chicken from the bones in each piece (save these and the skin to make chicken stock for soup, sauces, etc, in the cooker afterwards or, if chicken is bought the day before, bone it and make the stock straight away for this dish) and skin them. Take a little of the cream, brush the chicken pieces with it and roll them in seasoned flour. Wash the mushrooms and slice them lengthwise, stalks and all. Lift the trivet from the cooker, heat the butter, brown the slices of ham on both sides and lift out. Brown the chicken all over until a golden colour only and lift out. Add the hot stock (if added cold, allow the cooker to cool), put back the ham and on each slice a piece of chicken, placing them close together so that they touch. Lay the mushrooms in a thick layer on the top, dot with butter and cover with a piece of greaseproof paper. Bring to pressure in the usual way, cook for 5 minutes and reduce the pressure with cold water. During this cooking, make the sauce but do not add the cream or egg. Lift each piece of ham with its own chicken and mushrooms on to a serving dish and keep hot. Reboil the sauce, check seasoning; mix the cream with the beaten yolk and add, away from the heat, cooking for a further 2 minutes but without allowing the sauce to boil otherwise it will curdle. Pour round the dish and garnish each portion with a sprig of parsley.

Sherry to taste, may be added to the sauce, just before serving, for extra richness.

HASTY CHICKEN CURRY

These two hurry-along recipes would be just the thing if friends invite themselves at the last minute and you still have time to pop into your local shop before it closes.

Pressure Cooking Time: 5 minutes

4 portions of chicken, fresh or frozen; 3 tablespoons olive oil or butter; 3 medium onions; 2 eating apples; 1–1½ tablespoons curry powder or to taste; ¾ pint of stock (use a chicken cube); 2–3 oz sultanas; salt and pepper; 1 cup of rice, 2 cups of water; 1 tablespoon flour for thickening; 1–2 tablespoons redcurrant jelly; choice of chutney to hand separately; banana if available to garnish rice.

Skin the chicken pieces, dust in salt and pepper; chop the onion and apple finely and make the chicken stock. Lift the trivet from the cooker, put in the oil or butter and when hot, quickly brown the chicken pieces and lift out. Fry the onions until golden brown then add the curry powder and cook for 2 to 3 minutes. Stir in the stock and bring to the boil; put back the chicken pieces and add the apple, sultanas and seasoning. Put in the trivet and then a solid container with the rice and salted water, covered with greaseproof paper. Bring to pressure in the usual way, cook for 5 minutes and allow the pressure to reduce at room temperature. During this cooking, pre-heat the oven to Gas No 3, 325° F. Lift out the rice, rinse with boiling water, put on a baking sheet and into the oven, turn off the oven and leave the rice to dry. Add the thickening and redcurrant jelly to the curry, reboil, taste and correct seasoning and cook for 2 to 3 minutes. Make a ring of rice on the serving dish, pour the curry into the centre and garnish the rice with strips of banana or a few sultanas or lemon slices. Hand the chutney separately.

This recipe could also be used for fresh lamb or veal; or if cooked pieces of chicken, turkey, ham, cubed beef is to be curried, then add after pressure cooking the sauce and rice and cook for 2 to 3 minutes with the thickening to heat through thoroughly.

QUICKIE CHICKEN CASSEROLE

Pressure Cooking Time: 5 minutes

4 pieces of fresh or frozen chicken; 3 oz butter or fat; 2 medium onions; 2 medium carrots; $\frac{1}{4}$ lb mushrooms or selection of any other vegetables such as celery, cucumber, a little turnip; 1 pint of chicken stock (made from cube); a good pinch of mixed herbs; seasoning; 2 tablespoons of tomato ketchup or other savoury sauce; flour for thickening; a little sherry if available and parsley for garnishing.

Wipe and skin the chicken pieces, season well. Dice the onions and other vegetables if used or slice the mushrooms. Lift the trivet from the cooker, heat the fat, brown the chicken pieces all over and lift out. Brown the onions, add the hot chicken stock (if cold, allow the cooker to cool), put in the mushrooms, the seasonings and the sauce. Bring to pressure in the usual way, cook for 5 minutes and reduce the pressure with cold water. Lift out the chicken and keep hot. Add the thickening, reboil and cook for 2 to 3 minutes. Taste and correct seasoning and pour in sherry if liked. Pour the sauce over the chicken and sprinkle thickly with parsley.

SOUTHERN CHICKEN CASSEROLE

Pressure Cooking Time: 15–20 minutes

$3\frac{1}{2}$–4 lb fowl; 4 slices of streaky bacon, thick cut; 2 carrots; 1 green pepper and 2 medium onions or 6 shallots; 4 firm tomatoes; $\frac{1}{2}$ pint hot water; $\frac{1}{4}$ pint chili sauce; salt, celery salt; flour for thickening if required.

Ask your supplier to cut the fowl into four to six portions; wipe the chicken pieces, skin them and roll in seasoned flour; cut the bacon into large dice. Coarsely chop the carrots and the shallots if used. Wash the pepper, cut in half, remove all seeds and slice finely. Skin and halve the tomatoes and remove the pips. Lift the trivet from the cooker, put in the bacon and cook until nicely brown and the fat runs out. Add the chicken and brown the pieces evenly all over. Lift out the chicken, put in the prepared vegetables and cook for 3 to 4 minutes. Add the hot water (if cold, allow the cooker to cool), the chili sauce and the chicken in layers, sprinkling each lightly with the salts. Bring to pressure in the usual way, cook for 15 to 20 minutes according to the size of the joints, reduce the pressure with cold water. Lift the chicken into a casserole dish, add the thickening, if required, to the sauce, bring to the boil again, taste and correct seasoning and pour into the dish.

BRAISED DUCKLING WITH CHERRIES

Pressure Cooking Time: 10–12 minutes per pound

1 duck, cleaned and trussed; a bed of 4 slices of streaky bacon, 2 medium sliced onions, 2 medium carrots cut in rounds, 2 or 3 cubes of turnips, a sliced stick of celery, a bay leaf; $\frac{1}{2}$ pint brown stock; a dish of maraschino cherries.

Wipe the duck and weigh. Lift the trivet from the cooker, put in the bacon and allow to cook until the fat runs out. Carefully brown the breast of the duck only, on both sides, lift out and dust with seasoned flour. As it is essential to have a brown stock for this dish, if you have none ready cook the onions now until really dark brown. Put in the liquid, the rest of the vegetables and then the duck. It would make it extra special if you had a small glass of white or red wine to pour over the duck but if not, spoon over a little of the juice from the cherries. Bring the cooker to pressure in the usual way, cook for the required time, reduce the pressure by standing the cooker in a deep bowl of cold water. During the cooking, preheat the oven to Gas No 5, 375° F, and have ready a roasting tin with a little hot fat in it. Lift out the duck (but leave the cooker in cold water), baste with the hot fat and put as near to the top of the oven as possible to brown. When the cooker contents are nearly cold, skim off as much fat as possible, then sieve, return this thick gravy to the pan, reheat, taste and correct seasoning, then pour into a deep casserole. Put the duck on top; it may be served whole as it will be so well cooked that it will joint easily, but you may prefer to cut it into portions before taking it to table. Hand the cherries separately.

DUCKLING BIGARADE

Pressure Cooking Time: 10 minutes

1 duckling; butter and seasoning; peel of 1 bitter orange; 3 slices of streaky bacon; a pinch of mixed herbs, a little fresh chopped parsley and chives, a pinch of nutmeg; 2 sliced onions; 2 sliced carrots; $\frac{1}{2}$ pint of white stock; seasoning; 1 tablespoon butter, 1 tablespoon flour, a little orange juice for the sauce; a small glass of white wine would still further improve this dish, if available; watercress for garnish.

Wipe the duckling and put a knob of butter and a large piece of orange rind inside it. Cut the bacon slices in half; mix the herbs together. Lift the trivet from the cooker, fry the bacon lightly until the fat runs out and while still hot roll in the mixed herb mixture. Brown the breast of duck on both sides, lift out, season well with salt and pepper and lay the prepared bacon slices over the breast. Put into the cooker the stock and vegetables and then the duck (if using wine pour it over now), bring to pressure in the usual way, cook for the required time, reduce the pressure in a deep bowl of cold water. During this cooking, shred the rest of the orange peel very finely, put two tablespoons of water in a small saucepan and when boiling put in the shreds, boil quickly for 2 to 3 minutes and drain. Melt the butter in the saucepan, add the flour and cook gently for a minute or two. Lift out the duck and keep hot. Strain the stock and beat gradually into the saucepan, return to the heat and cook for 2 to 3 minutes. Check for a pouring consistency, add the cooked peel and a little strained orange juice, taste and correct seasoning and hand separately. Garnish the duck with the watercress.

BLANQUETTE OF RABBIT

Pressure Cooking Time: 20–25 minutes

1 small rabbit, jointed; 2 medium onions; 2 or 3 cloves; bouquet garni; strip of lemon peel; $\frac{1}{2}$ pint of stock (a chicken cube can be used); 2 tablespoons butter, 2 tablespoons flour, $\frac{1}{2}$ pint milk, 1 egg yolk, 2 tablespoons cream for sauce; bacon rolls (p. 297) or 2 tablespoons chopped ham, sprigs of parsley, slices of lemon for garnish.

Joint the rabbit and clean thoroughly. Lift the trivet from the cooker, put in the stock, the sliced onions, seasonings and joints, bring to pressure in the usual way, cook for the required time and reduce the pressure with cold water. During this cooking, make the sauce with the butter, flour and milk. Lift out the rabbit and keep hot in a casserole dish. Strain the stock and add sufficient to the sauce to give a coating consistency. Reheat, taste and correct seasoning, add the mixed cream and egg yolk and cook again but without reboiling. Pour over the rabbit joints and garnish with the bacon rolls or chopped ham, parsley and lemon slices.

FRICASSEE OF RABBIT

Pressure Cooking Time: 20–25 minutes

This dish can be made a real delicacy if the rabbit joints are first marinated for a couple of hours in $\frac{1}{2}$ pint of white wine or cider. They should be turned over 2 or 3 times whilst marinating.

1 rabbit jointed (and marinated); 3 finely sliced onions; 2 tablespoons of dripping; $\frac{1}{2}$ pint of white stock or the liquor from the marinade; 2 slices of streaky bacon; a piece of lemon rind if stock is used; 2 slices of fried bread, chopped parsley as garnish.

Wipe the rabbit joints and season well. Lift the trivet from the cooker, heat the diced bacon until the fat runs out, then brown the joints and the onions. Add the liquid, lemon rind and seasoning, bring to pressure in the usual way, cook for the required time and reduce the pressure in cold water. During this cooking, fry the bread, cut into triangles and dip half of each in the chopped parsley. Lift the joints into a casserole dish and keep hot. Boil the contents of the cooker rapidly until reduced and thick, taste and correct seasoning, pour over the joints and garnish with the fried triangles of bread.

BRAISED OR JUGGED HARE

Pressure Cooking Time: 30–40 minutes

1 hare; 2 tablespoons of dripping or lumps of bacon fat; seasoned flour; 2 chopped onions; a crushed clove of garlic; a blade of mace; $\frac{1}{4}$ pint brown stock; seasoning; a small glass of red wine; 1 or 2 field mushrooms; the blood of the hare, if liked; 2 slices of fried bread, redcurrant jelly.

Joint the hare and clean thoroughly. Lift the trivet from the cooker, melt the fat and brown the joints, lift out and toss in seasoned flour. Brown the onions, drain away the fat, add the sliced mushrooms, the stock and wine, the seasonings and the joints, bring to pressure, cook for the required time and reduce the pressure with cold water. During this cooking, fry the bread and cut in triangles. Lift the joints into a casserole dish and keep hot. Boil the contents of the pan until well thickened and if the blood is to be used, add it now but do not allow the sauce to reboil. Taste and correct the seasoning and pour over the joints. Dip one point of each triangle in redcurrant jelly and serve as garnish.

SALMIS OF PARTRIDGE

Pressure Cooking Time: 15–25 minutes

2 small to medium partridges; 2 small onions stuck with a clove each; 3 slices of streaky bacon; 2 tablespoons of dripping; $\frac{1}{2}$ pint of brown stock strongly flavoured with tomato purée; bouquet garni and a sprig of rosemary if available; chopped parsley or watercress for garnish.

Wipe the partridges, clean carefully, put an onion inside each and dust with seasoned flour. Lift the trivet from the cooker, melt the fat, fry the bacon slices until golden brown but not crisp and lift out. Gently brown the partridges all over, lift out, lay a bacon slice down the centre, then parcel each carefully but loosely in a piece of greaseproof paper. Drain the fat from the cooker, put in the liquid and the seasonings, the trivet and then the parcels. Bring to pressure in the usual way, cook for the required time, reduce the pressure with cold water. During this cooking, prepare four slices of fried bread and lay ready in the serving dish. Lift out the parcels, turn upside down to open so that the juices run over the partridges as they stand on the fried bread, and keep hot. Lift out the trivet, boil the liquid rapidly until the sauce is thickened, then pour round the dish or hand separately.

BRAISED PHEASANT CHARTREUSE

Pressure Cooking Time: 7–10 minutes

1 large or 2 small pheasants; 2 oz dripping; $\frac{1}{2}$ pint brown stock or water; 1 large white cabbage; 4 frankfurter or cocktail sausages; 2 thick bacon rashers; 2 medium carrots; 1 medium sliced onion; flour for thickening; a little red wine, if liked, to enrich the gravy; a small bunch of watercress.

Wipe the pheasant and see it is securely trussed. Cut the cabbage into quarters, the carrots in four lengthways and the bacon slices in four pieces. Lift the trivet from the cooker, heat the bacon until the fat runs out, carefully brown the pheasant all over, lift out and dust with salt and pepper. Lightly fry the onions, then drain off the fat, put in the liquid, the cabbage, the onion and carrots, the pheasant on top and the sausages around it. Bring to pressure in the usual way, cook for the required time and reduce the pressure with cold water. Lift the pheasant out and put on one side. Put the cabbage quarters on the serving dish, the pheasant on top and the sausages, bacon and carrots around as garnish. Strain the stock, removing any fat by drawing small pieces of absorbent paper across the surface; add the thickening, reboil, cook for 2 to 3 minutes, taste and correct seasoning and add the red wine if available. Put the watercress in a bunch on the dish, hand the sauce separately.

COLD MEATS

BRAWN

Pressure Cooking Time: 35 minutes

$\frac{1}{2}$ salted pig's head (cow head or pig's cheek could be used instead); small knuckle of veal; 2 small onions; 2 small carrots; $\frac{1}{2}$ teaspoon of nutmeg; blade of mace; 3 cloves; a few peppercorns; a pinch of meat or mixed herbs; seasoning; 1 pint cold water; 1 hard-boiled egg and gherkin or cucumber slices for garnish.

Lift the trivet from the cooker, put in the meats and the water, bring to the boil in the open pan and skim until there is nothing more coming to the surface. Add the rest of the ingredients, bring to pressure in the usual way, cook for 35 minutes and allow the pressure to reduce. Lift out the joints, remove all the meat and cut into ½-inch dice. Strain the stock, boil rapidly with the bones in the open pan until reduced to about half a pint, taste and correct seasoning. Put back the meat and reboil then turn into a wetted mould or basin to three-quarters fill it, cover completely with the stock and leave to set. Turn out, just before serving, by dipping quickly in and out of boiling water.

Serve, garnished with overlapping alternate slices of hard-boiled egg and gherkin or cucumber.

CHICKEN LIVER PATÉ

This should be made a day or two before required so that it can mature.

Pressure Cooking Time: 3 minutes

½ lb chicken livers; 1 tablespoon melted butter; 1 tablespoon brandy and 1 of sherry; 2 tablespoons butter; 2 tablespoons cream cheese; salt, pepper; a pinch of mixed spice and a pinch of herbs such as thyme, basil, rosemary, marjoram as available; ½ pint water for the cooker with a little vinegar or lemon juice.

Wipe the livers and put into a deep saucer or dish that will fit into the cooker with one tablespoon melted butter, covering with a piece of greaseproof paper. Put the water, trivet and livers in the cooker, bring to pressure in the usual way, cook for 3 minutes and reduce the pressure with cold water. During this cooking, mix the butter, cheese, herbs and seasoning to a smooth consistency. Lift the livers from the cooker, strain the stock into the brandy and sherry and whisk well. Sieve the livers or put through a liquidiser, combine all the ingredients together, beat well, smooth into a 1-lb loaf tin or small soufflé dish and refrigerate until firm. Serve with slices of hot toast in individual portions garnished with crisp heart of lettuce leaves.

GALANTINE OF BEEF

Pressure Cooking Time: 35 minutes

1 lb minced lean beef; ¼ lb raw ham; ¼ lb sausage meat; 1 small onion; ¼ lb fresh white crumbs; 2–3 large mushrooms; 2 tablespoons fresh chopped parsley; a dash of Worcester or HP Sauce; 1 egg; seasoning; 2 hard-boiled eggs if liked; ¾ pint water for cooker; golden crumbs for coating.

Mince together the meats, chop the mushrooms and onion very finely. Mix all the ingredients together and bind with the beaten egg. Put into a seamless 1-lb loaf tin or suitable container rinsed in cold water and tie down with a double thickness of greaseproof paper or form into a roll and tie in a triple thickness of greaseproof paper, pleating this to allow for the roll expanding. If hard-boiled eggs are used, lay these end to end in the middle of the mixture. Lift the trivet from the cooker, put in the water, if the galatine is in a container, add a little lemon juice or vinegar and then the trivet; if in a roll, put directly into the water. Bring to pressure in the usual way, cook for 35 minutes and allow the pressure to reduce at room temperature.

Lift out the container, take off the paper, put on a clean piece and press under heavy weights. (If a loaf tin has been used, a carton of sugar, on its side, usually forms a good base for the weights.) If a roll has been made, reroll very tightly in clean paper and press between two large plates.

When cold, coat in golden crumbs and serve with salad.

GALANTINE OF VEAL CHAUDFROID

Pressure Cooking Time: 25 minutes

$\frac{1}{2}$ lb breast or fillet of veal; $\frac{1}{4}$ lb pork sausage meat; $\frac{1}{4}$ lb streaky bacon; 6 tablespoons breadcrumbs; seasoning; a pinch of nutmeg; $\frac{1}{2}$ teaspoon powdered mixed herbs; 2 tablespoons of stock (a dissolved chicken cube can be used); 1 egg; 2 thin slices of cooked ham or tongue; 1 pint water for the cooker; a small bottle of mayonnaise (approx. 5 oz); 1 tablespoon single cream; 1 packet of aspic jelly; gelatine; slices of cucumber and radish, chopped aspic, crisp green lettuce and watercress for garnish.

Wipe, trim off all fat from the veal and mince finely. Cut the bacon rashers and the ham or tongue in fine lengthwise strips. Combine the veal, sausage meat, bacon, breadcrumbs, seasonings and herbs, add the stock and beaten egg and mix well together. Spread the mixture into an oblong about $\frac{1}{2}$ inch thick on a triple thickness of greaseproof paper, lay the strips of ham or bacon side by side down its length, then roll up like a Swiss Roll and tie very firmly in the paper. Put the water, trivet and roll in the cooker, bring to pressure in the usual way, cook for 25 minutes and reduce the pressure with cold water. Lift out the roll, and press, still in the paper between two boards or plates, using at least 4 lb in weights. On the morning of the day for serving, make up the aspic jelly as instructed on the packet. Dissolve a $\frac{1}{4}$-oz packet of gelatine in one tablespoon of the warm aspic. Beat the mayonnaise well, add the cream and then the aspic with the gelatine and put on one side until setting to a smooth, thick coating consistency, then coat the roll evenly and allow to set. Decorate down the centre with overlapping slices of cucumber and radish and baste with thickening aspic to coat the roll and set the decorations. Put the rest of the aspic jelly to set. For serving, trim the edges of the roll, using a knife dipped in hot water, put on a flat dish and garnish with alternate green salading and small piles of the aspic jelly chopped finely, again with a knife dipped in hot water.

This galantine of veal can also be served cold but plain; sprinkle the paper and the roll with golden crumbs before pressure cooking, then press in the usual way.

PRESSED TONGUE

Pressure Cooking Time: 15 minutes per pound

1 ox tongue; 2 dessertspoons vinegar; 12 peppercorns; 2 or 3 cloves; a bay leaf; cold water to cover.

The easiest way to handle the tongue is to tie it loosely in a piece of butter muslin. If the tongue has been smoked, soak overnight in cold water. Lift the trivet from the cooker, put in the tongue and other ingredients, add sufficient water to half fill the cooker or just cover the tongue, whichever is the less, bring to pressure in the usual way, cook for the required time and allow the pressure to reduce at room temperature. Lift the tongue on to a large dish, untie, skin carefully and remove all the small bones. While still hot, curl the tongue into a basin or a soufflé dish which is just a little too small for it, put a saucer or plate which just fits inside the container on top and press with weights from the household scales (or packets of sugar, etc). Leave overnight, then to turn out the tongue, dip the dish just to the level of the top, in boiling water, count to about twenty, then turn on to the serving dish and give a shake.

Serve with new potatoes and a mixed or green salad.

PRESSED VEAL

Pressure Cooking Time: 30 minutes

2 lb knuckle of veal on or with the bone; salt, pepper; 3 cloves, 6 peppercorns, 1 bay leaf or 1 teaspoon of pickling spice; 1 tablespoon of lemon juice or vinegar; $\frac{1}{2}$ pint of chicken stock, made from a cube or water.

If the veal is in one piece, ask your butcher to chop it into two or four pieces. Wipe the meat and trim off fat. Lift the trivet from the cooker, put in the water, meat, seasonings and herbs, bring to pressure in the usual way, cook for 30 minutes and reduce the pressure with cold water. Lift out the meat, cut it all away from the bones, chop it finely and leave to cool. Boil the stock rapidly in the open pan until reduced by half, strain, then add the lemon or vinegar and taste to correct seasoning. Put the meat into a loaf tin or mould rinsed with cold water; it should be of a size so that the meat is very tightly packed. Add sufficient stock to fill the mould, cover with a piece of buttered paper and press with heavy weights for at least 12 hours. Before serving, unmould by dipping quickly in and out of boiling water; suggested garnishes would be lettuce, quartered hard-boiled eggs and halved tomatoes, cut decoratively and filled with cooked peas.

MADE-UP DISHES

CHICORY WITH HAM BRUXELLOIS

6–8 cooked chicory; 6–8 thin slices of cooked ham; ½ pint white sauce (p. 291); grated cheese; golden crumbs; rolls of thin brown bread and butter; sprigs of parsley.

Wrap each chicory in a slice of ham and lay them, head to tail, in a shallow, ovenproof serving dish. Coat with the white sauce which should have plenty of pepper but not too much salt, sprinkle thickly with grated cheese and finely with golden crumbs and brown under a hot grill. Hand round separately, slices of brown bread cut very thinly, with the crusts removed, plenty of butter, rolled up and arranged in a pile with sprigs of parsley for decoration.

COQUILLES OF CHICKEN MORNAY

Slices of cooked chicken; ½ pint cheese sauce (p. 292); grated cheese, knobs of butter.

Cut sufficient slices of chicken for four and put into individual scallop shells or in a shallow ovenproof serving dish. Make the cheese sauce using a little chicken stock as well as milk, if available. Coat this over the chicken slices, sprinkle thickly with grated cheese, dot with butter and brown under a hot grill.

HAM MAILLOT

Pressure Cooking Time: 4 minutes

Potatoes, carrots, turnips, fresh or frozen peas for garnish; slices of cooked ham sufficient for four people; 1 level tablespoon butter, 1 level tablespoon flour, salt and pepper, ½ pint cooking sherry or Madeira; ½ pint water for the cooker; a little chopped parsley for garnish.

Preheat the oven to Gas No 4, 350° F. Peel the vegetables and cut into even sizes, shaping as nearly as possible to look like large olives

—about twelve of each vegetable. Put the water and the trivet in the cooker, put the well-salted carrots, turnips and potatoes in three piles, bring the water to the boil and when the pan is filled with steam put in the salted peas in a perforated container. Bring to pressure in the usual way, cook for 4 minutes and reduce the pressure with cold water. During this cooking, melt the butter in a small pan, add the flour and seasoning and cook allowing it to turn a light brown colour. Add the wine, reheat and cook, stirring all the time for a minute or two. Lay the slices of ham, overlapping in a deep dish, coat with the sauce and put in the centre of the oven to heat through. Before serving, check the sauce and if thicker than a coating consistency add a little more heated wine. Lift out the vegetables; pile the peas at each end of the dish and the other vegetables in alternate heaps on either side facing each other. Sprinkle the ham only, lightly, with the chopped parsley.

OX TONGUE WITH CHERRIES

Medium thick slices of cooked ox tongue; thin slices of unpeeled cucumber; a small tin of red cherries; a pint of made-up aspic jelly; a green salad with dressing to choice.

Lay the slices of tongue overlapping on a shallow serving dish with a little of a cucumber slice just showing between each and surround with a complete circle of the strained cherries. Have the aspic really cold but still liquid, and use sufficient to cover the tongue and cherries. Allow to set, then serve with the dressed green salad.

SECTION V

Cereals, Rice and Pastas

This particular group of foods is probably not as popular as it used to be since there has been so much talk and discussion over the last few years of the advantages to health in keeping to a diet light in starchy foods and with the swings in fashion which require, from time to time, those sylph-like figures which are so difficult to achieve. But unless on medical orders, or as a matter of choice, a very strict diet is being followed, a reasonable amount of carbohydrate will not do all that much harm and for the younger members of the family, active and growing, it remains an essential item of the daily food intake. While pressure cooking cereals and other such foods do not represent quite such a spectacular saving in time as for meats, vegetables, soups and so on, it does mean that rice, for example, can be pressure cooked at the same time as many of the dishes it is to accompany; this represents quite a considerable saving in fuel as it does away with a second saucepan which in itself means less work too for the cook and washer-up. Nowadays there are so many varieties and forms of these foods, with new ones coming on to the market every day, that it is not possible to mention them all. However, the timetable and recipes in the following section should give a good idea of average times from which to work out the correct one for a particular type, without too much trouble.

There are also many new varieties specially treated for quick-cooking and with these, unless the time given on the packet is considerably longer than the pressure cooking time, it is probably more sensible to cook them on their own, following the instructions given on the packet.

It is, however, true to say that the completeness of the cooking under pressure does bring out an extra good taste in cereals such as oatmeal and ensures that macaroni, spaghetti, rice are really swollen and soft and very absorbent of other flavours such as cheese, tomato, garlic which may require to be added to them.

You are sure to find that serving a choice of rice, macaroni, spaghetti, noodles will add a very welcome as well as nourishing variety to your family's diet and can substitute most satisfactorily for those daily servings of potatoes which even the best of housewives can find monotonous, to prepare, to cook—and to eat.

GENERAL INSTRUCTIONS

The trivet is not used for any of these foods as all require to be cooked in plenty of salted water or sauce as they must swell and absorb liquid during cooking. As a general rule, pastas such as macaroni, spaghetti, noodles, etc, will require approximately one-third of the normal cooking time when pressure cooked, eg:

Normal cooking time: 8–10 minutes; pressure cooking time: 3–4 minutes.
Normal cooking time: 10–15 minutes; pressure cooking time: 5–6 minutes.
Normal cooking time: 15–25 minutes; pressure cooking time: 8–10 minutes.

If the recipe being followed requires further cooking of the pasta when other ingredients are added, then the first pressure cooking time should be cut by 2 to 3 minutes.

As these foods usually require to be plunged into boiling salted water, do not try to put the cover on with the weight on or the valve closed. As the pan will be filled with steam it may be difficult or even impossible to close the cover completely and therefore safely; once the cover is correctly closed the weight can be put on or the valve be closed immediately.

As all cereals tend to froth and boil up during cooking, the pan must never be more than one-third full when ready to be brought to pressure. Use **High** pressure and allow to reduce at room temperature.

During the actual pressure cooking the heat can be kept a little lower than normal and, if the contents of the pan begin to boil through the valve, just keep an eye on it to make sure that the steam still continues to escape. As the cooking is so short and the meal usually waiting to be dished up it is not difficult to do this. Should a floury-looking liquid begin to boil out of the valve, take the cooker away from the heat for a moment, give it a good shake backwards and forwards, then put it back on the heat and continue for the rest of the cooking time, still watching it carefully.

In the following recipes, the small cereals, pastas and the rice are measured in cups: 1 full teacup = 6 oz approximately; the larger cereals and those cooked in lengths are weighed in ounces. For most dishes, 2 oz should be allowed per person.

CEREAL	AMOUNT	WATER	PRESSURE COOKING TIME
Barley			
pearl	1 cup	4 cups, 1 teaspoon salt	20 minutes
Macaroni			
2-inch lengths	8 oz	2 pints (4 cups), 1 tablespoon salt	4–5 minutes
elbow	8 oz	2 pints (4 cups), 1 tablespoon salt	5–6 minutes
Noodles			
fine	8 oz	2 pints (4 cups), 1 tablespoon salt	2–3 minutes
medium	8 oz	2 pints (4 cups), 1 tablespoon salt	3–4 minutes
alphabet	1 cup	3 cups, 1 tablespoon salt	3–4 minutes
small shells	1 cup	4 cups, 1 tablespoon salt	3 minutes
Rice			
long grain	1 cup	2 cups, ½ teaspoon salt	5 minutes
Oatmeal			
coarse	1 cup	4 cups, ½ teaspoon salt	15–20 minutes
Spaghetti			
fine	8 oz	2 pints (4 cups), 1 tablespoon salt	3–4 minutes
regular	8 oz	2 pints (4 cups), 2 tablespoons salt	5–6 minutes
Vermicelli	8 oz	2 pints (4 cups), 1 tablespoon salt	3–4 minutes

BARLEY

This is most usually added to clear soups such as vegetable or chicken to give them plenty of bulk and to make them more of a meal in themselves. It is an excellent food too, for invalids and can be made into a cream soup or barley water, recipes for which will be found in the appropriate section.

MACARONI

To serve as a course of a meal, allow 2 oz per person. After pressure cooking, reduce the pressure with cold water and drain through a colander.

MACARONI CHEESE

8 oz macaroni; 2 tablespoons butter; 1 pint cheese sauce (p. 292); 3 tablespoons grated cheese; paprika pepper; croûtons of fried bread (p. 298).

Cook the macaroni as directed and during this cooking make the cheese sauce and have the butter ready, melted in a large saucepan. Turn the macaroni into the saucepan, toss until well coated with the butter. Add the cheese sauce, stir and put into a buttered ovenproof dish. Sprinkle thickly with the cheese, dot with knobs of butter and while it is browning lightly under the grill, fry the bread. Sprinkle with paprika and garnish with triangles of fried bread.

MACARONI RAREBIT

4 oz macaroni; 1 tablespoon butter; ½ pint cheese sauce (p. 292) with mustard and Worcester Sauce; slices of tomato; 1 tablespoon grated cheese; 2 slices streaky bacon; a little chopped chives.

Cook the macaroni as directed. During the cooking, make the cheese sauce but add a quarter teaspoon of mustard to the flour and a good dash of Worcester Sauce with the milk; fry the diced streaky bacon until crisp, in its own fat; cut the tomato slices. Toss the macaroni in a saucepan with the melted butter then divide into four individual buttered ovenproof dishes or scallop shells. Pour over the sauce, sprinkle with cheese, arrange the tomato slices and brown under a hot grill. Garnish with the fried bacon and chives.

SAVOURY MACARONI

8 oz macaroni; 2 tablespoons butter; 1 finely chopped onion; 4 tomatoes; some strips of red or green pepper if available; 2 oz sliced mushrooms; $\frac{1}{4}$ pint brown stock or gravy; 8 oz cooked ham, meat, chicken or sausages; dash of Worcester Sauce; seasoning.

Cook the macaroni as directed, pile on the serving dish to keep hot. During this cooking, heat the butter in a frying pan and gently cook the onions, mushrooms and peppers if used. Add the quartered tomatoes, cook for a moment or two, stir in the liquid, seasonings and finally the cooked meat. Cover and leave over a low heat until ready to serve. Add the Worcester Sauce, taste and correct seasoning and pour over the macaroni. Serve piping hot, with or without grated cheese handed separately.

NOODLES

To serve as a course of a meal, allow 2 oz per person. After cooking, reduce the pressure with cold water and drain through a colander.

The larger, broader, kinds of noodles may replace macaroni in the recipes already given and the finer types replace spaghetti in those following. Alphabet and shell noodles may be served in thin or clear soups such as chicken, vegetable, etc, when they give an attractive as well as a nutritious addition.

Fine noodles would make an excellent accompaniment for a pot-roast, Swiss steak, Swedish meat balls, etc, and as they do not take long to cook it does not mean keeping these dishes hot for too long. If served, in place of dumplings, with a boiled meat such as silverside or mutton they can be added to the cooking liquid, 3 to 4 minutes before the end of the full cooking time.

BUTTERED NOODLES

8 oz fine noodles; 3 tablespoons butter; chopped parsley or chives.

Cook the noodles as directed. Have ready the melted butter, which should be allowed to turn brown over a low heat.

Serve the noodles, pour over the browned butter and garnish with the parsley.

NOODLE SUPPER

8 oz medium or broad noodles; 2 tablespoons butter; salt, pepper and nutmeg; 4 oz grated cheese, cheddar and parmesan mixed; a crisp green salad to accompany.

Cook the noodles as directed. Melt one tablespoon of butter in the cooker, put back the drained noodles and toss until they are well coated. Stir in the cheese, the rest of the butter, the seasoning and a pinch of nutmeg and reheat. Serve piping hot, with individual green salads.

SHRIMP SHELLS

4 oz small shell noodles; 1 tablespoon butter; a packet of frozen shrimps; 2 tablespoons of mayonnaise and 1 tablespoon thin cream or top of the milk; a squeeze of lemon juice; a little grated cheese; golden crumbs; lemon butterflies (p. 299) and sprigs of parsley.

Cook the shells as directed. During the cooking, wash the thawed out shrimps quickly in cold water. In a small saucepan heat the mayonnaise with the cream over a low heat, stir in the shrimps and add pepper and lemon juice to taste. Put the noodles back into the cooker with the butter and toss until well-coated and glistening. Arrange the noodles in buttered individual ovenproof dishes or scallop shells leaving a shallow well in the centre of each. Fill this with the shrimp mixture, sprinkle with the cheese and golden crumbs and brown under a hot grill. Garnish each with a lemon butterfly and a sprig of parsley.

OATMEAL

Now that quick-cooking oats are so popular it is really only for the coarse, whole oatmeal that pressure cooking is such a time-saver. Be sure to stir the oatmeal well after adding to the boiling water and watch the pan during the cooking to make sure that it is not frothing up to block the valve. Allow the pressure to reduce at room temperature and if the porridge is not quite thick enough, it can be boiled while stirring in the open pan until the desired consistency is reached.

RICE

One cup of rice will give approximately four cups when cooked, so allow one full teacup, approximately 6 oz, for two people as an accompaniment or as part of a complete dish.

If cooked on its own, the rice should be thrown into the salted boiling water in the cooker and the pressure should be reduced with cold water.

In many of the recipes, the rice is cooked with other ingredients and it is then put into a solid container in the proportion of two cups of water to one of rice, the container being covered with a piece of greaseproof paper. At the end of the cooking time, the pressure is allowed to reduce at room temperature to ensure that the rice will absorb all the water.

With either method, the rice should be finished off as given in the following recipe:

BOILED RICE AS AN ACCOMPANIMENT

Cook long-grain rice as directed but add half a lemon to the water. During the cooking preheat the oven to Gas No 3, 325° F, and boil a kettle of water. As soon as the rice has been strained, pour the boiling water over to separate the grains. Put into a hot dish and then in the oven on the middle shelf. Turn off the oven and leave to dry out for a few minutes.

BUTTERED RICE

Cook the long-grain rice as directed and leave to dry out in the oven for a few minutes as explained for boiled rice. Melt 2 tablespoons of butter in a saucepan, stir in the rice, add a beaten egg, a sprinkling of chopped parsley or chives, reheat and serve piping hot with a bowl of grated cheese handed separately.

There are so many varied ways of serving rice that it is only possible to give a few suggestions here but as nearly all such recipes require cooked rice as a basis for the dish, this would be pressure cooked to save time and then the particular recipe be followed from then on.

A particularly attractive way to serve rice is to form it into a ring on the serving dish, leaving a large well in the centre into which the other ingredients can be filled. The ring can be plain or buttered rice or one of the following variations and should be dried in the pre-heated but turned-off oven as given for **Boiled Rice**.

CURRIED RICE

For serving with cooked chicken, veal or lamb heated in a White Cream or Tomato Sauce.

After rinsing, put back in the pan, add a teaspoon of curry powder which has been heated in a tablespoon of melted butter and stir until mixed through.

YELLOW RICE

For vegetarian dishes, using mixed vegetables, hard-boiled eggs, in Tomato or a Curry Sauce.

While the rice is cooking, melt a little butter or oil in a frying pan, add a finely diced onion and cook gently. When the rice has been rinsed and dried, add to the frying pan and stir slowly until the rice turns golden brown.

ARABIAN RICE

Delicious with cooked poultry or game reheated in a rich, brown gravy or Espagnole or Madeira Sauce.

When the rice has been rinsed, stir in 2 tablespoons of melted butter, 2 oz sultanas or small raisins and 2 oz of finely shredded, blanched almonds and mix well together.

RICE—CHINESE STYLE

While the rice is cooking, beat an egg and scramble it very lightly in butter, in a frying pan. Add a cup of diced fresh or tinned lobster or crab meat and the drained rice and allow to cook gently for 3 or 4 minutes without browning. Stir in 1 teaspoon of soy sauce, season using fresh-ground black pepper if possible and serve piping hot.

RICE—SPANISH STYLE

While the rice is cooking, melt 2 tablespoons of butter or oil in a frying pan, add a finely chopped onion, a clove of garlic (or a squeeze of garlic juice), 2 tablespoons of diced green peppers and cook gently until soft. Add 3 or 4 large peeled, chopped tomatoes, a crushed bay leaf and seasoning, and simmer gently until the drained rice is ready. Stir in the rice, reheat and serve piping hot.

JAMBALAYA

Pressure Cooking Time: 8 minutes

2 slices of bacon; 2 tablespoons of olive oil or butter; 1 medium onion; 1 clove of garlic; a stick of celery; 2 tablespoons green pepper; 1 large tin of tomatoes; $1\frac{1}{2}$ pints of chicken stock; a selection of herbs such as bayleaf, thyme, ground cloves; 8 oz rice; seasoning and a small pinch of cayenne pepper; 4 oz cooked chicken; 4 oz of fresh prawns; a small glass of dry, white wine.

Dice the bacon, onions, garlic, celery and peppers. Lift the trivet from the cooker, heat the oil or butter and cook the bacon until the fat runs out and it is golden. Add the onion and cook until transparent, then put in the rice and stir over a low heat until it is golden. Add the rest of the vegetables, the herbs and seasonings and lastly the tomatoes and stock. Bring to the boil, stir well, bring to pressure in the usual way, cook for 8 minutes and reduce the pressure with cold water. During this cooking, dice the chicken and cut the prawns into two or three. The Jambalaya should now be thick, with very little liquid and the rice should be tender but still in separate grains. Add the chicken and prawns, and lastly the wine, taste and correct seasoning and reheat very carefully so that the grains of rice remain apart.

RISOTTO

Pressure Cooking Time: 6 minutes

This dish should always be made with Italian or the round-grain rice. It is not really satisfactory if made with the long-grain rice as this type is not sufficiently absorbent to give the desired result.

2 tablespoons of olive oil; 1 finely sliced medium onion and a clove of garlic; 1 cup of rice; 4 cups of boiling, well-seasoned chicken stock; 4 heaped tablespoons grated Parmesan cheese.

Lift the trivet from the cooker, heat the oil and cook the onion until just turning brown. Add the garlic and rice and stir until the rice begins to look transparent. Pour in the boiling stock, stir for a moment or two until the liquid is boiling again, bring to pressure in the usual way, cook for 6 minutes and allow the pressure to reduce at room temperature. The rice should have absorbed all the stock but if it has not, allow it to cook for a moment or two in the open pan. Stir in the grated cheese and serve at once, piping hot and piled high on the serving dish.

RISOTTO WITH MUSHROOMS

During the cooking as given in the preceding recipe, gently cook a $\frac{1}{4}$ lb of finely sliced button mushrooms in a little oil and add these to the rice in the cooker just before serving. The grated cheese should be handed separately.

RISOTTO WITH CHICKEN LIVERS

During the cooking of the rice as given for **Risotto**, thinly slice 3 chicken's livers and fry them very carefully so that they do not dry up, in 1 tablespoon of mixed butter and olive oil, then lift out. Add the strained juice of half a lemon or 1 tablespoon of white wine to the juices in the pan, then $\frac{1}{4}$ pint of thickened brown stock or chicken gravy. Taste and correct seasoning, put back the livers, reheat without boiling and serve piled into the centre of a rice ring.

PILAFF

Pressure Cooking Time: 5 minutes

2 oz butter; 2 tablespoons of chopped onion; 1 cup of long grain rice; 2 cups of hot chicken or veal stock; a little paprika pepper or chopped parsley for garnish.

Lift the trivet from the cooker and lightly cook the onion in the melted butter, but without allowing it to colour. Add the rice and stir until it begins to look transparent. Add the hot stock, allow to boil again stirring well, cover, bring to pressure, cook for 5 minutes and allow the pressure to reduce at room temperature. Return to the heat and flick with a fork until each grain is separate. Arrange in a ring or as a bed on the serving dish with any of the following accompaniments:

Diced cooked turkey in a cream sauce, the rice garnished with bacon rolls.

Diced cooked lamb or mutton in a cream sauce, with raisins stirred into the rice.

Add some diced celery with the onions in the frying pan.

Diced cooked duck in a cream sauce, the rice garnished with slices of peeled oranges or cooked, stoned prunes.

SPAGHETTI

As a complete dish, spaghetti is usually cooked in the long lengths in which it is sold. To do this, wait until the salted water in the cooker is boiling fast, then taking a fistful of spaghetti, plunge the ends in the water but don't let go. As the spaghetti softens, it can be bent until it all slips under the water and the cover can then be fitted on easily. After reducing the pressure with cold water, the spaghetti should be strained and should be tender but still quite firm.

SPAGHETTI BOLOGNAISE

Pressure Cooking Time: 10 minutes and 5 minutes

$\frac{3}{4}$ lb spaghetti; 3 tablespoons olive oil or butter; 1 onion; 4 oz lean minced raw beef (or 2 oz beef, 2 oz chicken livers); 2 oz mushrooms (stalks only will do); a little diced carrot and celery if liked; a piece of lemon rind, a bayleaf or a little basil if available, salt, pepper, a pinch of nutmeg as seasonings; 2 good tablespoons of tomato purée or paste stirred into $\frac{1}{4}$ pint of brown stock (made with beef cube); a clove of garlic or squeeze of garlic juice; 2 lumps of sugar; $\frac{1}{4}$ pint dry white wine; a little olive oil or butter; 2 tablespoons of grated Parmesan cheese.

Lift the trivet from the cooker, heat the oil and gently brown the diced onion. Add the meat, chopped mushrooms and other vegetables if used. Cook for 2 to 3 minutes only, stirring all the time as the meat must not be allowed to harden. Pour in the wine and boil rapidly for a moment or two, then add the seasonings, sugar and the tomato liquid, stir again, bring to pressure, cook for 10 minutes and reduce the pressure with cold water. Turn the sauce into another saucepan and while it is cooking very gently, without a lid, to reduce it to a really creamy consistency, rinse out the cooker and prepare the spaghetti as directed. While it is draining, put a little oil or butter in the cooker, allow it and the cooker to warm thoroughly, put back the spaghetti and stir it around off the heat until it is well coated. Serve in a deep, really hot dish, pour over the sauce and hand the cheese separately.

SPAGHETTI MILANAISE

Pressure Cooking Time: 5–6 minutes

$\frac{3}{4}$ lb spaghetti; 2 tablespoons olive oil or butter; 6 oz of mixed strips of cooked ham and tongue; 1 tablespoon of strips of tinned button mushrooms; 2 tablespoons of tomato purée or paste added to $\frac{1}{4}$ pint beef stock (made with cube); seasoning; 2 tablespoons grated cheese; chopped parsley.

Cook the spaghetti as directed, drain and rinse with boiling water. Heat the oil in the cooker, put back the spaghetti and stir with a fork until well coated. Add the meat, mushrooms and the tomato liquid, heat thoroughly stirring gently, correct seasoning and serve piping hot in a deep dish, sprinkled with the cheese and parsley.

QUICK SPAGHETTI SAVOURY

Pressure Cooking Time: 5–6 minutes

4 oz spaghetti; $\frac{1}{2}$ pint cheese sauce (p. 292); 4 large tomatoes; seasoning; 4 circles of fried bread; 2 tablespoons grated cheese; chopped parsley.

Cook the spaghetti as directed. During the cooking, grill the halved, seasoned tomatoes; fry the circles of bread and put ready on four individual dishes with the tomatoes on top and keep hot. Make the sauce and when the spaghetti is drained stir it in, reheat, season well and pile on to the tomatoes. Sprinkle with the cheese and chopped parsley.

SECTION VI

PUDDINGS, BREAD AND CAKES

In these days of rush and bustle many housewives, and particularly those who work outside the home, just do not have sufficient time before the family is clamouring for its meal, to prepare the great variety of steamed puddings and hot sweets which used to be such a great standby in grandmother's and even mother's day and which were so delicious and welcome on cold winter evenings and such a good way to satisfy the hungry adults and growing children's appetities. Then again, because of the long time necessary for steaming sponge and suet puddings and the length of time that the oven must be on for milk puddings cooked in the usual way, the cost of the fuel used had to be taken into consideration. But a pressure cooker means that now you can include these welcome additions to the family menus again, with speedy cooking, great economy of fuel, and no need to watch over the stove to see the saucepan is not running short of water and with hardly any steam to add to the problem of condensation in the kitchen.

If you are serving cold meat or grilling for the first course, then your pressure cooker would be free for one of these puddings and they can also be a great help in providing extra bulk to a meal which may have to be a little light or scanty of the more expensive foods such as meat, fish or poultry.

In the following recipes you will find a selection of the different kinds of puddings which are suited to pressure cooking both at home and outdoors where you can still end the meal with a flourish even when no oven is available.

STEAMED PUDDINGS

The method of pressure cooking these corresponds to the usual way of steaming or boiling on top of the stove but there are one or two points to remember which will ensure complete success from your very first attempt.

Any type of bowl or container in metal, china, ovenglass or boilable plastic can be used as long as it is watertight and it should be well greased.

It should not be more than two-thirds filled to allow room for the pudding to rise during the cooking.

A fitted lid is not recommended as this does not allow the release of the steam nor the quick penetration of the heat which is essential if the super-heated steam under pressure is to do its work properly.

A double thickness of greased greaseproof paper is recommended and is all that is required for the covering. If it is a little difficult to put the bowl in and lift it out when hot, the string tying the paper firmly down should be taken loosely across from one side to the other and tied, to form a handle.

Sufficient water must be put in to the cooker before the pressure cooking starts to last the cooking time. The minimum required is $\frac{1}{4}$ pint for every $\frac{1}{4}$ hour or part of $\frac{1}{4}$ hour's cooking plus $\frac{1}{2}$ pint to make quite sure. This must be boiling before putting the pudding in and should have a little lemon juice or vinegar added to prevent the darkening of the metal in hard-water areas. Do not put the water on and allow it to boil rapidly while you are making the pudding as this could mean, if you were delayed, that while you might have put the right amount in to start with too much could have boiled away and the pan might then boil dry before the cooking time was up.

The trivet should be used to stand the pudding on.

All mixtures, puddings, breads and cakes which contain a raising agent and which should have a light texture when cooked must be allowed to steam gently as in an ordinary steamer before beginning the pressure cooking. This is because if the cooker was brought to pressure in the usual way the pressure of steam building up in the pan would prevent the raising agent working and the mixture would remain heavy and you would be disappointed. The exact steaming time needed is given in the sample recipes and this must be done over a low heat so that the steam is just puffing gently out of the open vent which ensures that the pan is full of steam and the water only simmering. If, during this preliminary steaming time, the heat is left unnecessarily high, then too much water will be driven off as steam and this will lead to the pan boiling dry before the full pressure cooking time is up.

The recommended pressure for all mixtures is **Low** (5 lb) which will give the perfect result of a light, open texture with the mixture risen to the fullest extent. If your pressure cooker is fitted with a fixed pressure, then it would be worth while to apply to the manufacturer to see if it is possible to buy and fit a variable pressure control, particularly as you will certainly want to use your cooker for this purpose now you can see all the advantages.

However, if you have only the fixed pressure, excellent results can still be obtained if the quantity given in the following pudding recipes is divided into four, being cooked in individual bowls or ordinary teacups. This cuts down the cooking time so that the extra pressure does not have too much chance to affect the desired result.

When the cooking time is up, the pressure should be allowed to reduce at room temperature and then if you are not quite ready to serve the pudding just remove the weight or open the valve but leave the lid on and the pudding will remain hot for at least 10 to 15 minutes.

If some pudding is left over and is to be served again, just put $\frac{1}{2}$ pint of hot water in the cooker, then the pudding covered as before; bring to pressure and allow the pressure to reduce at room temperature which will be sufficient to heat it through.

It is not advisable to pressure cook steamed mixtures with other foods. This is because they require a lot of water which would swamp meat, fish, vegetables and so on, and they do not take kindly to being disturbed during the cooking or having the water taken off the boil which would have to be done to open the cooker as they have a longer cooking time than most other foods which would be served for the same meal. If the pressure cooker is needed, as it probably will be, to prepare part of the first course, then the pudding should be cooked first and kept hot either with the serving dishes or by being stood in a pan of boiling water over a low heat on the back of the stove.

If you want to adapt your favourite recipes to pressure cooking or are using packet mixes, then between half and one-third of the normal cooking time would be about the average, for example:

NORMAL COOKING TIME	PRESTEAMING TIME AND PRESSURE COOKING TIME AT LOW (5 LB)	
30 minutes	3 minutes	5 minutes
45 minutes	5 minutes	10 minutes
1–1¼ hours	15 minutes	25 minutes
1¼–2 hours	15 minutes	35 minutes
2–3 hours	20 minutes	50–60 minutes

If increasing the quantities as given in the following recipes, then a general rule is to increase the pressure cooking time by 10 minutes for every 2 oz extra flour, the other ingredients being increased in proportion.

These times do not apply to Christmas Puddings, for which a special table is given on p. 231.

The recipes in this section are to serve four people. The quantities for these recipes, where accuracy is important are given in ounces, but if you have no scales you can refer to the table of measurements in spoonfuls given on p. 22.

INSTRUCTIONS FOR PRESSURE COOKING STEAMED PUDDINGS

Have the right amount of boiling water ready in the cooker with a little lemon juice or vinegar added and the trivet.

Always leave a little space in the bowl or container for the pudding to rise.

Tie the bowl down securely with a double thickness of greased, greaseproof paper.

When the pudding is in the cooker, put on the cover, turn the heat high and wait until the steam escapes freely through the open vent.

Next, lower the heat and cook gently with the vent open and the steam just puffing out for the steaming time as given in the recipe.

When this time is up, raise the heat again to high, put on the Low or fixed weight as recommended—and wait for the hissing sound and the second escape of steam to show that pressure has been reached.

Lower the heat again and pressure cook in the usual way for the required time.

Remove the cooker from the heat and allow the pressure to reduce at room temperature.

Lift out the bowl, take off the paper, loosen round the edges, put the hot serving dish over the top, turn upside down, give the container a good shake and lift off.

BASIC RICH PUDDING MIXTURE

Cooking Time: In one bowl 15 minutes steaming; 25 minutes at **Low**
In four individual bowls, 5 minutes steaming; 10 minutes at **High**

CANARY PUDDING

3 oz margarine or butter; 3 oz caster sugar; grated rind of 1 lemon; 1 large egg or 2 small; 6 oz self-raising flour with a pinch of salt; a little milk if necessary; $1\frac{1}{4}$ pints water for the cooker; Custard, Jam or Fruit sauce (p. 297) handed separately.

Grease a $1\frac{1}{2}$ pint bowl or container and the greaseproof paper for covering. Put the cooker with the trivet and water on a low heat, to boil. Cream the fat with the grated lemon rind until quite soft, add the sugar and continue beating until creamy and white. Add the lightly beaten egg, a little at a time, beating well between each addition so that the mixture does not curdle. Fold in the sieved flour and salt, then add a little milk if necessary to give a soft, dropping consistency. Put into the container, smooth the top and tie down securely with the greaseproof paper. Continue as given in the instructions on p. 159. Serve the sauce separately or, if a Lemon sauce, a little may be poured over the pudding before being taken to table.

VARIATIONS

Chocolate: 2–3 oz of cocoa or drinking chocolate sieved with 4 oz flour or 3 oz grated chocolate added with milk and vanilla essence to taste. Serve with a chocolate sauce (p. 296).

College: With two tablespoons raspberry jam put into the bottom of the container before the mixture. Serve with a raspberry jam or redcurrant jelly sauce (p. 297).

Coconut: 2 oz desiccated coconut folded in with flour. Serve with a jam sauce (p. 297).

Fruit: 3–4 oz of dried fruit such as raisins, sultanas, currants with one teaspoon of mixed spice, added with the flour.

Ginger: Two teaspoons ground ginger sieved with the flour. Serve with a white sauce (p. 296) in which can be stirred some finely chopped crystallised ginger, or a thin custard (p. 297).

CHERRY CUP PUDDINGS

Cooking Time: 4 individual: 5 minutes steaming;
10 minutes at **High**

4 oz margarine or butter; 5 oz caster sugar; 2 small eggs; 4 oz self-raising flour; 2 tablespoons milk; 1 small tin of red cherries; $\frac{3}{4}$ pint water for the cooker; 1 teaspoon cornflour with a little cochineal to colour and maraschino essence to flavour, for the sauce.

Grease four large cups and a double sheet of greaseproof paper. Make the pudding as given in the previous recipe, adding the strained, chopped cherries with the milk. Put the cooker on a high heat with the trivet and water to bring to the boil. Divide the mixture into the cups, smoothing the tops. Put the cups on the trivet, lay the piece of greaseproof paper over the top and continue as given in the instructions on p. 159. Make the sauce, using the juice from the cherries and adding the colouring and flavouring as required. Hand separately.

For a special occasion, the **Compôte of Cherries**, p. 185, could be handed as an accompaniment, with pouring or whipped cream.

ORANGE CASTLES

Cooking Time: 4 individual: 5 minutes steaming;
10 minutes at **Low**

2 eggs and their weight in butter, sugar, self-raising flour; the grated rind of a large orange and 1 tablespoon strained orange juice; halved cherries and small pieces of angelica to decorate, $\frac{3}{4}$ pint water for the cooker; 1 tablespoon water, 1 tablespoon sugar, 1 tablespoon orange marmalade, rest of juice of orange for the Marmalade sauce.

Grease four large cups very well and put a halved cherry and a small diamond of angelica as a leaf, in the bottom of each. Make the mixture, using the orange juice instead of the milk, and cook as given in the instructions on p. 159.

To make the sauce, melt the sugar in the water being careful to stir until dissolved, boil with the marmalade and add the orange juice to give a pouring consistency. These Orange Castles should be served on individual dishes with the sauce poured round.

CARAMEL PUDDING

Cooking Time: 15 minutes steaming; 35 minutes at **Low**

For the caramel: 2 oz granulated sugar, 2 tablespoons water; for the pudding: 3 oz margarine or butter, 3 oz caster sugar, 2 large separated eggs, 6 oz self-raising flour, 4 tablespoons milk; 1½ pints water for the cooker; single cream to hand separately.

To make the caramel: put the sugar and water in a small saucepan over a low heat, stir and do not allow to boil until the sugar has dissolved. Stop stirring and continue boiling rapidly until the syrup begins to turn golden brown. Quickly pour into the warmed bowl and turn it round and round, coating the sides right up to the top.

Make the pudding: by creaming together the butter and sugar; beat in the yolks only, then fold in the flour and milk alternately, a little at a time. Put the cooker on with the water and trivet and bring to the boil. Whisk the egg whites until stiff and fold into the mixture. Put into the bowl, smooth the top and tie down with a double sheet of greased, greaseproof paper, pleated down the centre to allow for the pudding to rise. Continue as given in the instructions on p. 159. Turn the pudding on to the serving dish when the pressure has reduced, but leave the bowl in position over the pudding until ready to serve so that all the caramel will run out. Hand the cream separately.

(If any caramel should be left in the bottom of the bowl, just leave it to soak overnight with a little water. The syrup thus made can be used for stewing fruit.)

EVE'S PUDDING

Cooking Time: 15 minutes steaming; 20 minutes at **Low**
In 4 individual: 5 minutes steaming; 10 minutes at **High**

Seasonable fruit; 6–8 oz gooseberries, ½ lb peeled, cored cooking apples, 6 oz apricots, 2 tablespoons sugar or to taste for sweetening.
For the sponge mixture: 2 oz margarine or butter, 2 oz caster sugar, 1 standard egg, 4 oz self-raising flour with a pinch of salt, 2 tablespoons milk; a little brown sugar; 1¼ pints water for the cooker.

Use a soufflé dish or small casserole about 7 inches wide and 2¾ inches deep as this pudding will have to be taken to table in the dish in which it is cooked. The fruit for this dish can be fresh, bottled or tinned.

Grease the dish well with butter, put in a spoonful of brown sugar and turn the dish around so that the sides are coated. Prepare the fruit, if fresh, as for stewing; if bottled or tinned, strain off the juice. Put a layer of the fruit with sugar in the bottom of the dish. Put on the cooker with the water and bring to the boil. Make the mixture as for **Canary Pudding** (p. 160) and pile it over the fruit, smoothing over the top and leaving a slight well in the centre. The dish must not be more than two-thirds full. Cook as given in the instructions on p. 159. Lift out the dish, sprinkle with brown sugar and put under a hot grill, but watch carefully to see it does not burn.

PINEAPPLE SPONGE

Cooking Time: 15 minutes steaming; 25 minutes at **Low**

2 eggs and their weight in butter, sugar and self-raising flour sieved with a pinch of salt; 1 tablespoon finely chopped pineapple; 1 tablespoon pineapple syrup; $1\frac{1}{4}$ pints water for the cooker; some pieces of pineapple and angelica for decoration.

For the sauce: pineapple juice, a little chopped pineapple, a squeeze of lemon juice, 1 tablespoon sherry, 1 teaspoon arrowroot, a little sugar to taste.

This pudding would make an attractive dinner party sweet if cooked in a seamless ring mould. Cut a piece of greased greaseproof paper to fit the bottom and on this put a decoration of pieces of pineapple and angelica. Put the cooker with the water and trivet on to boil. Make the mixture as given for **Canary Pudding** (p. 160), gently fill the mixture into the mould, smooth the surface, cover and cook as given in the instructions on p. 159.

To make the sauce, blend the arrowroot with a little of the pineapple juice, boil the rest, add to the arrowroot and then reboil until clear. Just before serving, add the chopped pineapple, the lemon juice, a little sugar if necessary and the sherry.

Turn the pudding out carefully, lift off the paper and pour the sauce around it.

BASIC PLAIN PUDDING MIXTURE

SPICED SULTANA PUDDING

Cooking Time: 15 minutes steaming; 30 minutes at **Low**
In 4 individual: 5 minutes steaming; 10 minutes at **High**

6 oz self-raising flour with a pinch of salt; 3 oz margarine; 2 oz sugar; 3–4 oz sultanas; 1 level teaspoon mixed spice; 1 egg; 2–3 tablespoons milk; $1\frac{1}{2}$ pints water for the cooker; melted golden syrup to hand separately.

Grease the bowl and a double sheet of greaseproof paper. Put the cooker with the water and trivet to boil. Sieve the flour with the pinch of salt, rub in the fat until the texture of fine breadcrumbs, add the sultanas, the sugar and spice and mix to a soft dropping consistency with the beaten egg and milk. Put into the bowl, smooth the surface, tie down securely with the paper and cook as given in the instructions on p. 159 for the required time. Serve with warmed golden syrup, handed separately.

VARIATIONS

Marmalade: Leave out the fruit and spices. Put two tablespoons marmalade in the bottom of the bowl before putting in the mixture or stir three tablespoons of marmalade into a little less milk to mix the pudding. Serve with a Fruit or Marmalade sauce (p. 161).

Ginger: Leave out the fruit and spices. Add one teaspoon ground ginger and mix two tablespoons of golden syrup or treacle into a little less milk to mix the pudding. Serve with warmed syrup or custard.

Black Cap Pudding: Leave out the fruit and spices. Put two tablespoons of blackberry jelly in the bottom of the bowl first; add half teaspoon almond essence with the beaten egg. Serve a matching jam sauce (p. 297).

SUMMER CURRANT PUDDING

Cooking Time: 15 minutes steaming; 40 minutes at Low

1 lb prepared, stewed black- or redcurrants; 4 oz self-raising flour; pinch of salt; 6 oz melted margarine or butter; 4 oz fine breadcrumbs; 1 large egg; milk to mix; sugar for sweetening, juice of 1 lemon; $1\frac{1}{2}$ pints of water for the cooker; a little arrowroot or cornflour to make the sauce.

Grease a bowl and a double thickness of greased greaseproof paper. Strain the blackcurrants, keeping the juice. Sieve the flour and salt, mix in the melted margarine, stir in the breadcrumbs and mix to a stiff dough with the beaten egg and milk as required. Roll two-thirds of the dough into a circle, flour well, fold in quarters, lift into the basin and spread it out to line it evenly, pressing it firmly against the base and sides. Put in the currants, adding sugar as necessary and a little lemon juice. Trim the pastry and damp the edges. Add the trimmings to the one-third of pastry left, roll into a circle to cover the top of the pudding and squeeze the edges together. Tie down securely with the greaseproof paper and continue the cooking as given in the instructions on p. 159.

Boil the juice from the fruit with a tablespoon of sugar and thicken with blended cornflour or arrowroot. A tablespoon of sherry added to this sauce will make it even more delicious.

FRUIT PUFFS

Cooking Time: 5 minutes steaming; 12 minutes at **Low** or **High**

A little sugar and cinnamon for coating the container; 4 oz self-raising flour with a pinch of salt; 2 oz margarine or butter; 1 tablespoon sugar; a little milk to mix; about 4 dessertspoons of cooked, bottled or tinned fruit, sweetened and strained; 1 pint of water for the cooker; a little cornflour or arrowroot and sugar to thicken the syrup.

Grease four teacups or individual moulds, put a little mixed sugar and cinnamon in each and shake to coat the bottom and sides. Have the boiling water and trivet ready in the cooker. Sieve the flour and salt, rub in the margarine, add the sugar and sufficient milk to give a soft dough. Divide into four, put into the moulds and make a deep hollow in the middle with the floured handle of a spoon. Put a spoonful of the fruit into each and draw the dough together again to seal it in. Put the containers on the trivet, lay the greaseproof paper over and continue as given in the instructions on p. 159.

Thicken the fruit syrup with a little blended cornflour or arrowroot, adding a little more sugar and colouring as necessary. Serve the fruit puffs on individual hot dishes and pour the sauce round.

A delicious sauce to accompany these, for a special occasion would be a **Sweet–Sour Cream Sauce** as follows:

To ½ pint of soured cream add ½ tablespoon of strained lemon juice, ¼ teaspoon of cinnamon and 3 tablespoons of thin honey and beat all well together.

FRUITY DUMPLING

Cooking Time: 15 minutes steaming; 45 minutes at **Low**

8 oz self-raising flour with a pinch of salt; 4 oz margarine; 2 tablespoons sugar; 2 oz mixed dried fruit; ½ teaspoon each ground ginger, mixed spice, cinnamon; 1 tablespoon treacle, ½ tablespoon golden syrup with a little milk to give a soft dough; 1¾ pints water for the cooker; custard sauce to hand separately.

Put the cooker on to boil with the water and trivet. Line a pudding cloth with a piece of greased greaseproof paper. Sieve the flour and salt, rub in the margarine, stir in the sugar, fruit and spices and mix to a soft but not sloppy dough with the warmed treacle, syrup and a little milk. Form into a dumpling, tie loosely but securely in the cloth, put in the cooker and continue as given in the instructions on p. 159. When the dumpling is lifted out it should be left on a deep plate for a few minutes to drain before being opened and lifted out. Serve with a custard (p. 297), handed separately.

CINNAMON PUDDING

Cooking Time: 10 minutes steaming; 45 minutes at **High**

4 oz breadcrumbs, preferably brown; 4 oz self-raising flour sieved with a pinch of salt; 3 oz margarine; 3 oz granulated sugar (brown if using white bread); 4 oz sultanas; 1 level tablespoon cinnamon; 1 large egg; milk as required; $1\frac{1}{2}$ pints water for the cooker; warmed syrup or custard to accompany.

Grease a $1\frac{1}{2}$-pint bowl and a double thickness of greaseproof paper. Put the cooker on to boil with the water and trivet. Rub the margarine into the flour, stir in the dry ingredients and the fruit and mix to a dropping consistency with the beaten egg and a little milk. Continue as given in the instructions on p. 159. Serve with a warmed syrup or custard.

FLUFFY BREAD PUDDING

Cooking Time: 5 minutes steaming; 10 minutes at **High**

This pudding is best made in a small seamless loaf pan and should be made in time to leave in the oven for 10 minutes before serving.

4 teacups (4–6 thick slices) of stale bread soaked for 20 to 30 minutes in hot water; 2 tablespoons of margarine or butter; 3 tablespoons brown sugar; 3 oz dried fruit, currants, raisins, sultanas or mixture; 1 teaspoon nutmeg or mixed spice; 1 large egg; sufficient milk to give a soft consistency; 1 pint of water for the cooker; custard or vanilla white sauce (p. 296) to hand separately.

Grease a loaf pan and a double thickness of greaseproof paper. Put the cooker on to boil with the water and trivet. Squeeze all the water out of the bread and beat with a fork until broken up and smooth. Melt the fat with the sugar, pour over the bread, add in the dried fruit and spice, mix with the beaten egg and sufficient milk to give a soft mixture. Fill into the pan leaving at least 1 inch space at the top. Tie down securely and cook as given in the instructions on p. 159. During the cooking, preheat the oven to Gas No 4, 350° F. Lift off the paper and leave in the oven, as near the top as possible, while the first course is being eaten. Serve with a sauce to choice.

SUET PUDDINGS

The basic **suet mixture** from which these recipes are made is in the proportion of twice as much flour as shredded suet, a pinch of salt and sufficient cold water to mix to an elastic dough with sugar and flavourings added according to the recipe. The quantity is always referred to by the weight of flour, e.g. 6 oz of suet crust would be 6 oz of self-raising flour sieved with a pinch of salt, mixed with 3 oz shredded suet and any sweetening or flavouring required and then sufficient water added to give a stretchy dough, neither sticky so that it cannot be easily handled with floured hands or rolled on a floured board yet not so stiff that it will break up when shaped or rolled.

BOILED FRUIT PUDDING

Cooking Time: 15 minutes steaming; 30 minutes at **Low** or **High**

8 oz suet crust; 1½–2 lb of fresh fruit such as apples, plums, damsons; 3–4 tablespoons of sugar to taste; 1 tablespoon of water; 1½ pints boiling water for the cooker; custard or cream to hand separately.

Make the suet crust, roll two-thirds into a circle, flour well, fold in flour, lift carefully and line the basin with it, pressing the crust firmly against the basin at the bottom and round the sides. Put in half the fruit, prepared as for stewing, 1 tablespoon of water and the sugar, then fill in the rest of the fruit. Trim the edges, add these to the one-third of pastry left and roll this into a circle the size of the top of the basin. Damp the edges of the pastry lining the basin, put on the circle and press the edges together well all round. Cover with a double thickness of greased, greaseproof paper. Put into the cooker and continue as given in the instructions on p. 159 for the required time. Turn carefully on to a hot dish and hand custard or cream separately.

VARIATIONS

Apple: Slice the apples finely, flavour with lemon rind, cloves or cinnamon; golden syrup could be used for sweetening instead of the sugar.

Plums: If small these may be cooked whole, but prick each once or twice with a fork. If large, halve and stone.

Damsons: If very hard these should be brought to pressure in the cooker first as they may not cook completely inside the suet crust.

Blackcurrants: These must be packed very tightly or the pudding will collapse when turned out as this fruit shrinks a lot when cooked.

Blackberry and Apple: Put a layer of each alternately and a little extra sugar as blackberries are very tart.

JAM LAYER PUDDING

Cooking Time: 15 minutes steaming; 40 minutes at **Low**
10 minutes steaming; 30 minutes at **High**

6 oz self-raising flour with a pinch of salt; 3 oz shredded suet; 3 oz sugar; 3 tablespoons of milk; 3–4 tablespoons jam; 1½ pints water for the cooker; jam sauce handed separately.

Sieve the flour and salt, mix in the sugar and suet. Make a well in the centre, put in the milk and stir until well mixed. Roll out the pastry thinly, cut into four or five rounds and spread all but one with jam. Put the cooker on to boil with the water and trivet. Put a little jam in the bottom of the basin, then pile the rounds one on top of the other with the plain round on the top, leaving at least 1-inch space for the pudding to rise. Tie down securely with a double thickness of greased greaseproof paper and continue the cooking as given in the instructions on p. 159. Turn carefully on to the hot serving dish and hand the jam sauce (p. 297) separately.

GOLDEN CRUMB PUDDING

Substitute for the jam, three tablespoons breadcrumbs mixed with four tablespoons of syrup and a squeeze of lemon juice.

This recipe may be used as a simple Jam, Golden Syrup or Lemon Curd Pudding, putting the jam or syrup into the bottom of the bowl, then the suet mixture flattened to fill it. A jam, golden syrup or lemon sauce (p. 297) should be handed separately.

JAM ROLY-POLY

Cooking Time: 10 minutes steaming; 25 minutes at **Low**

8 oz suet crust (see p. 167); jam; 1½ pints water for the cooker; custard (p. 297) to hand separately.

Put the cooker on to boil with the water and trivet. Make the suet crust and roll out thinly to a width at least 1 inch less than that of the cooker. Spread with jam, moisten round the edges with water or milk and roll up. Wrap in a double thickness of greaseproof paper or in aluminium foil or a pudding cloth lined with greaseproof paper and make the ends secure. Put the roll in the cooker and continue as given in the instructions on p. 159. Serve with a custard sauce, handed separately.

VARIATIONS

Orange Delight: Spread the roll with marmalade instead of jam and put a layer of thinly sliced, peeled oranges with all pips removed. Serve with the marmalade sauce on p. 297.

Spiced Apple: Spread the roll with finely chopped cooking apples mixed with 2 oz currants, a teaspoon of mixed spice and 2 oz brown sugar.

Spotted Dog: Spread the roll with 3 oz of mixed dried fruit, chopped peel and a little grated lemon rind.

MILK AND EGG PUDDINGS

To many people this heading will simply mean memories of rice puddings from childhood—and not very happy memories at that. But this is where you can really score with your pressure cooker; rice puddings can come in many guises and so can all the delicious hot and cold sweets made with a basis of milk and eggs with an endless choice of fruits, flavourings and additions to give both winter and summer dishes that will soon be family favourites—and for you, minutes instead of hours of slow oven cooking.

Milk puddings, on their own, should be cooked directly in the pressure cooker, without the trivet so that the milk is then the liquid supplying the steam to build up pressure. Cooked this way the puddings will be thick, creamy and delicious and as they will usually fit best into the cooking time-table for the meal if they are prepared first they can be left to brown off either under a grill or in the oven while the first course is being cooked and eaten. Use **High** pressure.

CREAMY RICE PUDDING

Pressure Cooking Time: 12 minutes

2 big tablespoons pudding rice; 2–3 tablespoons sugar; a good knob of margarine or butter; 1 pint of milk less 2 tablespoons; a slice of lemon rind for the cooking if liked; nutmeg to dust the top after cooking.

Lift the trivet from the cooker, put in the margarine and let it melt to grease the bottom of the pan. Pour in the milk and bring to the boil on a high heat. Do not go away and leave the cooker for, as soon as the milk boils and begins to rise in the pan you must put in the rice and sugar, stir until the milk reboils, then straight away lower the heat to between medium and low until the milk is simmering well but not rushing up to the top and put on the cover. The steam will now be seen to be escaping straight away, so put on the weight or close the valve and bring the cooker to pressure but without altering the heat. This will take a little longer than usual but after no more than 2–3 minutes you should hear the hissing sound to tell you that pressure is up, so start the cooking time and lower the heat further if the cooker is hissing unnecessarily loudly. When the cooking time is up, allow the pressure to reduce at room temperature for at least 5 minutes. Stir the pudding well, put into a dish, sprinkle with nutmeg, dot with a little butter and set to brown under a low grill or at the top of a warming oven or put on one side to cool if required as the basis for another sweet.

VARIATIONS

Vanilla: Flavour with a vanilla pod put in for the cooking and removed before serving.

Sultana: 1 to 2 oz sultanas added for the cooking.

Coconut: 1 dessertspoon desiccated coconut added with the rice.

The rice for the following recipes can be cooked at any time when the cooker is not in use for a meal and be kept in a cool place until required.

HOT FRUIT CONDÉ

Pressure Cooking Time: 12 minutes
Oven Time: 20 minutes

Rice pudding as in previous recipe; a little vanilla essence; 6–8 fruits such as cooked halved pears; tinned halved apricots or peaches, pineapple slices; 2 small eggs; $1\frac{1}{2}$ tablespoons caster sugar; a spoonful of granulated sugar; halved glacé cherries and small pieces of angelica to decorate.

Preheat the oven to Gas No 3, 325° F. While the rice pudding is cooking, strain the fruit but leave whole; butter a pie dish well; separate the yolks and whites of the eggs. Flavour the rice pudding with vanilla essence to taste, beat in the egg yolks and pour into the dish. Lay the fruit on top. Beat the whites until stiff, fold in the caster sugar and pile on top of the fruit. Bake on the middle shelf of the oven for 20 minutes or until pale golden. Arrange five or six halved cherries each with a leaf of angelica on the meringue and serve quickly.

PEAR CONDÉ

A cooked rice pudding as in recipe; vanilla essence for flavouring; 4 halved, strained, cooked bottled or tinned pears; 4 stalks of angelica; for the sauce: 2 tablespoons of apricot jam, 2 teaspoons arrowroot, $\frac{1}{4}$ pint water, a little red colouring, 1 teaspoon of sherry if liked or a spoonful of sugar and a little lemon juice.

When the rice is cooked, add vanilla essence and chill. Spoon equally into four individual dishes, laying a halved pear, flat side down in the centre of each and placing the angelica as the stalk. Make the sauce by boiling the jam and water, adding the blended arrowroot and boiling until clear. A little colouring may be added and then the sherry or the lemon juice and sugar. Leave the sauce until it cools a little and then when thickening coat the pears and the surface of the rice evenly. The dishes, for a special occasion, can be piped with whipped cream decorated with very small pieces of crystallised cherry.

For children, a raspberry jelly, instead of the sauce, can be spooned over the pears and rice when it is thickening, just before it sets.

APRICOT CREOLE

A cooked rice pudding as in recipe; about $\frac{1}{2}$ teaspoon ground ginger; 3 oz currants; 2 oz mixed peel; 6–8 strained, halved cooked, bottled or tinned apricots; apricot sauce as in previous recipe.

When the rice is cooked and chilled, stir in the ground ginger to give a definite 'hot' taste, add the currants and mixed peel and pile in the centre of a serving dish. Arrange the apricots to stand up against the sides of the rice and, when the sauce is really thickening, spoon over the apricots to coat them evenly.

For a special occasion, the prepared rice can be pressed firmly into a decorative mould rinsed out in cold water, thoroughly chilled, then turned out on to the serving dish and decorated as before.

RICE CUSTARD

Pressure Cooking Time: 5 minutes and 5 minutes

1 cup of rice with 2 cups of water; $\frac{1}{2}$ pint water for cooker with a little lemon or vinegar; 2 oz seedless raisins; 2 eggs; 4 tablespoons sugar; 1 teaspoon vanilla essence; $\frac{1}{2}$ pint hot milk; a little nutmeg.

Cook the rice as given in the instructions on p. 150. During the cooking, beat the eggs with the vanilla essence and sugar, heat the milk and pour over, stirring all the time. Butter a soufflé or casserole dish that will fit in the cooker. Stir the raisins into the rice, then mix thoroughly with the custard and put into the dish, stand on the trivet and cover with a double thickness of greaseproof paper. Bring to pressure in the usual way, cook for 5 minutes and allow the pressure to reduce at room temperature. Sprinkle with nutmeg and brown lightly under the grill.

LEMON RICE

Pressure Cooking Time: 5 minutes and 5 minutes

1 cup of rice and 2 cups of water; $\frac{1}{2}$ pint water for the cooker with a little lemon or vinegar; 1 large egg; 4 tablespoons sugar; juice and grated rind of 1 lemon; 3–4 tablespoons of lemon curd; a handful of chopped nuts.

Cook the rice as given in the instructions on p. 150. During the cooking, separate the yolk and white of egg; grate the lemon rind and strain the lemon juice. Beat the egg yolk, lemon juice and rind into the cooked rice. Whip the egg white very stiffly and fold into the rice lightly and carefully. Put into a buttered soufflé or casserole dish, stand in the cooker on the trivet and cover with a double piece of greaseproof paper. Bring to pressure in the usual way, cook for 5 minutes and allow the pressure to reduce at room temperature. During this cooking, warm the lemon curd and chop the nuts. Lightly spread the curd over the pudding and just before serving sprinkle with the chopped nuts.

LEMON SNOW

Pressure Cooking Time: 7 minutes

1 pint water; 2 tablespoons golden syrup; grated rind and juice of 2 lemons; 2 good tablespoons of sago; a little sugar if necessary; the whites of 2 eggs; a little whipped cream, a few cherries and pieces of angelica or small ratafias for decoration.

Lift the trivet from the cooker, put in the water and syrup and stir in the open pan until boiling. Add the lemon rind and juice, reboil, throw in the sago. Continue as in the instructions for **Rice Pudding** (p. 169). Stir the sago well, put into a large bowl and leave until cold. Taste and add more sugar if liked then gently fold in the stiffly beaten whites. Pile into a large or individual serving dishes, decorate with the whipped cream, cut cherries and angelica or ratafias.

Other cereals for milk puddings should be made following the instructions for **Rice Pudding** (p. 169), in the proportion of 2 large tablespoons (2 oz) of cereal, 3 tablespoons of sugar, to 1 pint of milk. Flavourings such as vanilla, a piece of lemon rind, a bay leaf can be added as required.

Large-grain cereal: Rice, Pearl Barley, 12 minutes.
Small-grain cereal: Tapioca, Sago, Semolina, 7 minutes.

HOME-MADE EVAPORATED MILK

Pressure Cooking Time: 10 minutes

If you are following a recipe calling for evaporated milk and find, at the last moment, that there is none in your store cupboard or you fancy some to serve with stewed fruit, porridge or cereal, here is a quick and economical way to do it with a delicious result.

Lift the trivet from the cooker, put in ½ pint fresh milk bring to 15 lb pressure in the usual way, cook for 10 minutes and allow the pressure to reduce at room temperature. Sugar or flavouring can be added to taste.

EGG PUDDINGS

Do not be surprised to find these puddings and those given in the following recipes in a book on pressure cooking. Steaming was always an accepted method of cooking these sweets and all that has to be done is to cut down by at least two-thirds the normal cooking time to achieve the most perfect results. Eggs are plentiful, not an expensive item of the family budget and can provide easily digested, concentrated protein while being served in a guise that will please the young and old who have a sweet tooth.

In all these custards and crêmes where whole eggs are used, a more extravagant and rich sweet can be served by increasing the proportion of eggs to milk to 1 egg for each ¼ pint of milk and even more so if 2 yolks are taken as 1 egg. Use High pressure.

BASIC EGG CUSTARD

Pressure Cooking Time: 5 minutes

2 large eggs; 2 tablespoons of sugar or to taste; ¾ pint milk; vanilla essence to taste; ½ pint water with lemon or vinegar for the cooker; nutmeg for the top.

Butter a soufflé dish or casserole in which the custard can be taken to table. Beat the eggs, sugar and vanilla gently but not to a froth; warm the milk but do not allow to boil. Pour on the eggs, stirring all the time, then turn into the prepared dish. Have the water and trivet ready in the cooker, put in the dish covered with a double thickness of greaseproof paper, bring to pressure in the usual way, cook for 5 minutes and allow the pressure to reduce at room temperature. Carefully lift off the paper, sprinkle nutmeg over the top.

This egg custard may be served hot or cold with any stewed, bottled or tinned fruit.

It may be cooked with the stewed fruit as a complete dessert, see p. 183.

When cold, it may be whisked well, either plain or with a little half-whisked cream stirred in, and be used as a base in sponge flans, fruit pastry flans and tartlets, for trifles or beaten and sieved to make fruit fools.

VARIATIONS

Honey: Replace sugar with two good tablespoons of thin honey, heating it with the milk.

Coffee: Add two tablespoons strong coffee in place of two tablespoons milk or one tablespoon coffee essence. Sprinkle top of custard with chopped nuts.

CHOCOLATE CREAM

Pressure Cooking Time: 5 minutes

2 eggs and 1 yolk; 3 dessertspoons sugar; small bar of plain chocolate or 2 tablespoons cocoa; $\frac{3}{4}$ pint milk; vanilla to taste; chocolate sauce to hand separately; a little sweetened whipped cream with pieces of cherry and angelica to decorate.

Butter a china or earthenware bowl; grate the chocolate and take a little to sprinkle in the bowl and turn it around to coat the sides. Beat the eggs, sugar, essence and grated chocolate lightly, pour on the heated milk, turn into the prepared bowl. Continue as for **Egg Custard** (p. 173). Chill thoroughly.

Make the chocolate sauce and allow to get cold (an excellent chocolate sauce can be made from Chocolate Instant Whip. Use half the packet and add a tablespoon of strong sweetened coffee to give it extra flavour and a pouring consistency). Turn out the cream, decorate with whirls of sweetened whipped cream each with a small piece of cherry and angelica and hand the sauce separately.

CRÊME REGENCE

Pressure Cooking Time: 5 minutes

As for **Chocolate Cream** but replace the chocolate and vanilla with six crushed macaroons stirred in to the cream with maraschino or almond flavouring to taste. Decorate with whipped cream and browned almonds and hand chilled apricot sauce separately.

CRÊME CARAMEL

In 4 individual: Pressure Cooking Time: 3 minutes

For the caramel: 3 tablespoons sugar; 3 tablespoons water; for the crême: 2 eggs and 1 yolk; $\frac{3}{4}$ pint milk; 2 tablespoons sugar; vanilla essence to taste; $\frac{1}{2}$ pint water with lemon or vinegar for the cooker; pouring cream to hand separately.

Put four teacups to warm or use four individual boilable plastic bowls. To make the caramel: put the water and sugar in a small saucepan, stir over a very low heat without boiling until the sugar is dissolved. Boil rapidly, without stirring but shaking the saucepan occasionally until the sugar begins to turn a deep gold. Carefully but quickly divide into the cups or bowls and smartly turn each around to coat the sides. With cups, butter any parts which do not get coated, once the caramel has cooled.

Beat the eggs, sugar and essence, heat the milk in the saucepan used to make the caramel and pour over the eggs, stirring all the time. Fill into the cups or bowls. Continue as for **Egg Custard** (p. 173), using just one big piece of doubled greaseproof paper to cover all the cups. Chill the crêmes, and when ready to serve, gently loosen round the edge of each and turn into an individual dish. Hand the cream separately.

If there is room in your cooker, you can double this recipe and cook the crêmes, standing four directly in the water in the cooker covered with greaseproof, then the trivet and four more covered on the top again.

CRÊME ECOSSAISE

In 4 individual: Pressure Cooking Time: 3 minutes

As in previous recipe but without the caramel and flavouring the crême with whisky to taste.

When the crêmes are served on individual dishes, coat with a thick apricot sauce well laced with whisky.

CRÊME BRULÉE

See recipe on p. 197.

GOLDEN CRUMBLE

Pressure Cooking Time: 10 minutes

1 pint milk; $\frac{1}{2}$ lb fine bread or stale cake crumbs; 2 large eggs; 2 oz currants; 1 teaspoon almond flavouring; 3 tablespoons sugar; $\frac{1}{2}$ pint water with lemon or vinegar for the cooker; warmed golden syrup.

Warm the milk, pour over the crumbs and allow to stand for 15 minutes. Stir in the beaten eggs, currants, flavouring and sugar, and put into a greased bowl. Continue as for **Egg Custard** (p. 173). Allow to stand a moment or two on lifting out of the cooker, turn on to a hot serving dish and coat with the warmed syrup.

ORANGE CRUMBLE

Pressure Cooking Time: 10 minutes

As above, leaving out the currants and almond flavouring and substituting the grated rind and juice of one orange; serve coated with Marmalade sauce (p. 297).

BREAD AND BUTTER PUDDING

Pressure Cooking Time: 6 minutes

3–4 thin slices of buttered bread; 3 tablespoons mixed dried fruit; a pinch of cinnamon or nutmeg; 2 large eggs; $\frac{3}{4}$ pint milk; 2 tablespoons sugar; $\frac{1}{2}$ pint water with lemon or vinegar for the cooker; a little brown sugar for the top; pouring cream to hand separately.

Fill a soufflé dish or casserole with alternate layers of bread cut into four, sprinkled with nutmeg or cinnamon and put in buttered side down, and the fruit. Continue as for **Egg Custard** (p. 173) and when the dish has been lifted from the cooker, sprinkle lightly with brown sugar and crisp up the top by browning carefully under a hot grill.

CHOCOLATE BREAD AND BUTTER PUDDING

Make as in the previous recipe, but before heating the milk take a spoonful in a small saucepan with a small bar of plain chocolate broken up and heat gently until the chocolate is dissolved. Then add the rest of the milk and continue as for **Bread and Butter Pudding**.

APPLE CHARLOTTE

Pressure Cooking Time: 12 minutes

2 large cooking apples; 8–10 slices of thinly cut white bread; 2–3 tablespoons of margarine or butter; 1 teaspoon cinnamon; 4 tablespoons demerara sugar; $\frac{1}{2}$ pint water with lemon or vinegar for the cooker; custard or pouring cream to hand separately.

Butter a soufflé dish or bowl. Peel, core and slice the apples. Cut two circles of bread to fit the top and bottom of the dish and trim enough slices to line it. Heat the butter, stir in the cinnamon and lightly fry the slices, except the one for the top, on both sides until golden brown. Line the basin with them, fill it with alternate layers of apple, sugar and the rest of the bread, finishing with the large circle. Continue as for **Egg Custard** (p. 173), allow to stand for a minute or two after lifting out of the cooker, then turn on to a hot serving dish.

Hand the custard or cream separately.

CABINET PUDDING

Pressure Cooking Time: 7 minutes

4 sponge cakes lightly soaked in a little sherry or liqueur; some chopped crystallised fruits such as cherries, angelica, pineapple, orange and lemon slices if available; 2 large eggs and 2 yolks; 2 tablespoons of sugar; ¾ pint milk; apricot sauce (p. 297).

Put a little liqueur or sherry into a shallow dish, put in the broken up sponge cakes, leave a little, then turn over until all has been absorbed. Pile into a buttered bowl with the chopped crystallised fruit. Continue as for **Egg Custard** (p. 173). Make a thick apricot sauce during the cooking. Allow to stand for a minute or two when lifted out of the cooker, turn gently on to the hot serving dish and coat with the sauce.

This really special pudding is even more delicious for a summer meal if, at the very last moment, thin slices of ice-cream are laid over it.

QUEEN OF PUDDINGS

Pressure Cooking Time: 5 minutes

The grand idea behind this recipe is that the basic pudding can be made well in advance, even overnight and in your cooker instead of having to light the oven, and can be kept covered with foil or a plate in a cool place ready to be finished off while you are preparing the rest of the meal. It is an excellent way to get ahead for a family party or when you have guests coming.

½ pint milk; some strips of lemon rind; 3 large tablespoons of fine breadcrumbs; 1 knob of butter; 1 tablespoon of sugar; 1 large egg; ½ pint water with lemon or vinegar for the cooker; 2 tablespoons of red jam; 1 dessertspoon caster sugar; pouring cream to hand separately.

Choose a soufflé dish or casserole that can go in the oven and to table and butter it well. Put the breadcrumbs in a bowl, boil the milk, butter and lemon rind and pour over. Cover and leave to stand for half an hour. Stir in the yolk of egg and sugar and put into the prepared dish. Continue as for **Egg Custard** (p. 173). When ready to finish off, preheat the oven to Gas No 3, 325° F. Take out the lemon rind, spread the jam over the top. Beat the egg white very stiffly, fold in half the sugar, pile on to the pudding and sprinkle with the rest of the sugar. Bake in the centre of the oven, 20 to 30 minutes, until turning golden.

BREAD AND CAKES

You will probably not think it worth while to make these in your pressure cooker as long as you have an oven available but should you ever want to 'bake' and only have the facilities of top-of-the-stove cooking you will find how successful these recipes can be and the results will in no way detract from your reputation as a cake-maker. To ensure their lightness, these mixtures with raising agents should properly be pressure cooked at Low (5 lb); at the higher pressures the texture may be found rather too close and dry.

YORKSHIRE SPICED LOAF

Cooking Time: 15 minutes steaming; 30 minutes at **Low**

8 oz self-raising flour; 1 level teaspoon baking powder; pinch of salt; 3 oz margarine; 3 oz sugar; 4 oz seedless raisins or sultanas; 2 oz walnuts; 2 level teaspoons mixed spice or 1 teaspoon nutmeg; 1 large egg; a little milk; $1\frac{1}{4}$ pints water with lemon or vinegar for the cooker.

Grease a suitably sized loaf pan and a double thickness of greased greaseproof paper and fold a pleat down it lengthways. Put the cooker with the trivet and water on to boil. Sieve the flour, salt and baking powder. Rub in the margarine until like fine breadcrumbs, stir in the sugar, spices, fruit and all but four of the walnuts roughly chopped, leaving a well in the centre. Into this put the beaten egg and two tablespoons of milk and blend until a stiff dough is made. A little more milk may be added as necessary. Put into the pan, pushing the mixture well into the corners and leaving a slight depression down the centre. Lay the four walnuts along this. Tie down securely with the paper and continue as given in the instructions on p. 159. Lift from the cooker, remove the paper, brush with a syrup made from one tablespoon of sugar boiled with one teaspoon of water and brown under a hot grill, watching carefully to see it does not burn. Allow to cool, turn out of the pan and when cold, keep in an airtight tin for at least 24 hours. This loaf is delicious sliced and buttered. If no grill even is available, boil one tablespoon sugar with one tablespoon water to make caramel as given on p. 175 and brush the loaf with this to give it an attractive appearance.

GINGERBREAD

Cooking Time: 15 minutes steaming; 35 minutes at Low

8 oz self-raising flour; $\frac{1}{2}$ teaspoon bicarbonate of soda; a pinch of salt; 1 teaspoon ground ginger; 1 level teaspoon cinnamon, $\frac{1}{2}$ level teaspoon nutmeg optional; 2 oz brown sugar; 2 oz margarine; 3 good tablespoons of golden syrup; 1 egg; about $\frac{1}{4}$ pint milk; $1\frac{1}{2}$ pints water with lemon or vinegar for the cooker.

Grease a suitably sized loaf or cake pan and a double thickness of greaseproof paper, pleated lengthways down the middle. Warm the fat, sugar and syrup until dissolved, stir well and allow to cool slightly. Sieve the flour, soda, salt and spices, make a well in the centre, put in the beaten egg and the cooled liquid, beat, then add sufficient of the milk to give a slack dough rather like a thick batter. Pour into the pan, tie down securely with the greaseproof and continue as given in the instructions on p. 159. When the gingerbread is lifted out, remove the paper and treat as suggested in the preceding recipe.

MARMALADE CAKE

Cooking Time: 15 minutes steaming; 35 minutes at Low

6 oz self-raising flour; 1 level teaspoon baking powder; pinch of salt; 2 level tablespoons of sugar; 4 oz mixed dried fruit; 2 level tablespoons of marmalade; 3 tablespoons of golden syrup; milk to mix, about $\frac{1}{4}$ pint; a piece of citron peel; $1\frac{1}{2}$ pints water with lemon or vinegar for the cooker.

Grease a suitably sized cake pan and a double thickness of greaseproof paper, pleated down the centre. Sieve the flour, salt and baking powder. Add the sugar, dried fruit, the marmalade and the warmed syrup and sufficient milk to mix to a dropping consistency. Put into the pan, leaving a slight depression in the centre in which lay the citron peel. Continue as given in the instructions on p. 159 and finish off as for the **Spiced Loaf** (p. 178).

CHOCOLATE CAKE

Cooking Time: 15 minutes steaming; 25 minutes at **Low**

4 oz self-raising flour; ½ teaspoon bicarbonate of soda; 1 tablespoon cocoa; 1 tablespoon margarine; 2 tablespoons sugar; 1 level tablespoon warmed golden syrup; a little milk; 1¼ pints water with a little lemon or vinegar for the cooker.

Grease a suitably sized cake pan (a ring mould if watertight would make an attractive cake) and a double thickness of greaseproof paper, pleated down the middle. Gently warm the sugar and syrup and set to cool. Sieve the flour, soda and cocoa, rub in the fat, make a well in the centre, pour in the liquid and mix well together, using milk as necessary to give a soft, dropping consistency. Put into the pan, tie down securely with the greaseproof and continue as given in the instructions on p. 159. When the cake is lifted out, remove the paper and continue as given for the **Spiced Loaf** (p. 178). If to be eaten at once, hundreds and thousands can be spinkled on the top while the syrup is still sticky or the cake can be left as it is until cold and then be iced with chocolate icing, ready-made packets of which are now available.

FRUIT CAKE

Cooking Time: 15 minutes steaming; 35 minutes at **Low**

3 oz margarine, 3 oz brown sugar, 3 oz mixed dried fruit boiled gently together for 3 minutes and allowed to cool; ½ lb self-raising flour sieved with 1 teaspoon of mixed spice and 1 level teaspoon of baking powder; a little milk; 1½ pints water with a little lemon or vinegar for the cooker.

Add the cooled ingredients to the dry ones, stir well and add sufficient milk to give a soft, dropping consistency. Continue as for previous recipes.

SECTION VII

Fruits and Desserts

FRESH FRUITS

As it would be difficult not to overcook the soft fruits if they were put loose into a pressure cooker, as is done in an ordinary saucepan, the recommended method is to cook them in a heat-proof container such as a soufflé or casserole dish so that they can be taken straight to table. This must, of course, be of a size which can be easily put in and taken out of the cooker and it should be covered with a double thickness of greaseproof paper. If being cooked on their own, pressure can be reduced in cold water but if an accompanying sweet, such as an egg custard is being done at the same time, as is explained in the recipe section, the pressure must be allowed to reduce at room temperature.

For large, hard fruits, pressure cooking is an easy and quick way, ensuring good colour and flavour and a delicious, concentrated syrup, as only a minimum amount of water need be put in for the short cooking time. In fact, as will be seen from the following recipes, many can be cooked in their own juice with sugar and flavouring added. The trivet is not required and the

PREPARING FRESH FRUITS

Pressure Cooking Time: 5 minutes

FRUIT	PREPARATION	METHOD OF COOKING
Apples	Peel, core, slice, rinse under cold water, do not drain	Pack in layers in container, sprinkling each with brown sugar, a strip of lemon peel, a little nutmeg or cloves to taste
Apricots	Halve and stone. Some of the stones can be cracked, the kernels blanched and cooked with the fruit for extra flavour	Basic sugar syrup in container
Blackberries	Alone; with sliced apples	Basic sugar syrup, in container; pack in layers in a container sprinkling each with a little water and a spoonful of sugar
Cherries	Whole or stoned	Basic sugar syrup in container with a little red colouring to improve the appearance
Currants	String and wash, do not drain	Pack in layers in container sprinkling each with sugar
Gooseberries	Top and tail, wash	Use only two tablespoons of water when making syrup, in container
Greengages, Plums, Damsons	Cook whole, prick each once or twice with fork, or halve and stone	Basic sugar syrup, in container
Peaches	Plunge for 1 to 2 minutes in boiling water, peel, stone and slice	Basic sugar syrup, in container
Pears		
Hard, stewing	Peeled, halved, cored	Basic sugar syrup, in container or in cooker without trivet: 8 minutes
Dessert	Peeled, halved, cored	Basic sugar syrup, in container, using $\frac{1}{2}$ pint and coloured with a little cochineal sometimes for variety
Raspberries	Rinse in cold water, do not drain	Sprinkle each layer with sugar, in container
Rhubarb	Cut in lengths, rinse in cold water, do not drain	Sprinkle each layer in container with sugar, a little cinnamon or piece of lemon peel to taste

pressure can be reduced with water or be allowed to reduce at room temperature, depending on the particular result required or the recipe being followed. Use High pressure.

Where fresh fruit of any kind is being cooked for pulping or purée, the trivet is not required and the fruit can be put directly into the cooker with a little water, with the sugar added or not—again depending on the recipe being followed.

INSTRUCTIONS FOR FRESH FRUITS

It is difficult to give any hard-and-fast rule as to the amount of water and sugar required to make the syrup, as this will depend on the ripeness and sweetness of any particular fruit. A basic syrup would be $\frac{1}{4}$ pint water boiled rapidly with 3–4 tablespoons of sugar in a small saucepan until beginning to thicken, then poured over the fruit.

If in a great hurry, the water can be put first in the bottom of the container and the sugar be sprinkled over the fruit as it is packed in layers.

STEWED FRUIT AND EGG CUSTARD

Pressure Cooking Time: 5 minutes

For this easy dessert two heatproof containers such as soufflé or casserole dishes would be best as they could then be taken straight to table, but they must be chosen so that they will stand one on the other without interfering with the vent and to allow the closure of the cover.

Stewed Fruit: Plums, gooseberries, apricots, apples, rhubarb prepared and sliced, halved or cut into lengths layered in the dish with plenty of sugar. No water need be added except for fruits such as pears which do not make much juice of their own.

Egg Custard: As given in recipe on p. 173.

Lift the trivet out of the cooker, put in $\frac{1}{2}$ pint water with a little lemon or vinegar, then the dish with the stewed fruit covered with a double thickness of greaseproof paper, then the trivet and on top the dish with the egg custard, also with a double thickness of greaseproof paper laid on top. Bring to pressure in the usual way, cook for 5 minutes, allow the pressure to reduce at room temperature. Lift out and serve at once or allow to chill thoroughly.

As this sweet does not mind being kept waiting, it can always be prepared before the meat course and be put on one side until required.

APPLE CLOUD

Pressure Cooking Time: 2 minutes

1 lb of cooking apples; 3–4 tablespoons sugar; a squeeze of lemon juice; 2 good tablespoons condensed milk; 2 egg whites; a little cochineal if available.

Peel, core, slice the apples, dip in cold water, then strain. Lift the trivet from the cooker, put in the apples, lemon juice, sugar and cook on a low heat until the bottom is covered with juice and the sugar dissolved. Bring to pressure in the usual way, cook for 2 minutes and allow the pressure to reduce at room temperature. Take out the apples, stir in the condensed milk, add a little colouring if liked, taste to see if more sugar requires to be added, pour over apples and leave until cold. In a large bowl, beat the egg whites until stiff, then gently fold in the apple mixture and pile into the serving dish.

SPICED CARAMEL APPLES

Pressure Cooking Time: 2–3 minutes

1 medium-sized eating apple per person; $\frac{1}{4}$ pint water, 6 oz loaf sugar, 1 clove, a pinch of cinnamon, juice of 1 lemon for the syrup; 4 slices of pineapple, $\frac{1}{4}$ pint double cream, a teaspoon of caster sugar, pieces of cherry and angelica, chopped nuts for decoration; $\frac{1}{2}$ pint water with a piece of lemon for the cooker.

Peel the apples very thinly and core. Put into a shallow plate or dish which will fit into the cooker. Put the ingredients for the syrup into a small saucepan, stir over a low heat until the sugar has dissolved, then boil rapidly until thick and turning golden brown. Pour immediately over the apples. Put the water, trivet and dish into the cooker and cover with a piece of buttered greaseproof paper. Bring to pressure in the usual way, cook for the required time and allow the pressure to reduce at room temperature. Lift out the dish, strain off the juice and immediately spoon it back over the apples to coat them evenly. Chill in the refrigerator or leave until quite cold. Whip the cream until stiff, fold in the sugar and the small pieces of cherry and angelica. Put a slice of pineapple in four individual dishes, stand an apple on each, fill the centre with the cream mixture and sprinkle with the chopped nuts.

STEWED APPLES

Pressure Cooking Time: 2 minutes

Do not fill the cooker more than one-third full as apples tend to froth up.

Cooking apples; white or brown sugar to taste; a piece of lemon peel or unusual flavourings such as rose petals, rosemary, a sprig of elderflower or a tablespoon of orange-flower water.

Peel, core and slice the apples or cut up roughly. If adding any of the unusual suggested flavourings, lift the trivet from the cooker, put in $\frac{1}{4}$ pint water and the flavourings, boil in the open pan for 3 to 4 minutes, then lift out the flavourings before putting in the sugar and allowing it to dissolve. If using orange-flavour water, put into the cooker with the sugar, stir until dissolved and boil for 2 to 3 minutes. Otherwise, rinse the apples with cold water, put into the cooker with the sugar and lemon, bring to the boil slowly in the open pan until sufficient juice has run out to cover the bottom of the pan. Bring the apples to pressure in the usual way, cook for 2 minutes and allow the pressure to reduce at room temperature. If there is too much juice with the apples strain them; beat thoroughly with a potato masher or wooden spoon, taste to see if more sugar is needed, add a good knob of butter and stir until melted.

This method should be used for all fruits which are to be pulped or pureéd for use as tart fillings, for sweet omelettes or fruit fools.

COMPÔTE OF CHERRIES

Pressure Cooking Time: 1 minute

$\frac{1}{2}$ lb bright red cherries; $\frac{1}{4}$ lb white sugar; 2 tablespoons water; a squeeze of lemon juice; 1 big teaspoon of redcurrant jelly; cochineal; 1 tablespoon of Kirsch; whipped cream, flavoured with Kirsch.

Wash and stone the cherries. Lift the trivet from the cooker, put in the water, lemon juice and sugar, stir until dissolved and boil rapidly until beginning to thicken, put in the cherries, bring to pressure in the usual way, cook for 1 minute and allow the pressure to reduce at room temperature. Lift the cherries with a straining spoon into a deep bowl. Pour the syrup into a small saucepan, add the jam and colouring and boil until really syrupy, skimming from time to time to keep the syrup clear. Remove from the heat, stir in the Kirsch, pour over the cherries and put to chill thoroughly. About 5 minutes before serving, put stemmed glasses in the refrigerator, serve the cherries into them, decorating with a swirl of the flavoured whipped cream.

Any suitable fruits prepared this way are excellent for serving over ice-cream, or for the filling of meringue cases.

GOOSEBERRY FOOL

Pressure Cooking Time: 2 minutes

1 lb of gooseberries (½ pint purée) with a little extra sugar and a little green colouring added after sieving; ½ pint milk, 1 dessertspoon cornflour, sugar to taste, 1 egg for custard (or ½ pint custard made from custard powder).

Prepare the gooseberry purée as in preceding recipe, adding the extra sweetening and a little green colouring, if necessary. To make the custard, mix a spoonful of the milk with the cornflour, boil the rest, add the blended cornflour, return to the heat and reboil. Stir in the yolk of egg and cook for a minute or two but without boiling. Add sugar to taste and allow to cool. Beat the white of egg and fold in, alternately with the gooseberry purée. Put into a serving or individual dishes and, at the last moment, decorate with whipped cream, cherries, angelica, baby ratafias as desired.

ORANGE DELIGHTS

Pressure Cooking Time: 5 minutes

4 seedless oranges; ½ pint water for the cooker; 1 tablespoon hot water, 4 tablespoons brown sugar, pinch of cinnamon, pinch of nutmeg, 2 tablespoons golden syrup, a few chopped dates and nuts for the syrup.

Lift the trivet from the cooker, put in the water and the whole, washed, unpeeled oranges. Bring to pressure in the usual way, cook for 3 minutes and reduce the pressure in cold water. When cool, peel the oranges, put in a shallow dish that will fit easily into the cooker and pour over the mixed ingredients for the syrup. Bring to pressure again, cook for 2 minutes and reduce the pressure with cold water. Strain off the syrup and boil rapidly until thick in a small saucepan. Serve the oranges with the syrup poured over.

These Orange Delights may be served sliced as a dessert with pouring or whipped cream or with cottage or cream cheese in a salad.

PEACH ROYAL

Pressure Cooking Time: 2–3 minutes

4 whole peaches; ¼ pint water; 4 tablespoons sugar; juice of ½ lemon; ¼ pint double cream; 1 tablespoon brandy if liked; caster sugar to taste; 1 small punnet of firm, small strawberries; finely chopped or shredded almonds to decorate.

Lift the trivet from the cooker, put in the water and sugar, bring to the boil stirring to make sure the sugar dissolves, boil for 2–3 minutes, put in the washed peaches, bring to pressure in the usual way, cook for 3 minutes and allow the pressure to reduce at room temperature. When cool, skin, halve, stone, put in a shallow dish, sprinkle with the lemon juice and chill in the refrigerator. For serving, whip the cream, fold in the brandy, a little caster sugar and lastly the halved strawberries. Pile this on to the cut side of the peach halves, decorate with the nuts and serve in individual dishes.

PEACH FLAMBÉ

Pressure Cooking Time: 2–3 minutes

4 peaches cooked as in previous recipe; 1 small glass of Kirsch.

When the peaches have been lifted out, skin and stone them. Boil the syrup rapidly in the open cooker until reduced to about two tablespoons and put back the peaches. Warm the Kirsch (or brandy if preferred) in a small saucepan, set light to it with a match and quickly pour over the peaches. As soon as the flames are out, put the cover on the cooker and leave to stand for 10 minutes. Serve at once or after thorough chilling in the refrigerator.

GOLDEN PEARS

Pressure Cooking Time: 4–8 minutes

1 or 2 pears per person; 4 oz soft brown sugar; thinly peeled rind of an orange; a small bottle or tin of apple juice; double cream and sugar for sweetening; cherries, angelica, chopped nuts to decorate.

Peel the pears very thinly, leave whole and with the stalk on. Lift the trivet out of the cooker, put in the sugar, orange rind and apple juice, stir until the sugar is dissolved and boil rapidly for 5 minutes. Put in the pears standing upright and lay the trivet on top to keep them in position. Bring to pressure in the usual way, cook 4 minutes for dessert pears, 8 minutes for hard, cooking pears and leave the pressure to reduce, with the cover on for 20 minutes or longer if possible. Lift out the pears and again stand upright in a large serving dish. Put the syrup into a small saucepan, boil until syrupy, then coat each pear. Chill and just before serving, whip the cream, sweeten, stir in small pieces of cherries and angelica and the chopped nuts, put into a small dish and stand in the centre of the pears for serving.

COCONUT PEARS

Pressure Cooking Time: 2–3 minutes

4 pears cooked as in previous recipe; a little cochineal if liked; 4 tablespoons of sultanas stirred into 2 tablespoons of golden syrup; coconut; shredded almonds.

A little cochineal may be added to the syrup before cooking to colour the pears.

Lift out the pears halve and place, cut side up, on the grill pan. Fill the golden syrup into the hollows, sprinkle with the coconut and shredded almonds and grill, watching carefully that the coconut does not burn.

MARSHMALLOW PEARS

Pressure Cooking Time: 2–3 minutes

4 dessert but not over-ripe pears; $\frac{1}{4}$ pint water; 4 tablespoons sugar; piece of lemon rind and a squeeze of lemon juice or a teaspoon of ground ginger or cinnamon to taste; 4 pink, 4 white marshmallows; pouring cream to hand separately.

Lift the trivet from the cooker, put in the water, sugar and flavourings, bring to the boil, stirring until the sugar is dissolved, and boil until thick. Put in the peeled, halved and cored pears, cut side up, bring to pressure in the usual way, cook according to ripeness and reduce the pressure with cold water. Carefully lift the pears out with a straining spoon, place cut side up on the grill pan and place a marshmallow on each. Grill very gently until the marshmallows have melted, but watch them carefully to see they do not burn. Serve the pears, arranging the colours alternately or serving each person one white and one pink in an individual dish. Hand the single cream separately.

PINEAPPLE CARMELITE

Pressure Cooking Time: 1 minute

1 pineapple giving 5–6 slices; one layer 7-inch sponge cake, topped with vanilla glacé icing; 1 large tub of vanilla ice-cream; $\frac{1}{4}$ pint water, 4 oz white sugar for syrup.

Cut the pineapple into even slices (saving the top with the green leaves); trim off the outside, cut away any black pieces, remove the centres with an apple corer. Lift the trivet from the cooker, put in the pineapple and syrup, bring to pressure in the usual way, cook for 1 minute and allow the pressure to reduce at room temperature. Lift out the slices and leave to thoroughly drain. In a small saucepan, boil the syrup until thick and put to cool. When ready to serve, lay the slices around the top of the sponge cake leaving a space in the centre. Beat the ice-cream, fill into the centre and cap with the pineapple top. Hand the syrup separately.

DRIED FRUITS

These fruits are very often neglected as they are always thought to require long soaking and even longer cooking and therefore seem to be too much trouble, but a pressure cooker does away with all that. The super-heated steam quickly softens and swells the fruit while bringing out all the sweetness and flavours in a matter of minutes so that, even when fresh fruits are not available, you can serve a dish of stewed fruit or a delicious dessert full of nutritive value and with many variations.

INSTRUCTIONS FOR DRIED FRUITS

Wash the dried fruits with hot water, put into a bowl, pour over boiling water in the proportion of 1 pint to 1 lb of fruit, making sure that all the fruit is under water, cover with a plate and leave for 10 minutes.

The trivet is not required.

Add two to three tablespoons of sugar per pound of fruit and use the soaking water for the cooking.

Use High pressure and reduce at room temperature.

FRUIT	FOR COOKING	PRESSURE COOKING TIME
Apple Rings	Shreds of lemon peel, or cloves	6 minutes
Apricots	Add a little orange juice to ¾ pint water	3 minutes
Figs	Cut off dried stalks	10 minutes
Peaches	Add a little orange juice	5 minutes
Pears	Add 1 or 2 cloves to ¾ pint water	10 minutes
Prunes	Add a shred of lemon or orange peel	10 minutes
Fruit Salad	Add a shred of lemon or orange peel	10 minutes

APRICOT MALLOW

Pressure Cooking Time: 2 minutes

6 oz dried apricots; $\frac{1}{4}$ pint water; 2 tablespoons orange juice; 18 marshmallows; 2 egg whites; 3 tablespoons sugar; sliced marshmallow and shredded almonds to decorate.

Presoak the apricots using only $\frac{1}{4}$ pint boiling water, as directed. Lift the trivet from the cooker, put in the apricots, soaking water and orange juice, bring to pressure in the usual way, cook for 2 minutes and allow the pressure to reduce at room temperature. Strain off the juice, chop the apricots and put them with two tablespoons of juice and sixteen of the marshmallows into a saucepan. Fold the mixture over and over on a low heat until the marshmallows are beginning to melt, remove from the heat, continue folding until the mixture is smooth and spongy and allow to cool. Beat the white of eggs stiffly, fold in the sugar, then fold this into the apricot mixture. Serve in a deep dish or pile into individual dishes and when cool, decorate with sliced marshmallows and shredded almonds.

APRICOT SNOW

Pressure Cooking Time: 3 minutes

6 oz dried apricots; $\frac{1}{2}$ pint water; 3 whites of eggs; sugar to sweeten; browned almonds to decorate.

Wash, presoak and cook the dried apricots as given in the instructions. During this cooking, preheat the oven to Gas No 5, 375° F. Sieve the apricots and add about one dessertspoon of the juice to the purée. Taste and add sweetening if thought necessary. Fold in the stiffly beaten whites and put into a buttered, sugared heatproof serving dish. Bake until golden for 15 to 20 minutes.

To brown the almonds, blanch and shred them, then put on a baking tray and leave on the bottom of the oven while the pudding is cooking, until golden brown. Sprinkle over the pudding just before serving. Boil the syrup in an open saucepan until thick and hand separately. It may be sharpened, if preferred, with a little lemon juice.

FRUIT SALAD

Pressure Cooking Time: 10 minutes

1 packet of dried fruit salad; water and sugar in proportion; 2 tablespoons seedless raisins; $\frac{1}{4}$ orange, unpeeled and finely sliced; $\frac{1}{4}$ lemon unpeeled and finely sliced; blended cornflour for thickening with a little cochineal for colour.

Wash, presoak and cook the fruit salad, with the orange, lemon and raisins as given in the instructions. Lift the fruit into the serving dish, add the blended cornflour to the syrup, boil for a moment or two to thicken, add the colouring as necessary and spoon over the fruit.

If a clear syrup is preferred, use arrowroot for the thickening.

PRUNE WHIP

Pressure Cooking Time: 10 minutes

$\frac{1}{2}$ lb prunes; $\frac{1}{2}$ pint water; strip of lemon peel; 2 large tablespoons of marmalade; a squeeze of lemon juice; 2 egg whites with 2 tablespoons of sugar; crushed crystallised violets or roses, sugar strands or hundreds and thousands for decoration.

Wash, presoak and cook the prunes with the lemon rind according to the instructions (p. 189). Strain the prunes, stone and mash to pulp. Add the lemon juice and marmalade and allow to cool. Beat the whites stiffly, fold in the sugar, then fold into the prune mixture. Pile into individual glasses and just before serving decorate to give a touch of colour.

For a children's sweet, use the prune juice made up to 1 pint with cold water to dissolve a lemon jelly. Stir in the mashed prunes and marmalade and, when cool, add a little sugar if necessary, fold in the stiffly beaten whites and put into a serving dish. Decorate as for **Prune Whip**.

SECTION VIII

Regional and Continental Dishes

Nowadays when all the world and his wife have many more opportunities to travel on business or take the family on holidays abroad everyone is becoming more familiar with the regional and national dishes of other countries. It is therefore a pleasant reminder of new places, sunny skies, lazy days to make these in your own home, to offer them to your guests, for they can add variety and spice to the family menus and serve as excellent conversation pieces for your dinner parties.

Many of them can be adapted to pressure cooking and, if some of the ingredients are not those usually found on your kitchen shelf when that special occasion comes along, you will find a wide variety and choice of herbs, sauces, vegetables, packaged foods available in your local shops which will never be wasted; try them with your own favourite dishes to give that extra dash that will make your family sit up and take notice—and congratulate you on a new dish.

ENGLAND

STEAK AND OYSTER PUDDING

Steaming Time: 15 minutes
Pressure Cooking Time: 55 minutes

For cooking instructions, follow the recipe for **Steak and Kidney Pudding** (p. 121).

1 lb stewing steak; $\frac{1}{2}$ lb mushrooms; 8–12 oysters; seasoning; a little flour; 8 oz suet crust; 1$\frac{1}{2}$ pints boiling water with lemon juice or vinegar, for the cooker.

Wipe the meat, trim away all fat, cut into small pieces and toss in seasoned flour. Peel the mushrooms and cut into thin slices lengthways, including the stalk. Open the oysters and wash well. Continue as given on p. 121.

IRELAND

CRUBEENS

Pressure Cooking Time: 30 minutes

2 fresh pig's trotters per person; $\frac{1}{2}$ pint water; seasoning; 1 large crisp green cabbage; potatoes can be cooked with this dish if liked.

Wash and scrub the trotters thoroughly, lift the trivet from the cooker, put in the water and trotters, bring to pressure in the usual way, cook for 25 minutes and reduce the pressure with cold water. During this cooking, peel the potatoes if they are to be served as well, wash the cabbage and shred roughly tossing it well in plenty of salt and pepper. Pack the cabbage down into the liquid, put the trivet on top and the potatoes, cut to cook in 5 minutes. Bring to pressure again, cook for the last 5 minutes and reduce the pressure with cold water. Serve the potatoes, and the trotters dished on the strained cabbage. Taste and correct seasoning, boil the liquor in the open pan for 2 to 3 minutes to reduce it, then pour into the dish.

SCOTLAND

POTTED HAUGH

Pressure Cooking Time: 1 hour

1 lb of haugh (shin of beef); 2 lb of nap bone (foot or could be marrow bone); 1$\frac{1}{2}$ pints water; $\frac{1}{2}$ teaspoon of peppercorns, $\frac{1}{2}$ teaspoon mixed spice, $\frac{1}{2}$ teaspoon powdered or piece of mace, tied in a piece of double muslin; seasoning.

Lift the trivet from the cooker, put in the water, the nap bone and the bag of spices, bring to the boil, skim well, bring to pressure in the usual way, cook for 40 minutes and allow the pressure to reduce at room temperature. Leave to stand a while, then remove as much fat as possible. Bring to the boil again in the open cooker, add the well-seasoned meat, bring to pressure again, cook for a further 20 minutes and allow the pressure to reduce at room temperature. Lift out the meat and strain the stock. Shred the meat or cut small or put through a mincer and fill into bowls or moulds rinsed in cold water. Remove the fat again from the stock, return to the cooker, taste and correct seasoning, boil rapidly for 5 minutes and fill the bowls. Put on one side, stirring occasionally as the stock sets to make sure the meat is evenly distributed. Leave until set, then turn out by dipping quickly in hot water and serve with a green or mixed salad.

WALES

CAWL MAMGU

Pressure Cooking Time: 20 minutes

It is recommended to scald the meat the night before so that the fat can be removed.

2 lb best end of neck of Welsh lamb; ½ lb carrots; 1 small swede; 1 lb medium potatoes; 2 large leeks; 1 tablespoon chopped parsley; seasoning; ¾ pint water; blended flour for thickening.

Wipe the meat, lift the trivet from the cooker, put in the joint and the water, bring slowly to the boil in the open pan and skim carefully or allow to stand overnight and remove the fat just before starting the cooking. Bring to pressure in the usual way, cook for 15 minutes and reduce the pressure with cold water. During this cooking, prepare the vegetables, cutting the carrots in half, the swede and leeks in slices, the potatoes in quarters and add with the parsley to the cawl. Bring to pressure again, cook for the last 5 minutes and reduce the pressure with cold water. Lift out the meat, divide into portions and serve into individual bowls or plates with a selection of the strained vegetables. Taste the cawl and correct the seasoning, add the blended flour, allow to cook for a minute or two while stirring and pour into the dishes.

AMERICA

CHICKEN PAPRIKA

Pressure Cooking Time: 7 minutes

1 young, roasting chicken about 2½ lb; 4 tablespoons butter; 4 medium onions; 2 medium tomatoes; 1–1½ tablespoons of paprika; ¼ pint water; 1 tablespoon flour, 2 tablespoons sour cream for thickening; seasoning; 1 cup of rice, 2 cups of water in solid container; a little more paprika for garnish.

Joint the chicken into portions; chop the onions finely, quarter the tomatoes. Lift the trivet from the cooker, heat the butter and gently fry the onions until just turning colour but not brown. Add the paprika, stir until well mixed, then put in the tomatoes, the water and the chicken. Put the trivet on top and the covered container of rice. Bring to pressure in the usual way, cook for 7 minutes and allow the pressure to reduce at room temperature. During this cooking, boil a kettle of water and heat oven. Blend the flour and cream. Lift out the rice and finish as instructed. Serve the chicken and vegetables and keep hot. Gradually add the strained stock to the cream, taste and correct seasoning, reheat but do not allow to reboil and pour over the chicken. Hand the rice separately sprinkled with a little paprika.

BROWN APPLE BETTY

Pressure Cooking Time: 10 minutes

6 oz soft white crumbs; 2–3 tablespoons of melted butter; 4 oz brown sugar; ½ teaspoon each of nutmeg and cinnamon; 4–5 large cooking apples; a little lemon juice if apples are not of the sour variety; a teaspoon of grated lemon rind; ½ pint water with a little vinegar or lemon juice added, for the cooker; pouring or whipped cream handed separately.

Butter a soufflé dish or suitable-sized heatproof bowl. Combine the crumbs with the melted butter, sugar and spices; peel, core and slice the apples. Put in alternate layers of the crumb mixture and apples, starting and finishing with the crumbs and leaving at least 1-inch space at the top as the crumbs will swell during the cooking. Put the water into the cooker with the trivet and the dish covered with a double thickness of greased, greaseproof paper. Bring to pressure in the usual way and cook for 10 minutes and allow the pressure to reduce at room temperature. Serve in the dish or allow to stand for 2 to 3 minutes and unmould.

Serve with pouring or whipped cream.

BELGIUM

CARBONADES FLAMANDES

Pressure Cooking Time: 20 minutes

$1\frac{1}{2}$ lb good stewing steak; 2 large onions; 2 tablespoons of dripping; 1 bay leaf; $\frac{1}{2}$ pint beer or brown ale, $\frac{1}{4}$ pint brown stock; seasoning; pinch each of sugar and nutmeg; chopped parsley for garnish.

Cut the meat into large squares and season well; chop the onions. Lift the trivet from the cooker, heat the fat and quickly sear the meat all over, keeping it on the move. Brown the onions, drain off any surplus fat, take the cooker away from the heat and allow it to cool. Add the liquids, the seasonings and the bay leaf, bring to pressure in the usual way, cook for 20 minutes and reduce the pressure with cold water. Lift out the bay leaf, serve the meat and onions and keep hot. Boil the liquid in the open pan until thick, taste and correct seasoning and pour over the meat. Sprinkle thickly with chopped parsley.

To give a sharp taste, a teaspoon of wine vinegar can be stirred into the sauce, just before serving.

If a lot of sauce is preferred, thicken in the usual way with a little blended flour instead of reducing by rapid boiling.

CHICOREE À LA ROYALE

Pressure Cooking Time: 3 minutes and 5 minutes

4 chicory; 2 tablespoons butter and 2 tablespoons water; seasoning; 2 eggs; $\frac{1}{2}$ pint milk; salt and pinch of nutmeg; a little butter; $\frac{1}{2}$ pint water with a little lemon juice or vinegar for the cooker.

Wash the chicory well but do not cut it in any way. Lift the trivet from the cooker, put in the butter, allow to melt, add the water and chicory, bring to pressure in the usual way, cook for 3 minutes and reduce the pressure with cold water. During this cooking, warm the milk and pour on to the seasoned, beaten eggs. Lift the chicory into a greased soufflé or heatproof dish, pour over the custard and dot with butter. Rinse the cooker, put in the water, the trivet and the dish covered with a double thickness of greased, greaseproof paper. Bring to pressure in the usual way, cook for 5 minutes and allow the pressure to reduce at room temperature. Serve garnished with sprigs of watercress, or the top may be sprinkled with grated cheese and lightly browned under a hot grill.

FRANCE

POT AU FEU

Pressure Cooking Time: 20–25 minutes

2 lb topside of beef; 2 legs and 2 wings of chicken; a large piece of marrow, shin bone or knuckle of veal; 2 pints water; 4 whole small onions; 4 whole medium carrots; 2 small, halved turnips; 4 leeks using white part only; 1 clove of garlic; 1 bay leaf, sprig each of parsley and thyme; salt and pepper; crisp French bread as accompaniment; mustard or horseradish sauce handed separately.

Lift the trivet from the cooker, put in the meat, the bone and the water. Bring to the boil in the open pan, skim well. Bring to pressure in the usual way, give all but 8 minutes of the cooking time and reduce the pressure with cold water. Skim again if necessary, put in the chicken, vegetables and seasonings, bring to pressure again, give the rest of the cooking time and allow the pressure to reduce at room temperature. Lift out the meat and serve, with the skinned chicken on a hot dish. Strain the broth, lift out the vegetables, arrange round the serving dish and keep hot. Skim the fat from the broth with kitchen paper, return to the pan, taste and correct seasoning, reheat and serve in individual bowls, with the crisped French bread handed separately. The meat may be carved before being taken to table; lay out in slices with a chicken piece to form a portion, each being accompanied by a selection of the vegetables. Hand the mustard or horseradish sauce (p. 291), which would be delicious made with sour cream, separately.

CRÊME BRULEE

Pressure Cooking Time: 4 minutes

¾ pint double cream with 1 tablespoon milk; 3 tablespoons sugar; 3 yolks of large eggs; about 1 teaspoon vanilla essence or more to taste; 3 tablespoons light brown sugar; ½ pint water with lemon or vinegar for the cooker.

Put the milk and then the cream into a small saucepan and warm very gently over a low heat, stirring all the time, pour over the beaten yolks and sugar and stir again. Add the vanilla to taste, then pour the cream into a buttered soufflé dish. Have ready in the cooker the water and the trivet, put in the cream and lay on top a double piece of greaseproof paper. Bring to pressure in the usual way, cook for 5 minutes and allow the pressure to reduce at room temperature. Allow to cool first and then chill thoroughly. When ready to serve, light the grill; half fill the grill pan with crushed ice (to do this, take the cubes from the ice-box, put in a tea-towel and crush with a hammer or the heavy weight from a set of scales), put the crême in the middle and cover with the brown sugar. Set the cream under the grill and watch it all the time until the sugar melts and turns brown. Be very careful here or the sugar will burn. Serve at once or chill again and serve ice-cold.

GERMANY

SAUERBRATEN

Pressure Cooking Time: 20–25 minutes

Correctly the meat should be left to marinate for seven days, turning it over every day.

2 lb piece of topside of beef; 4 thin slices of fat pork belly; 1 large onion; bouquet garni; $\frac{1}{4}$ pint water, $\frac{1}{4}$ pint vinegar; 2 tablespoons dripping or cooking fat; 1 teaspoon flour; seasoning; $\frac{1}{4}$ pint sour cream; 1 teaspoon of sugar.

To make the marinade, boil together for 5 minutes the chopped onion, the water and vinegar. Tie strips of the pork right round the joint, put it in a deep bowl with the bouquet garni and pour the marinade over. To keep the meat down in the liquid put a weighted saucer or plate on top. Leave as long as possible but turn the meat at least once during the soaking. When ready, lift the trivet from the cooker, heat the fat and brown the well-dried meat on all sides. Lift out and dust lightly with flour. When the cooker has cooled slightly, pour in half the strained marinade liquid, the sugar and the cream, put back the meat, bring to pressure in the usual way, cook for the required time and reduce the pressure with cold water. Lift out the meat and carve it; lay the overlapping slices on the serving dish and keep hot. Taste and correct the seasoning, reboil the sauce, pour a little over the meat and hand the rest separately.

HÜHNER FRIKASSEE

Pressure Cooking Time: 15–20 minutes

1 roasting chicken; seasoning; a little lemon juice; 2 tablespoons of butter; 12 button onions or shallots; 6 large field mushrooms; $\frac{1}{4}$ pint dry white wine; 1 tablespoon flour blended with a little milk for thickening; $\frac{1}{4}$ pint single cream; chopped parsley and bacon rolls (p. 297) for garnish.

Wipe the chicken, cut into joints and season well with salt, pepper and a sprinkling of lemon juice. Prepare the onions, leaving whole, cut the mushrooms into four. Lift the trivet from the cooker, heat the butter, fry the chicken pieces evenly until golden brown and lift out. Add the onions and mushrooms and cook gently for 2 to 3 minutes.

Lift the cooker from the heat, allow to cool, add the wine and put back the chicken portions. Bring to pressure in the usual way, cook for the required time and reduce the pressure with cold water. During this cooking, prepare the blended flour and make and grill the bacon rolls. Lift the chicken on to the serving dish and keep hot. Add the blended flour to the liquid, bring to the boil and cook for 2 to 3 minutes stirring all the time. Taste and correct seasoning, stir in the cream, reheat but without boiling and pour over the chicken. Garnish with chopped parsley and the bacon rolls. This dish is at its best when sour cream, rather than fresh, is used.

GREECE

KOTO AVGOLEMONO

Pressure Cooking Time: 25 minutes

1 chicken weighing 2½ to 3 lb; a large knob of butter; 1 lemon; an onion stuck with 2 cloves; a stick of celery; bouquet garni; crushed clove of garlic; a carrot; seasoning; 1 pint of chicken stock; a cupful of rice.
For the sauce: strained juice of the lemon; 2 yolks of eggs; 1 tablespoon of cold water; a little of the chicken stock; lemon quarters with parsley sprigs for garnish.

Put the giblets to soak in a little salted water. Wipe the chicken and stuff the body cavity with a slice of lemon peel, the knob of butter and plenty of seasoning. Rub the outside all over with the cut surface of the lemon and a little salt and pepper. Lift the trivet from the cooker and put in the chicken stock, the vegetables, the giblets, the seasonings and the chicken, bring to pressure in the usual way, cook for 20 minutes and reduce the pressure with cold water. Bring the stock to the boil in the open cooker, throw in the rice, bring to pressure again, cook for the last 5 minutes and allow the pressure to reduce at room temperature. Lift out the chicken, cut into portions and keep hot. Strain the stock, lifting away the bouquet garni, the vegetables and the giblets. Shake the rice left until all the liquid has drained off, pile on a serving dish, place the chicken pieces on top, cover with another dish or a piece of foil and keep hot in the oven. In a small bowl beat the yolks, add the lemon juice and water and two tablespoons hot stock. Put into a small saucepan and over a low heat, stir while the eggs cook. Do not allow to boil or the sauce will curdle and add a little more stock as the sauce thickens until a coating consistency is reached. Taste and correct seasoning, then pour over the chicken. Garnish the rice with the lemon quarters and sprigs of parsley.

PSARI ME KOLOKYTHIA

Pressure Cooking Time: 5–10 minutes

1 whole fish such as small, fresh haddock or 1 steak of cod, haddock, turbot, halibut, etc, per person; 2 tablespoons of olive oil; 2 medium sliced onions; 1 crushed clove of garlic; herbs to taste and to include dill, mint and chopped parsley; 4 ripe tomatoes; a teaspoon of sugar; seasoning and a pinch of cinnamon; $\frac{1}{4}$ pint water; 5 or 6 courgettes or 2 very young marrows; strained lemon juice to taste.

Lift the trivet from the cooker, heat the olive oil, put in the sliced onions, garlic, herbs and seasonings and the tomatoes, and cook for 2 to 3 minutes but without allowing to colour. Add the water and stir well. Put the unpeeled whole courgettes or the young marrows cut in half lengthways and with the seeds removed, on top of the vegetables, and on this bed lay the fish. Cover with a piece of buttered greaseproof paper, bring to pressure in the usual way, cook for the required time and allow the pressure to reduce at room temperature. Lift the fish out carefully, put the courgettes on a deep serving dish, then the fish back on top and keep hot. Reheat the sauce, add a little lemon juice, taste and correct seasoning, reboil rapidly in the open cooker to reduce to a coating consistency, then pour over the fish.

This dish, in Greece, is served either hot or cold.

HOLLAND

ZUURKOOL STAMPOT

Pressure Cooking Time: 9 minutes

1 lb of sauerkraut; 2 lb of potatoes; 1 large onion; 4 slices of streaky bacon; 6–8 oz continental sausage; $\frac{1}{4}$ pint water; salt and pepper.

Lift the trivet from the cooker, put in the chopped bacon and allow to fry until golden crisp but not brown, lift out. Add the hot water (if cold, allow cooker to cool), the sliced potatoes in layers, well sprinkled with salt and pepper, then a layer of sauerkraut and onion. Sprinkle with the fried bacon and lastly add the piece of sausage. Bring to pressure in the usual way, cook for 9 minutes and allow the pressure to reduce at room temperature. Lift out the sausage, slice and keep hot. Mash the vegetables or cut through roughly with a knife, taste and correct seasoning, reheat, serve into a deep dish and lay the sliced sausage on top.

KABELJAUW EN GARNALENRAGOUT

Pressure Cooking Time: 6 minutes

2 small cod or 4 steaks; 4 oz shrimps (fresh or frozen); $\frac{3}{4}$ pint of water; 1 tablespoon butter, 1 tablespoon flour for thickening; a little lemon juice; 2 tablespoons chopped parsley; seasoning.

Lift the trivet from the cooker, put in the water, the fish and the lemon juice and seasoning, bring to pressure in the usual way, cook for 6 minutes and reduce the pressure with cold water. During this cooking melt the butter in a small saucepan, add the flour and allow to cook without browning. Lift out the fish, add the stock to the flour in the saucepan stirring all the time, put in the shrimps, bring to the boil, taste and correct seasoning and cook for 2 to 3 minutes. Divide the fish into large pieces, removing all skin and bone, put back in the cooker, pour over the sauce and reheat. Serve, piping hot, in a deep dish, sprinkled thickly with parsley.

ITALY

MINESTRONE MILANESE

Pressure Cooking Time: 10 minutes

2 slices of thick, streaky bacon; 2 tablespoons olive oil or butter; 1 medium onion; 1 celery heart; $\frac{1}{4}$ large green cabbage; $\frac{1}{4}$ lb French or runner beans; 2 tablespoons of peas; 3 tomatoes; 1 potato; 1 crushed clove of garlic; 1 tablespoon chopped parsley; 2 courgettes or 1 small marrow; $1\frac{1}{2}$ pints of water; 4 oz rice; seasoning; grated Parmesan cheese may be handed separately.

Chop the bacon finely, saving the rinds; slice the onions into strips, the celery and potatoes into strips 2 inches long, shred the cabbage, cut the beans into thin diagonal slices and peel and chop the tomatoes. If courgettes are used, do not peel but slice, remove the seeds and cut into 2-inch strips; for a marrow, skin and cut as before. Lift the trivet from the cooker, heat the oil and gently fry the bacon, onions and celery until just turning brown. Add all the rest of the vegetables, the bacon rinds, the stock and seasoning and bring to the boil. Throw in the rice, bring to pressure in the usual way, cook for 10 minutes and allow the pressure to reduce at room temperature. Taste and correct the seasoning, reheat and serve in individual soup bowls, handing the cheese separately if liked.

OSSOBUCHI

This recipe should be made well in advance of the meal as it requires to stand for 2 to 3 hours.

Pressure Cooking Time: 20 minutes

3 lb of veal shank or shin, sawn by the butcher into $2\frac{1}{2}$-inch long pieces; 2 tablespoons of butter; seasoning; $\frac{1}{2}$ pint Marsala; water; 1 teaspoon flour; 1 beef or chicken cube; 1 clove of garlic; 2 or 3 strips of lemon peel; 1 teaspoon finely chopped anchovies; 1 tablespoon grated lemon rind, 1 tablespoon chopped parsley, 1 small teaspoon chopped garlic as garnish; risotto to hand separately.

Tie each piece of veal with thin string so that it will hold together. Lift the trivet from the cooker, heat the butter and brown the pieces until golden and lift out. Pour in the wine, add the seasoning, bring to the boil; put back the veal and boil, turning the pieces at least once, until the wine is well reduced. Sprinkle in the flour, put in the stock cube and sufficient water to not quite cover the pieces. Bring to pressure in the usual way, cook for 20 minutes and allow the pressure to reduce at room temperature. Turn into a covered dish and leave to stand for 2 to 3 hours.

About three-quarters of an hour before the meal, use the pressure cooker to cook the Risotto, p. 152, and keep hot in the oven. Put the Ossobuchi back in the cooker, add the garlic, lemon peel and anchovies and warm through gently until bubbling. Lift the pieces on to a hot serving dish, remove the clove of garlic and lemon peel and boil the sauce until a thick, coating consistency. Pour over the meat, garnish with the mixed lemon rind, parsley and garlic and hand the risotto separately.

MEXICO

CHILI CON CARNE

Pressure Cooking Time: 20 minutes and 10 minutes

8 oz small kidney beans (the red ones should be used if available); 2 pints water; 2 tablespoons of butter; 2–3 teaspoons chilli powder; 2 tablespoons bacon fat; 1 large chopped onion; 1 lb finely minced lean steak; $\frac{3}{4}$ pint brown stock; salt; cream crackers handed separately and pickled cucumbers if available.

Wash, soak and cook the beans according to the instructions on pp. 55, 63, 64 or 66. After straining, put back in the cooker and reheat with the butter and 1 teaspoon of the chilli powder. Lift out, take one-third of the beans and mash thoroughly. Rinse the cooker, heat the bacon fat and fry the onion until transparent. Add the meat, brown quickly stirring all the time, put in the hot stock (if cold, allow cooker to cool), the mashed beans, salt and the rest of the chilli powder, stirring all together well. Bring to pressure in the usual way, cook for 15 minutes and reduce the pressure with cold water. Add the rest of the beans, taste and correct seasoning, and allow to boil until the consistency is that of a thick stew. Hand the crackers and cucumbers separately.

This dish is often preferred flavoured with tomatoes: for this, use a tin of tomatoes with the juice and only $\frac{1}{2}$ pint of water. For quickness, a large tin of baked beans in tomato sauce could be used instead, with a little extra tomato purée or sauce.

SPAIN

GAZPACHO

Pressure Cooking Time: 5 minutes

This is served as an iced soup and must be prepared well in advance to allow plenty of time for it to be thoroughly chilled.

8 fresh tomatoes; 1 large onion; 1 cucumber; 1 green pepper; 1 tablespoon of butter; 1 crushed clove of garlic; 1 teaspoon of sugar; $\frac{1}{4}$ pint of white stock or water; $\frac{1}{4}$ pint red wine; seasoning; 2 tablespoons lemon juice; salt and cayenne pepper; $\frac{1}{4}$ pint tomato juice; 2–3 tablespoons olive oil; 1 tablespoon butter and diced bread for croûtons (p. 298).

Skin the tomatoes, put two on one side and cut the rest up roughly; chop the onion; wash the cucumber, put half on one side, cut the other into cubes; wash the pepper, remove seeds, put half on one side and chop the other roughly. Lift the trivet from the cooker, heat the butter, put in the onions and tomatoes and cook until the onions are transparent but not coloured. Add the cucumber, pepper, garlic, sugar, seasoning and liquids, bring to pressure in the usual way, cook for 5 minutes and reduce the pressure with cold water. Strain the soup through a fine sieve and put the liquid to one side. Sieve the soup and add just sufficient liquid to give a thick consistency to the soup. Put in the refrigerator and chill thoroughly. Just before serving, put the lemon juice and seasoning into a small bowl, stir in the tomato juice and the olive oil drop by drop until well blended and stir gently into the soup. Prepare the following and serve each in separate dishes to be handed round separately: the half cucumber, unpeeled, cut into cubes and tossed with the half green pepper cut into thin strips; the two tomatoes each cut into eight pieces; the croûtons of bread fried golden brown in the butter heated with a clove of garlic.

At the last moment, serve the soup into individual bowls and add a small ice cube to each.

PAELLA

Pressure Cooking Time: 8 minutes

This dish must be a combination of chicken and shellfish. If it is difficult to obtain fresh shellfish there is no reason why tinned or frozen should not be used.

1 young, roasting chicken 2½–3 lb; a mixture of shellfish, including about 4 Dublin Bay prawns, 10–12 mussels or oysters, 1 small cooked or tin of lobster; 2 tablespoons of olive oil; 1 medium onion; 1 green pepper; 1 clove of garlic; 1½ pints chicken stock; 6 oz rice; a good pinch of saffron; 2 tomatoes; salt, paprika pepper; pinch of marjoram; 1 teaspoon chopped parsley; 1 teaspoon of finely chopped leek if available.

Wipe the chicken, skin and cut into joints; cut the prawns, mussels and lobster into large pieces; chop the onion, the peeled tomatoes and the pepper. Lift the trivet from the cooker, heat the oil, gently brown the chicken pieces and lift out. Add the clove of garlic cut lengthwise, the onions and pepper and cook until the onions are just turning brown. Add the tomatoes, saffron, seasoning, parsley, leek, stir well together, put back the chicken pieces, pour in the hot stock, bring to the boil in the open cooker and throw in the rice. Put in the trivet and on it the shellfish, covered with a piece of greaseproof paper. Bring to pressure in the usual way, cook for 8 minutes and allow the pressure to reduce at room temperature. Lift out the shellfish and then the trivet, stir the paella which should be thick with almost all the liquid absorbed. If it is a little thin, boil rapidly in the open cooker. Serve in a deep casserole dish, laying the shellfish on top in an attractive pattern.

HUNGARY

GOULASH

Pressure Cooking Time: 15–20 minutes

1–1½ lb of good stewing steak such as chuck, or rump; 2 large sliced onions; 2 tablespoons dripping or butter; a clove of minced or crushed garlic if liked; ¼ pint stock or water; ¼ pint tomato juice; about 2 teaspoons paprika, salt; bay leaf; 4 thickly sliced potatoes; a little red wine; chopped parsley for garnish.

Wipe and trim the meat, cut into large cubes and toss in seasoned flour, shaking well to remove any surplus. Lift the trivet out of the cooker, heat the fat and fry the onions until golden brown, lift out, fry the meat, keeping it moving to colour evenly all over. Lift out the meat and away from the heat, add the hot liquids (if cold, allow the cooker to cool), stirring until all the brown bits have been lifted from the bottom. Put back the onions and the meat, then the garlic and bay leaf and paprika, bring to pressure in the usual way, cook for all but 4 minutes of the cooking time, and reduce the pressure with cold water. Check that there is still sufficient liquid remembering that the potatoes will take up about one-third of what there is and if necessary, add a little more. Put in the potatoes, stir the goulash well, taste to correct seasoning which should be on the peppery side, bring to pressure again and cook for the last 4 minutes, reducing the pressure with cold water. Lift out the bay leaf, stir in a little red wine to taste and serve, piping hot, garnished with chopped parsley.

WEST AFRICA

JOLIFF RICE

Pressure Cooking Time: 5 minutes

1 chicken weighing about 2½–3 lb; 2 tablespoons butter; 4 small onions; 1 green pepper; seasoning; ¾ pint of chicken stock; ¼ pint beer; 1 bay leaf; pinch of turmeric; 6 oz rice; 1 packet of frozen peas; strips of red pepper or chillies, black or green olives, plain or stuffed, for garnish.

Joint the chicken into portions, skin and season well with salt and pepper; chop the onions finely; remove pips from the pepper and cut into thin slices. Lift the trivet from the cooker, heat the butter, fry the joints all over until golden brown and lift out. Gently fry the onion, garlic and pepper strips, add the hot stock (if cold allow the cooker to cool), the beer and seasonings, stir well, allow to boil, throw in the rice and peas. Bring to pressure in the usual way, cook for 5 minutes and allow the pressure to reduce at room temperature. Serve in a deep dish, lifting out the chicken, rice and vegetables; boil the sauce until a thick consistency in the open pan, tasting and correcting the seasoning. Garnish with the strips of peppers and olives, dotted over the surface.

SPINACH STEW

Pressure Cooking Time: 15 minutes

1½ lb stewing beef or lamb; ¼ pint palm or vegetable oil; 4 onions; 4 tomatoes; 8 freshly ground black peppercorns; 2 oz ogusi seeds; 2 lb fresh spinach (2 × 12 oz frozen could be used instead); seasoning; ¼ pint water; 1 teacup of rice with 2 cups of salted water; 1 small tin of baked beans in tomato sauce.

Wipe the meat and cut into ½-inch cubes; slice the onions; peel and quarter the tomatoes. Lift the trivet from the cooker, heat the oil and lightly brown the meat. Lift out and sprinkle thickly with salt and pepper. Fry the onions and the tomatoes, add the hot water (if cold, allow the cooker to cool) and the seasonings, and bring to the boil. Put back the meat, bring to pressure in the usual way, cook for 10 minutes and reduce the pressure with cold water. During this cooking, cut the frozen spinach into small pieces; put the rice and salted water into one solid container and the baked beans out of the tin, into another. Add the spinach to the stew, put in the trivet and the rice and beans covered with a piece of greaseproof paper. Bring to pressure again, cook for a further 5 minutes and allow the pressure to reduce at room temperature. During this cooking, preheat the oven to Gas No 4, 350° F, and boil a kettle of water. Lift out the rice, rinse in a colander by pouring over the boiling water, spread on a baking tray, put into the oven and turn off the heat. Serve the baked beans into a separate dish and keep hot. Lift out the trivet, taste and correct the seasoning of the stew and leave on a low heat. Form a border of rice on the serving dish and pour the stew in the centre. Hand the baked beans separately.

SWEDEN

KÖTTBULLAR

Pressure Cooking Time: 10 minutes

$\frac{3}{4}$ lb finely minced steak; $\frac{1}{4}$ lb minced veal; $\frac{1}{4}$ lb minced pork or ham; 1 small finely chopped onion; 1 tablespoon butter; 3 tablespoons of fine white breadcrumbs soaked in $\frac{1}{4}$ pint sour cream; seasoning; pinch of cloves; 1 egg; 2 tablespoons brown sugar; 1 teaspoon dry mustard; $\frac{1}{4}$ pint water; $\frac{1}{4}$ pint vinegar.

Lift the trivet from the cooker, heat the butter and fry the onions golden brown. Lift out and mix with the meats, the breadcrumbs, seasoning and beaten egg to give a firm consistency that will form easily into meat balls. If the mixture is too dry, add a little milk as necessary. Form into eight balls and stand on one side for at least an hour. Put the vinegar and water into the cooker, add the mustard, sugar and cloves and boil, stirring all the time, until the sugar is dissolved. Toss the meat balls in seasoned flour, put into the liquid, bring to pressure in the usual way, cook 10 minutes and allow the pressure to reduce at room temperature. Lift the meat balls into a serving dish and keep hot. Boil the stock rapidly until thickening, taste and correct seasoning and pour into the dish.

SECTION IX

Vegetarian and Invalid Dishes

A section such as this in a general cookery book cannot cover the subject of the particular requirements of these two groups entirely, but the following recipes are just to give an idea of how useful your pressure cooker can be when special diets are a necessity or just a matter of choice.

For vegetarians, who have to ensure an adequate supply of proteins in their diet, the quick, complete cooking of the pulse vegetables such as beans, split peas, lentils is a guarantee of the full retention of their flavours and the softness which makes for easy digestion. Again, the shortness of cooking time for fresh vegetables leading to the higher retention of vitamins and other nutrients and the concentrated cooking liquid which need never be wasted, means that all the goodness is there to aid health and vitality. To make these dishes appetising and to give variety they should be well seasoned and pepped up a bit with herbs, spices, garlic, onions and so on, or something tart such as fruit sauces or, if permissible, sour cream. As they also lack fats, these should be added in the form of a vegetable oil either for preliminary frying of the ingredients or by addition before serving. To obtain a balanced diet, desserts to follow should be fresh, tinned or stewed fruit rather than further cereals.

For invalids, the many advantages of having a pressure cooker must by now be obvious. All the delicate dishes, tender, well flavoured to encourage a flagging appetite, with all their goodness to help build up strength can be done in a matter of minutes and even the small quantities which are all that is usually required present no problem as, using cups, small boilable plastic bowls, deep saucers, individual portions of savoury and sweet dishes can be done together and in the same time to lighten the work and the washing-up and leave more time for the extra care and nursing that having someone ill in the house always entails.

Many of the following recipes are interchangeable, many others suitable will be found in previous sections and for those who have been ill and are trying to get back to normal food, the suggestions for infant feeding might prove helpful.

VEGETARIAN STOCK

Pressure Cooking Time: 30 minutes

½ lb large haricot beans; the outside stalks of a head of celery; 1 large onion; 1 large carrot; bouquet garni; a few white peppercorns; salt; a strip of lemon peel; 2 pints of water.

Presoak the beans as given in the instructions on p. 64. Cut the vegetables up into rough ½-inch dice. Lift the trivet from the cooker, put in the water in which the beans were soaked, made up to 2 pints, the vegetables and seasonings and bring to the boil. Add the beans, stir, bring to pressure in the usual way, cook for 30 minutes and allow the pressure to reduce at room temperature. Strain the stock for use. The beans could be used for the **Bean Ring** recipe, p. 210.

CORN CHOWDER

Pressure Cooking Time: 4 minutes

2 tablespoons vegetable oil; 1 peeled or chopped onion; 1 pint of creamed sweet corn (p. 54); 2 large potatoes cut in ¼-inch dice; 1 pint of water; seasoning; ½ pint hot milk; 2–3 tablespoons of blended flour for thickening; a good knob of butter; chopped watercress for garnish; fried croûtons (p. 298) to hand separately.

Lift the trivet from the cooker, heat the oil and allow the onion to cook until golden. Add the corn, potatoes and water, stir well, bring to pressure in the usual way, cook for 4 minutes and reduce the pressure with cold water. Add the flour blended with a little milk, stir until boiling; put the knob of butter on the top and seasoning to taste and allow to cook for a minute or two. Serve, sprinkled thickly with chopped watercress and hand the croûtons separately.

PEANUT BUTTER SOUP

Pressure Cooking Time: 10 minutes

1 small onion, diced; 2 sticks of young celery, cut roughly; 1 tablespoon of vegetable oil; 1 pint white vegetable stock; seasoning and a pinch of celery salt if liked; 1 tablespoon flour with a little milk or stock for thickening; a small jar of peanut butter; lemon juice to taste; minced chopped watercress and peanuts for garnish.

Lift the trivet from the cooker, heat the oil and gently cook the onions and celery but do not allow to brown. Add the hot stock (if cold, allow the cooker to cool), the seasonings, bring to pressure in the usual way, cook for 10 minutes and reduce the pressure with cold water. Strain the soup (it may be sieved if liked), add the thickening, return to the cooker and reboil while stirring, then cook for 2 to 3 minutes. Add the peanut butter and lemon juice, taste and correct seasoning and serve, piping hot, garnished with the watercress and peanuts.

For added richness, two tablespoons of soured cream may be added just before the final reheating but do not then allow to boil.

VEGETABLE CHOWDER

Pressure Cooking Time: 5 minutes

1 teaspoon granulated sugar; 2 tablespoons vegetable oil; 2 diced onions; 2 diced carrots; ½ shredded white cabbage; 4 sticks of celery diced; 1 small diced turnip; ½ pint vegetable stock; ½ pint tomato juice; salt and pepper; 1 sour green apple, peeled and grated; extra stock if necessary.

Lift the trivet from the cooker, put in the sugar and, over a low heat, allow it to turn dark brown but without burning. Put in the oil and all the vegetables and cook, stirring gently until all are lightly browned. Add the stock, tomato juice and seasoning, bring to pressure in the usual way, cook for 5 minutes and reduce the pressure with cold water. Stir the soup, add a little more stock if necessary, taste and correct seasoning, stir in the grated apple, reheat and serve.

VARIATIONS

Rice would be excellent with this chowder; 1 cupful can be added after the liquid, which should be increased by $\frac{1}{2}$ pint and be allowed to boil before the rice is thrown in.

Dumplings would turn this soup almost into a meal on its own; make these in the usual way but add a little very finely diced onion and a $\frac{1}{4}$ teaspoon of thyme or marjoram to the suet mixture. After pressure has been reduced, bring the soup to the boil, drop in the dumplings and boil for 10 minutes with a plate on top to serve as a cover.

If this is to be a summer chowder, coarsely shredded French or runner beans, fresh peas and small, whole new potatoes could be added to the vegetables, but do not use leafy green vegetables as they would overcook.

BUTTER BEAN RING

Pressure Cooking Time: 30 minutes

$\frac{1}{4}$ lb butter beans; 2 large onions; 8 large cooked potatoes with an egg, a little peanut butter, milk, seasoning and a pinch of nutmeg; $\frac{1}{2}$ pint of white sauce (p. 291); sprigs of parsley.

Trim the onions, scrub well but leave skins on. Prepare and cook the butter beans, with the onions as given on p. 64. During this cooking, beat the peanut butter with the milk, add the cut up potatoes and mash until smooth and creamy. Add the seasoning, nutmeg and the egg and beat again. Grease a heatproof plate and pipe the mashed potatoes in a border round it. Brown lightly under the grill and keep hot. Make the white sauce. Lift out the onions, skin them, chop well and stir into the sauce. Strain the beans, put into the centre of the potato ring and pour the sauce over. Garnish with sprigs of parsley.

As a change of flavouring, the white sauce could be varied, a tomato or curry one being used instead.

CAULIFLOWER AMANDE

Pressure Cooking Time: 4 minutes

1 large cauliflower; 1 egg; $\frac{1}{2}$ pint white sauce (p. 291); fried breadcrumbs; chopped parsley; 2 oz shredded almonds; 1 tablespoon butter; $\frac{1}{2}$ pint water for the cooker.

Wash and trim the cauliflower, divide in half and cut away small triangles from the thick stems. Put the water and the trivet in the cooker, the halved cauliflower and the egg for hard boiling. Bring to pressure in the usual way, cook for 4 minutes and reduce the pressure with cold water. During this cooking, make the white sauce; fry the breadcrumbs and stir in the chopped parsley. Lift the halves of cauliflower on to the serving dish, fitting them together to look whole again, or serve portions on to individual dishes and keep hot. Chop the egg, add to the sauce, reheat and check seasoning, pour over the cauliflower, sprinkle thickly with the breadcrumbs and keep hot again. Melt the butter in a small pan and while it is still foaming stir in the almonds, then quickly spread them over the cauliflower and serve at once, piping hot. A salad of sliced tomatoes, sprinkled liberally with very finely chopped raw onions and sprinkled with chopped chives would go well with this dish and give an attractive colour.

CAPSICUM CURRY

Pressure Cooking Time: 5 minutes and 10 minutes

1 cup of rice, 2 cups of water, salt, ½ pint water with lemon juice or vinegar for the cooker; 1 tablespoon vegetable oil; 3–4 teaspoons curry powder; 1 finely chopped clove of garlic; 2 sliced onions; 1 chopped apple; 2 green peppers; 2 tablespoons sultanas; 2 tomatoes; 1 diced carrot; seasoning; ¼ pint water with vegetable extract to taste; 1 tablespoon of redcurrant jelly, chutney handed round separately.

Lift the trivet from the cooker, put in the water and the bowl of rice, water and salt, covered with a piece of greaseproof paper. Bring to pressure in the usual way, cook for 5 minutes and allow the pressure to reduce at room temperature. During this time, prepare the vegetables, wash the peppers, cut in half, remove the seeds and membranes and cut into ¾-inch strips. Turn the rice into a colander. Tip the water from the cooker, heat the oil, fry the onion and garlic until golden brown, add the apple and curry powder, cook for another minute, stirring all the time; away from the heat, add the hot liquid (if cold, allow the cooker to cool), reboil, put in the rest of the ingredients. Bring to pressure in the usual way, cook for 10 minutes, reduce the pressure with cold water. During this cooking, finish the rice as given on p. 151, form into a circle and keep hot in the oven. Taste and correct the seasoning for the curry, add the redcurrant jelly, reheat, pour in the centre of the rice ring and serve, piping hot, with the chutney handed separately.

CHESTNUT STEW

Pressure Cooking Time: 3 minutes and 8 minutes

6 oz medium noodles; $\frac{1}{4}$ lb chestnuts; 3 cups of water; 1 tablespoon of salt; 1 onion; 2 oz field mushrooms; 2 tomatoes; 2 tablespoons vegetable oil; 1 tablespoon flour; $\frac{1}{2}$ pint vegetable stock; 2 teaspoons redcurrant jelly or lemon juice; piquant sauce to taste; seasoning; a little more vegetable oil; chopped parsley for garnish.

Lift the trivet from the cooker, put in the water and salt and bring to the boil. Scrub the chestnuts very well, slit each with a pointed knife on both sides and put with the noodles into the cooker. Bring to pressure in the usual way, cook for 3 minutes and reduce the pressure with cold water. Strain into a colander, lift out the chestnuts, skin them and cut into slices. Heat the oil in the cooker, fry the sliced onion until brown, add the chopped tomatoes and sliced mushrooms and cook for a further minute or two. Add the flour, stir well with the vegetables, add the hot stock (if cold, allow cooker to cool), return to the heat and reboil while stirring. Add the seasoning and chestnuts, bring to pressure in the usual way, cook for 8 minutes and allow the pressure to reduce at room temperature. During this cooking, heat a little oil in another pan, fork the noodles in it until glistening, make into a deep bed on the serving dish and keep hot. Add the jelly or lemon juice and a dash of sauce to the stew, taste and correct seasoning, reheat and pour over the noodles. Garnish thickly with chopped parsley.

EGG AND MUSHROOM PIE

Pressure Cooking Time: 5 minutes

4 eggs; 1 cup of rice, 2 cups of water, salt; 4 oz button mushrooms with 2 tablespoons of butter; 1 pint of rich, cheese sauce (p. 292); a little grated cheese; a few golden crumbs; $\frac{1}{2}$ pint water for the cooker.

Lift the trivet from the cooker, put in the water, the eggs, and the rice and water in a covered bowl. Bring to pressure in the usual way, cook for 5 minutes and allow the pressure to reduce at room temperature. During this cooking, slice the mushrooms very finely and cook gently in the butter but without browning. Lift out, but leave the butter in the pan. Have some boiling water ready; light the grill; make the sauce. Drop the eggs into cold water. Put the rice in a colander, pour the boiling water over, shake well, turn into the frying pan and stir, over a low heat, until well coated with the butter. Shell the eggs and slice them. Into a greased ovenproof dish put alternate layers of rice, mushrooms and eggs, finishing with a layer of egg. Pour over the sauce, sprinkle with cheese and crumbs and leave under the grill until golden brown. This dish would be delicious served with a salad of hearts of lettuce and sprigs of watercress, with spoonfuls of redcurrant or cranberry jelly or mango chutney.

LENTIL ROLLETTES

Pressure Cooking Time: 20 minutes

6 oz lentils; 1 medium onion, 1 pint water for precooking, 1 yolk of large egg, seasoning, 1 level tablespoon nut butter for cutlets; beaten egg or a little milk, golden crumbs, fat for frying; fried parsley for garnish (p. 298); quick piquant sauce handed separately (p. 296).

Prepare, presoak and cook the lentils with the sliced onion as instructed on p. 64. When the lentils are strained, put back into the cooker and toss over a low heat until quite dry. Sieve, mix with the seasoning, nut butter, egg (if preferred, three tablespoons of dry mashed potato could be used instead) and seasoning, and form into small rolls. Allow to cool. Pass twice through the egg and golden crumbs, fry in hot fat until golden brown. Drain on kitchen paper, serve with the fried parsley.

VEGETABLE GALANTINE

Pressure Cooking Time: 20 minutes and 20 minutes

½ lb small haricot beans; 1 egg for hard-boiling; 2 diced onions, a little vegetable oil; 1 large tin of tomatoes; 4 oz stale bread soaked in a little milk; 1 egg; seasoning; ¾ pint boiling water with a little lemon juice or vinegar for the cooker; ½ pint tomato sauce with a little extra tomato purée; golden crumbs.

Prepare and cook the beans as given on p. 64. During this cooking, hard-boil the egg and fry the onions lightly in a little heated oil. Sieve the beans with the strained tomatoes (keeping the juice on one side) and beat well until really creamy. Squeeze the excess milk from the bread into the tomato juice; add the bread, onions, diced hard-boiled egg, seasoning and herbs to the bean and tomato purée and stir carefully with the yolk of egg. Beat the egg white until stiff and fold into the mixture. Grease a seamless loaf tin or mould, fill with the mixture and cover securely with a double sheet of greased, greaseproof paper. When the water in the cooker is boiling, put in the trivet and the galantine, bring to pressure, cook for 20 minutes and allow the pressure to reduce at room temperature for 10 minutes. During this cooking, use the tomato juice to make a tomato sauce, adding a little concentrated tomato purée to strengthen the flavour. Preheat the oven to Gas No 4, 375° F, and have ready the middle shelf. Carefully turn out the galantine on to the serving dish, coat with the golden crumbs and put into the oven while the accompanying green vegetables are pressure cooked. Pour the tomato sauce over the galantine or hand separately.

BARLEY BROTH

Pressure Cooking Time: 35 minutes and 20 minutes

The stock for this broth should be cooked in the evening for use next day.

1 lb neck of lamb; 1½ pints water; 1 onion, carrot, turnip; slice of celery; 2 tablespoons of barley; seasoning; chopped parsley for garnish.

Wipe the meat and cut into small joints. Lift the trivet from the cooker, put in the water and the joints, bring to pressure in the usual way, cook for 35 minutes and allow the pressure to reduce at room temperature. Lift out the joints, cut off the meat and keep covered in a cool place until required. Put the stock into a bowl and leave overnight. Next day remove the fat, put 1 pint stock into the cooker and bring to the boil. Throw in the barley and the finely diced meat and vegetables, add seasonings, bring to pressure in the usual way, cook for 20 minutes and allow the pressure to reduce at room temperature. Serve sprinkled with chopped parsley. This will give two appetising and nutritious helpings of broth which will be a meal in themselves.

BARLEY CREAM

As a variation with even greater food value, the rest of the stock can also be pressure cooked with barley and vegetables and, when pressure has been reduced and the seasoning corrected, a beaten egg can be added and the soup carefully reheated but without allowing to boil, otherwise it will curdle.

BARLEY WATER

Pressure Cooking Time: 45 minutes

3 oz pearl barley; 2 pints of water; 1 large lemon; sugar to taste.

Lift the trivet from the cooker, put in the water, bring to the boil, throw in the barley, bring to pressure in the usual way, cook for 45 minutes and allow the pressure to reduce at room temperature. Strain off the barley water, return to the cooker and boil rapidly for 5 minutes in the open pan. Add the strained lemon juice and sugar to taste. Allow to cool completely before drinking; keep in a covered container in a cool place.

BEEF TEA

Pressure Cooking Time: 30 minutes

$\frac{1}{4}$ lb of very lean beef; pinch of salt; $\frac{3}{4}$ pint water with a little lemon juice or vinegar for the cooker.

Wipe the meat, shred or scrape as finely as possible and put with the salt into a Kilner jar, or heatproof basin or boilable plastic bowl. Cover with a saucer, bring to pressure in the usual way, cook for 30 minutes and allow the pressure to reduce at room temperature. Lift out the container, press the meat against the sides with a wooden spoon, pressing as hard as possible to extract all the liquid. Put into a strainer and again press hard, but do not scrape the strainer as the beef tea should remain a clear liquid. Remove all traces of fat while hot with small pieces of jagged kitchen paper dragged across the top or allow to cool and lift off. Taste and correct seasoning, and reheat before serving with small fingers of dry toast.

SCALLOPED CHICKEN

Pressure Cooking Time: 8 minutes

You are sure to have some left-overs from a boiled chicken and this is a delicious way to disguise it and to vary the diet.

A spoonful of chopped celery; a small slice of soaked bread, well squeezed, or a spoonful of fresh breadcrumbs; a spoonful of parsley; a portion of sliced, cooked chicken; 1 egg; $\frac{1}{4}$ pint of chicken stock; seasoning; a few golden crumbs and dabs of butter; $\frac{1}{2}$ pint water with a little lemon juice or vinegar for the cooker; accompanying vegetables to choice.

Mix together the celery, bread and parsley; grease an individual deep dish, small bowl or cup, put in the chicken and mixture in layers. Beat the egg, add the hot chicken stock and seasoning and pour into the dish. Put the water and the trivet in the cooker, then the dish covered with greaseproof paper and the accompanying vegetables. (If you had a little steamed or rice pudding left over, this also could be reheated in a covered cup.) Bring to pressure in the usual way, cook for 8 minutes and allow the pressure to reduce at room temperature. Lift out the dish of chicken, put the cover back on the cooker to keep the vegetables hot. If the chicken is not in an individual dish, turn it out; sprinkle with golden crumbs, dot with butter and brown quickly for no more than a moment under a hot grill. Serve with vegetables which should be tossed in melted butter.

SOLE VERONIQUE

Pressure Cooking Time: 4 minutes

1 medium sole, filleted; 8 white grapes; $\frac{1}{4}$ pint milk; 2 oz button mushrooms; seasoning; a little lemon juice; 1 small tablespoon butter, 1 level tablespoon of flour for thickening; 1 spoonful of cream if liked; sprigs of parsley to garnish and a little coralline pepper if available, to add colour; $\frac{1}{2}$ pint water for the cooker.

Skin the fillets, sprinkle with salt, pepper, lemon juice on the skinned side, put a little knob of butter on each and roll up. Put the fish with the skinned and pipped grapes and mushrooms into an ovenproof dish that will fit in the cooker and add the milk. Put the water and the trivet in the cooker, then the dish covered with a piece of greaseproof paper, bring to pressure in the usual way, cook for 4 minutes and reduce the pressure with cold water. During this cooking, melt the butter in a small saucepan, add the flour and allow to cook for a minute or two without colouring. Lift out the dish, strain off the milk and add to the saucepan, stirring until the sauce thickens. Taste and correct seasoning and add cream. Reheat but do not allow to boil again.

Two fillets will probably be enough for one invalid meal so lift these on to a small serving dish, garnish with the grapes and mushrooms and pour over a little of the sauce, garnishing with sprigs of parsley and a line of coralline pepper.

The other two fillets, when cold, can be flaked, stirred into the remainder of the sauce and then for another meal, be piled into a scallop shell or individual heatproof dish, be sprinkled with grated cheese and dabs of butter and then grilled until golden brown. One or two slices of skinned tomatoes could garnish the top to add colour.

Complete Meal. To cook Sole Veronique as part of a complete meal, the dish when ready can be put directly into the water in the bottom of the cooker with the trivet on top and on this could go potatoes, a perforated separater with some green vegetable such as peas, beans, broccoli, asparagus, fresh or frozen, and then a cup of fruit and one or two cups of custard (for preparation, see **Infant Feeding**).

If extra potatoes were cooked, these could be mashed and piped around the **Fish Scallop,** prepared as already described, for another meal.

LAMB CUTLET WITH TOMATO

Pressure Cooking Time: 6 minutes

Season the cutlet well with salt and pepper, put in a deep saucer with a little butter and a slice of tomato on top. Cover with greaseproof paper and continue as for **Sole Veronique**, giving 6 minutes pressure cooking time. Take off the bone, mince the meat and tomato, moisten with a little of the stock and serve with accompanying vegetables, cooked at the same time, or piled on a buttered round of toast. A little meat extract may be added for extra flavour to the stock before mixing with the minced meat if it is to be served with vegetables or may be spread lightly on the toast after buttering.

TIMBALES OF FISH

Pressure Cooking Time: 5 minutes

This is another way to serve the sole fillets from the preceding recipe or a little cooked plaice, turbot or halibut from a family meal could be used instead.

A little cooked fish; 1 large egg; $\frac{1}{4}$ pint milk; seasoning; a little anchovy essence if liked; $\frac{1}{2}$ pint water with a little lemon juice or vinegar for the cooker; accompanying vegetables to choice; a tablespoon of mayonnaise or tartare sauce (p. 294).

Grease two cups well with butter. Beat the egg with the seasoning, heat the milk, add the anchovy essence if used and pour over the beaten eggs. Flake the fish and divide into the cups; pour the custard over and stir gently. Put the water and trivet in the cooker, then the cups of fish covered with greaseproof paper, and the accompanying vegetables. Bring to pressure in the usual way, cook for 5 minutes and reduce the pressure with cold water. Turn the timbale into the centre of an individual dish, surround with the vegetables; quickly heat the sauce without boiling, pour over the timbale and serve at once.

SECTION X

Infant and Child Feeding

It does not seem quite so necessary nowadays to prepare as much in the way of special foods for Baby or the very young child as it used to be as there are so many ready-made foods in such variety, easily obtainable and with the assurance of adequate food value but they do tend to be rather expensive, especially as quite a selection has to be bought each time to change the diet—but with your pressure cooker you can do all that is necessary with the minimum effort in work and time and with considerable economy and, as the small children eat their cooked meal at noon, it will still be available for the family's evening meal. Particularly if your youngest come back from school and having to fetch them means the time is short for cooking and eating the midday meal, your pressure cooker is going to be working overtime.

From the very first day make the most of it; if you want or need to sterilise the baby's bottles, teats and feeds you will find the instructions in the following section; when they grow a little older and need their food sieved or puréed you can cook a selection of different vegetables each day, a little chicken, liver or fish, prunes or other fruits so that they become accustomed to a wide range of flavours making it easier for them to join in the family meals later on and when they do reach this stage the pressure-cooked food will be so tender and full of flavour that they will easily become accustomed to it and you will know that it is full of nutrients to keep the child healthy with well-balanced meals.

Food for small children should be plain, with much less salt than for adults and it is generally helpful, for purées, pulps and dicing to cook the food just a minute or so longer than the times given in the rest of the book. Because pressure cooking is so quick and therefore less harmful to the nutrients in the food, there is no reason why suitable foods such as meat, fish, fruit, puddings set aside from the family's previous evening meal should not be kept, well covered, at the bottom of the refrigerator or in a cool place and be brought up to pressure only to reheat them through for the baby's meal next day. This does not apply to vegetables which are such a necessary source of vitamins and other food essentials in a baby's diet which should be cooked fresh each time and which it is only a matter of minutes to do in the pressure cooker.

The great standby for the mother, for this sort of feeding, is just ordinary teacups, or individual boilable bowls if food is to be kept over and the cups may be needed. Several composite meals for Baby using these are set out but these are only a very few of the many choices and combinations which you will soon discover for yourself as Baby gets older and can try out fresh flavours and foods as the days go by.

Nowadays, most mothers do not find it necessary to sterilise feeding bottles and baby foods, as there are so many suitable and safe disinfectants available and recommended but should this need to be done the following instructions have been tested and approved as giving complete safety. The feeding bottles and teats can be sterilised on their own or already filled with the correct amount for each feed, which can be made up from any type of milk or milk powder which will then be completely sterilised in a matter of minutes, with no more loss of vitamins or nutritional content than the longer process by ordinary heating. This sterilisation must be done in a cooker fitted with 10 lb pressure to give an internal temperature of 240° F, 115° C, and all the feeds for 24 hours can be done at the one time so that the cooker can be used for this just once each day when not required for the family meal. Just follow this simple procedure:

Wash the bottles and teats thoroughly. If sterilising the feeds as well, make these up according to the instructions and fill into the bottles. Put the teats into a cup or small bowl and cover lightly with a double piece of greaseproof paper.

Have ready in the pressure cooker $\frac{1}{2}$ pint water with a little lemon juice or vinegar and the trivet. Put in the bottles and cover across the top with a double thickness of greaseproof paper. Put the covered cup or bowl in the centre.

Bring to 10 lb pressure in the usual way, maintain this carefully for 5 minutes and allow the pressure to reduce at room temperature, being very careful, when moving the cooker from the heat, not to knock or jog it in any way.

Lift out the bottles, covering again quickly with the paper and a piece of muslin or a clean tea-towel to prevent any germs or dust entering.

It is best to have a small round tray or dish on which to lift out the bottles so that they can all be covered over at once and it is then possible to lift them into the refrigerator when cool or to stand on one side in a cool place, without uncovering them again.

Of course, if the bottles are provided with their own caps, these should be used and not be removed until required to be filled or to have the teat fitted. Leave the bowl of teats covered when lifted from the cooker.

It is not recommended to sterilise bottles with feeds with the teats in position as if the liquid boils up this may block them.

When a feed is due take out one of the bottles and fit the teat, taking care to replace the coverings at once. Stand the bottle in a jug of hot water until the required temperature is reached and shake the bottle well before using.

MEAT AND VEGETABLE BROTH

Pressure Cooking Time: 10 minutes

1 pint water; 4 oz finely minced beef; a little salt; a selection of vegetables such as carrot, potato, turnip, peas, beans, etc, using about 1 tablespoon of each, cut up very finely.

Lift the trivet from the cooker, put in the water, meat and salt, bring to pressure in the usual way, cook for 7 minutes, reduce the pressure with cold water. Strain off the meat, put back the stock and vegetables, bring to pressure again and cook for the last 3 minutes. Pass the vegetables through a sieve, return to the stock, stir well and warm just before feeding.

The mince can be used for an older child, stirred into gravy and served with fresh-cooked vegetables or could be added to stuffing for a marrow or with the addition of a little tomato sauce would be an excellent extra supper dish for one, on toast or with fried croûtons.

PURÉED VEGETABLES

Pressure cook as above but with a $\frac{1}{4}$ pint water or thin gravy, and use a little of the liquid to moisten the vegetables after they have been sieved.

COMPLETE MEAL—1

FISH WITH TOMATOES AND VEGETABLES; STEWED APPLE AND EGG CUSTARD

Pressure Cooking Time: 3 minutes

A small fillet of sole or plaice; a slice of tomato; a teaspoon of milk and a dab of butter; thin slices of potato, carrot, cabbage, beans, peas as available; a peeled, cored, sliced apple and sugar; 1 egg, $\frac{3}{4}$ cup of milk, a little sugar; $\frac{1}{4}$ pint water for the cooker.

Butter a saucer, put in the folded fillet with the slice of tomato, milk and butter and a pinch of salt. In another cup put the apple, without water but with a little sugar; in another buttered cup, beat the egg with a little sugar and add the heated milk. Put into the cooker a $\frac{1}{4}$ pint of water and the trivet. On it, put the saucer with the fish, the cups of apple and custard covered with a piece of greaseproof paper and the vegetables with a pinch of salt. Bring to pressure in the usual way, cook for 3 minutes and allow the pressure to reduce at room temperature. Lift out the fish and mash with a fork into the juice, accompanied by the vegetables mashed or put through a sieve. Serve half the custard and the apple, mashed or sieved, keeping the rest for the next day.

COMPLETE MEAL—2

DICED CHICKEN WITH VEGETABLES; RICE CUSTARD

Pressure Cooking Time: 4 minutes

Prepare this when you have a tablespoon of cooked rice left over from another dish.

A small piece of chicken breast brushed with butter; selection of vegetables, including pieces of potato, carrot, sprouts; 1 tablespoon of cooked rice, $\frac{3}{4}$ cup of milk, 1 egg and a little sugar; $\frac{1}{4}$ pint water for cooker.

Put the chicken brushed with butter on a saucer and add a spoonful of milk or white sauce if any is available. Prepare the vegetables. Heat the milk and pour slowly on to the beaten egg and sugar. Stir in the rice and if the child is old enough, a few seedless raisins can be added. Divide this into two buttered cups. Put the water and the trivet in the cooker, then the saucer of chicken, the vegetables and the two cups covered with a piece of greaseproof paper. Bring to pressure in the usual way, cook for 4 minutes and allow the pressure to reduce at room temperature. Cut the chicken finely, mix with the vegetables mashed or sieved and moisten with the liquid from the saucer. Serve one cup of rice custard, saving the other for another day.

COMPLETE MEAL—3

LIVER IN GRAVY WITH VEGETABLES; CHOCOLATE CREAM

Pressure Cooking Time: 3 minutes

A small piece of calf's liver, a little gravy and 2 slices of tomato; a selection of vegetables including thin slices of potato, carrot, a floweret of cauliflower or other green vegetable available; 1 egg, $\frac{3}{4}$ cupful of milk, 4–6 squares of plain or milk chocolate, a little sugar; $\frac{1}{2}$ pint water for the cooker.

Chop the liver finely and put in a cup with the gravy and tomatoes. Prepare the vegetables. Put the broken up chocolate into a small saucepan, add a drop of milk, stir over a low heat until melted, add the rest of the milk and heat, pour over the beaten egg and sugar and put into two buttered cups. Put the water and the trivet in the cooker, then the cups of liver and chocolate cream covered with a piece of greaseproof paper, and the vegetables with a pinch of salt. Bring to pressure in the usual way, cook for 3 minutes and allow the pressure to reduce at room temperature. Mash the vegetables in with the liver. Use one of the custards and put the other away for another day.

COMPLETE MEAL—4

EGG AND SPINACH WITH MASHED POTATO; STEWED APRICOTS

Pressure Cooking Time: 3 minutes

1 egg, 1 tablespoon of creamed spinach or other puréed green vegetable; a little cheese if the infant likes it; 5 or 6 dried apricots with sugar for sweetening; $\frac{1}{2}$ pint water for the cooker.

Soak the apricots in $\frac{1}{4}$ pint of boiling water for at least half an hour before required. Butter a cup, put in the spinach, break the egg in on top, put a pinch of salt and grated cheese, if liked. Cut the apricots up into very small pieces, put into two cups with sufficient of the soaking water to cover and add sugar to sweeten. Prepare the potatoes, slice very finely and put on a saucer with a knob of butter and a spoonful of milk. Put the water and trivet in the cooker, then the cups and saucer covered with a piece of greaseproof paper. Bring to pressure in the usual way, cook for 3 minutes and reduce the pressure with cold water. Mash the potatoes with the liquid. Turn out the egg and mash into the potatoes.

Feed the apricots as they are, mashed or puréed with a little top of the milk or thinned cream.

SECTION XI

Occasion Meals

SUGGESTIONS FOR COMPLETE AND SPECIAL MEALS

In this section are examples of how the pressure cooker can be used to prepare a complete meal.

With the present-day handy pressure cookers it is not usually practical, unless cooking very small quantities as for infants or an invalid, to prepare the whole meal at the same time but with a little forward planning sensibly combining the pressure cooker with the minimum use of the oven and choosing dishes which will follow each other easily to give an attractive, varied and nutritious menu an amazing amount of time and trouble can be saved.

The menus set out here are a little more special than every-day ones, but could be served at the week-end when everyone is at home with time to enjoy a family meal or when you are giving a small dinner party.

A SUMMER MEAL

Fish Scallops

Kidneys in Wine Sauce, New Potatoes and French Beans

Riz à l'Imperatrice

FISH SCALLOPS

Pressure Cooking Time: 4 minutes

1 large steak of turbot or halibut; 2 eggs; 2 tablespoons each diced French beans, new carrots, peas; 1 tablespoon each chopped gherkins and capers; 1 level tablespoon butter, 1 level tablespoon flour, 1 teaspoon dry mustard, seasoning, $\frac{1}{4}$ pint milk or fish stock, 2 tablespoons oil, vinegar, for mayonnaise sauce; $\frac{1}{2}$ pint water for cooker; 1 heart of lettuce, sprigs of parsley.

Put water and trivet in the cooker. Put the seasoned fish to one side covered with a small piece of greaseproof paper, the vegetables in a perforated container and the eggs broken into a buttered cup and also covered with a piece of greaseproof. Bring to pressure in the usual way, cook for 4 minutes and reduce pressure with cold water. During this cooking, melt the margarine in a small saucepan, add the flour and dry mustard and cook without colouring, add two tablespoons milk and leave on one side. Lift out the fish and flake it finely; lift out the vegetables and eggs. Add two tablespoons of stock to sauce and cook until smooth and, when cool, beat in the oil and sufficient vinegar to give tartness and a coating consistency. Take one spoonful and mix with fish, adding in the capers and gherkins. When preparing for serving, chop the eggs, slice the washed and dried lettuce finely. Put a bed of lettuce into four scallop shells or individual dishes, pile the fish in the centre of each and arrange a border of the mixed vegetables around the edge. Stir the mayonnaise well and check the consistency—if a little too stiff add oil, vinegar or a little cream as liked—and coat right over the shells. Sprinkle with the chopped eggs and garnish with parsley sprigs.

KIDNEYS IN WINE SAUCE

Pressure Cooking Time: 5 minutes and 4 minutes

$1\frac{1}{4}$ lb lamb's kidneys; $\frac{1}{4}$ lb streaky bacon; 1 tablespoon butter; $\frac{1}{4}$ lb button mushrooms; $\frac{1}{3}$ pint vin rosé; 1 tablespoon butter, 1 tablespoon flour, sour or fresh cream for sauce; seasoning; chopped parsley for garnish; small new potatoes, French beans for four to serve separately.

Prepare the bacon rolls (p. 299) and put on two small skewers. Skin kidneys, remove tubes and fat, cut in quarters and toss in salt and pepper, peel and slice the mushrooms finely. Lift out the trivet, heat the butter, gently fry the bacon rolls until brown and crisp, lift out and take off skewers. Brown the kidneys quickly but lightly, put in the bacon rolls, mushrooms and wine, bring to pressure in the usual way, cook for 5 minutes and reduce the pressure with cold water. During the cooking, warm the oven for the plates and serving dishes. Heat the butter in a small saucepan, add the flour and cook without browning for 2 to 3 minutes. Lift out the kidneys, mushrooms and rolls with a straining spoon and put in a covered dish. Add the liquid to the saucepan gradually, stirring all the time, reheat, taste and correct seasoning and without allowing to boil again add a little cream to give a coating consistency. Pour over the meat, cover and keep hot in the oven. The vegetables can now be cooked in the clean cooker. As this is a special meal, be extravagant when preparing the new potatoes trimming them all to the same size and shape about the size of a small plum. Slice the beans finely. Pressure cook these for 4 minutes in the usual way, reducing the pressure with cold water. Put a little butter in the container with the beans and toss or stir until it is melted, then serve. Lift out the potatoes and the trivet, strain out the stock, melt a little butter in the hot pan, put in some chopped parsley, toss the potatoes in it and serve. Just before taking to table, sprinkle chopped parsley on the kidneys.

RIZ À L'IMPERATRICE

Pressure Cooking Time: 10 minutes

¾ pint milk; a knob of butter; 2 oz pudding rice; vanilla pod or essence to taste; 2 tablespoons sugar; 2 yolks of eggs; ¼ pint double cream; ½ pint made up red jelly; Compôte of cherries, p. 185.

Make the Compôte of cherries. Take a spoonful of the liquid to add to the water and make up the ½ pint jelly. Use this to set a ½-inch layer in the bottom of a decorative jelly mould and leave to set. Make the rice pudding according to the instructions but giving the shorter cooking time. When the pressure is reduced, stir the pudding well, add the beaten yolks and cook gently for 3 to 4 minutes but do not allow to boil. Lift the pan from the heat, stir in the cream, check to see if any more sugar is required and put to cool. When the mixture is thickening and becomes really creamy, stir once more, fill gently into the mould and put to set. To unmould, dip the bottom ½ inch only in hot water to loosen the jelly and turn gently on to a large decorative dish. At the last moment, arrange the Compôte of cherries all around.

Suggested Preparation Schedule

Overnight or early in the day, prepare the fish scallops up to the point where the fish mixture and mayonnaise are ready to be filled into the scallops. Wash the lettuce and keep in a plastic bag. Chop the parsley for the fish and kidney dishes and prepare the vegetables and bacon rolls. Make the Compôte of cherries and finish the rice mould entirely, ready for serving.

In the early evening, prepare the kidneys and vegetables. About $\frac{1}{2}$ hour before serving the meal, start the kidney dish and while it is cooking finish the **Fish Scallops** and put ready on the table. While the vegetables are cooking, unmould the rice. Keep the kidney dish and vegetables hot while the first course is being eaten; put the Compôte round the rice just before taking to table.

A WINTER MEAL

Potage St Germain

Veal Marengo with Potato Croquettes

Cidered Apples

POTAGE ST GERMAIN

Pressure Cooking Time: 5 minutes

$\frac{3}{4}$ lb of frozen peas; 1 small onion; 1 tablespoon butter; sprig of fresh mint and parsley if available if not a pinch of mixed, dried herbs; 4 white peppercorns; seasoning; 1$\frac{1}{2}$ pints of white stock (a chicken cube could be used); $\frac{1}{4}$ pint single cream; fried croûtons (p. 298) to hand separately.

Allow the peas to thaw completely and drain well. Lift the trivet from the cooker, heat the butter and cook the peas, onion and herbs for a few minutes but do not allow to colour. Add the stock and the seasoning, bring to pressure in the usual way, cook for 5 minutes and reduce the pressure with cold water. Strain the soup, reserving the stock and put the peas only through a fine sieve. Return to the pan with half the stock, reheat, taste and correct the seasoning, and then continue adding more stock to obtain the correct consistency. Serve in individual bowls, and at the last moment pour a tablespoon of the cream in the centre of each bowl. Hand the croûtons separately.

If preparing this soup some time beforehand, keep any stock over in case a little more may be needed when reheating.

VEAL MARENGO

Pressure Cooking Time: 12 minutes

1 lb veal pieces; 2 tablespoons of olive oil; 3 medium onions; 2 oz fresh or small tin button mushrooms; $\frac{1}{4}$ pint white stock or water; bouquet garni; a piece of orange peel; 1 egg; 2–3 tablespoons tomato purée; lemon juice or white wine; 1 level tablespoon flour blended with a little milk for thickening; seasoning; 2–3 tablespoons of freshly chopped parsley; 1 tablespoon of brandy if liked.

Wipe, trim the meat and toss in plenty of salt and pepper. Skin and slice the onions and fresh mushrooms, or strain the tinned ones. Lift the trivet from the cooker, heat the oil and lightly cook the meat and onions until evenly golden brown. Lift out, drain off the oil, then put in the liquid, the tomato purée, onions, mushrooms, seasonings, the egg completely wrapped in aluminium foil and the meat on top. Bring to pressure in the usual way, cook for 12 minutes, reduce the pressure with cold water. Lift out the bouquet garni and then the egg, dropping it into a bowl of cold water. With a straining spoon lift the meat and vegetables into a deep serving dish and keep hot. Add the blended flour to the liquid, return to the heat, bring to the boil, stirring all the time, and cook for 2–3 minutes. Add the parsley and a little strained lemon juice or white wine to taste, correct the seasoning and pour the sauce over the meat. Shell the egg, slice and arrange down the centre of the dish as garnish.

POTATO CROQUETTES

Cook, strain, steam off and mash the potatoes as given in recipe on p. 52. To this purée add 1 beaten egg, 1 tablespoon melted butter, plenty of salt and pepper, beating all well together. Form into rolls about 3 inches long, dusting your hands lightly with flour to do so. Lightly beat together a white of egg and 1 tablespoon milk, leaving this in a deep plate or saucer. On a piece of greaseproof paper have ready some golden crumbs. Pass the croquettes through the egg and crumbs twice, coating them carefully all over. Leave for about 10 minutes, then fry in shallow fat until evenly golden brown. Serve on a plain doily garnished with sprigs of fried parsley (p. 298).

CIDERED APPLES

Pressure Cooking Time: to pressure only

2 lb of cooking apples; 3–4 tablespoons of brown sugar; $\frac{1}{4}$ pint cider; butter; single cream to hand separately.

Peel the apples, core and cut in quarters. Lift the trivet from the cooker, put in the sugar with a teaspoon of water and heat until the sugar dissolves, then allow to boil for a minute or two until it just begins to darken. Pour in the cider, put in the apples, bring to pressure in the usual way, remove from the heat and allow the pressure to reduce at room temperature. Open the cooker, turn the pieces of apple over in the syrup and put the cover back on. Heat the grill, lift the apples into a heatproof dish, dot with butter and put under a low grill until the butter melts and the apples begin to turn golden. While waiting, boil the syrup rapidly in the open cooker until thick, pour down the side of the dish and leave until quite chilled. Hand the single cream separately.

Suggested Preparation Schedule

Overnight or early in the day, the soup can be completely prepared except for the addition of the cream. The croûtons can be diced and kept in a plastic bag. The potato croquettes can be made and coated with the egg and breadcrumbs completely ready for frying.

The cidered apples can be completely prepared and left ready in the serving dish.

Early in the evening, put the soup into a saucepan ready for reheating. Prepare the meat, onions and fresh mushrooms or strain the tinned ones. Pick the parsley sprigs, wash and leave to dry in a clean tea-towel.

About three-quarters of an hour before serving, start the Veal Marengo. While it is cooking, preheat the oven to Gas No 1, 280° F, and put the serving dishes to warm in the bottom. Fry the potato croquettes, put on a baking tray lined with kitchen paper and keep hot in the oven. Finish off the Veal Marengo, serve in a covered dish and keep hot. Set the soup to reheat, checking for consistency and at the same time fry the croûtons. Keep these hot in the oven while frying the parsley which can then go in with the potato croquettes. Serve the soup, adding the cream and hand the croûtons separately.

Garnish the veal with the sliced egg and serve with the potato croquettes garnished with the parsley. Spoon the syrup over the apples and serve, handing the cream separately.

CHRISTMAS TIME

Christmas-time is obviously going to be a busy one for your pressure cooker, perhaps not so much on Christmas Day itself, though even then it is going to save you a lot of time and saucepan space on the top of the stove; but well beforehand the Christmas Puddings and preparation of stuffings, and afterwards in quick cooking of suppers and snacks with turkey left-overs, you are going to find it quite invaluable.

To get them out of the way and off your mind and to give them a chance to mature so that they are in perfect condition for serving on Christmas Day, the puddings should be made at least 6 to 8 weeks ahead, in fact, any time from September onwards when the new crop of dried fruit is fresh in the shops and you have time to get the ingredients together and your cooker is not in urgent demand would be the time to make them. Christmas Puddings once cooked and particularly pressure cooked which ensures their keeping quality, will last from one year to the next quite happily. With ordinary steaming or boiling at least 6 to 8 hours is necessary to give thorough cooking and the darkness and richness which is essential for this type of pudding but with your pressure cooker this time can be cut down to as little as 2 hours with a great economy of fuel and doing away with a kitchen filled with steam for the best part of a day.

Christmas Puddings should be made in china, earthenware, ovenglass, stainless steel or boilable plastic bowls; if aluminium bowls or foil containers are used they must first be lined with greaseproof paper as otherwise there may be a reaction with the acid content in the fruit which can give a bitter flavour.

The covering should be a triple thickness of greaseproof paper securely tied down for the cooking which, when the pudding is cold should be replaced with a clean double sheet of greaseproof and a piece of cloth again tied down or the covers of the plastic bowls, to prevent loss of moisture by evaporation.

The recipe which follows is a rich one and easy to make but if you have your own family favourite then make that and refer to the timetable for the steaming and pressure cooking times. An explanation of the steaming process is given on p. 157.

To decide the correct cooking time the weight of the actual pudding itself must be known. To do this, weigh the basin, decide what size pudding you are going to cook, then weigh this amount into the basin. A little room should be left in each basin for the pudding to rise.

The number of puddings that can be cooked at one time will depend on the size of your cooker and the height of the basins you are using. If there is room you can stand one basin on top of the other with the trivet in between but make sure that there is enough space between the top of the top basin and the vent so that, if the pudding should rise above the basin this will not become blocked and bring the safety plug into action through excess pressure being built up. If, for the pressure cooking, the amount of water necessary should come above the top of the basin, there is no need to worry as it will not harm the pudding at all providing that in this instance it is covered with a cloth as well as the greaseproof paper. In the old days before basins were thought of, Christmas Puddings were always cooked only in cloths and were plunged into a depth of boiling water—usually the clothes boiler or copper.

The following recipe will make approximately 4 × 1 lb by weight puddings but times for other weights would be as follows:

WEIGHT OF MIXTURE	WATER FOR COOKER	STEAMING TIME	PRESSURE COOKING AT HIGH
6 oz individual	1½ pints	10 minutes	50 minutes
1 lb	2¼ pints	15 minutes	1¾ hours
1½ lb	3 pints	20 minutes	2½ hours
2 lb	3½ pints	30 minutes	3 hours

A little lemon juice or vinegar should be added to the cooker unless the water will come over the top of the pudding.

The trivet should be used under the pudding or between two puddings, if one is stood on top of the other.

CHRISTMAS PUDDING

¼ lb flour; ½ teaspoon salt; ½ lb fine white breadcrumbs; ½ lb shredded suet; ½ lb raisins; ½ lb sultanas; ¾ lb currants; ¼ lb mixed peel; 2 oz almonds; ¾ lb brown sugar; grated rind and juice of 1 lemon; 1 teaspoon mixed spice; 1 teaspoon grated nutmeg; ½ teaspoon cinnamon; 2 tablespoons treacle; 2 tablespoons brandy; 1 tablespoon rum if liked; about ½ pint of stout or old ale or milk to mix; 2–3 eggs as liked.

Grease the basins well and prepare the coverings. Take 2 to 3 spoonfuls of the weighed flour and toss the dried fruit in it; leave the almonds to stand in boiling water for 2 to 3 minutes, remove the skins and shred finely; chop the peel; grate the lemon and strain the juice; warm the treacle and add the lemon juice; beat the eggs. Into a large bowl sieve the flour, salt and spices, stir in the suet, sugar and fruit, beat in the eggs, treacle, brandy and lastly, sufficient ale, stout or milk to give a firm, holding consistency. This pudding requires a great deal of stirring so that all the ingredients are thoroughly mixed, so you can allow all the family to take their turn and keep up a very old tradition of ensuring good luck for the year ahead for each member.

Weigh the mixture into the prepared basins, cover and tie securely and continue as given in the instructions, putting the puddings into boiling water in the pressure cooker. If liked, the mixture can be prepared and left covered overnight; next day give a final stir before continuing as above.

After the pressure has been allowed to reduce at room temperature, leave the puddings to cool. If more spirit is to be added, uncover, prick the pudding well with a skewer and pour over it two tablespoons of brandy, whisky or rum, recover and store in a cool place until required. This process can be repeated at least once more, if liked, before reheating on Christmas Day.

To reheat, have the trivet and 1 pint of boiling water with a little lemon or vinegar ready and pressure cook for 10 minutes for the individual puddings or 30 minutes for the larger puddings at **H**igh, the pressure being allowed to reduce at room temperature.

You may have had difficulty in previous years in getting the brandy to light around the pudding so that you can take it to table 'flaming'; the simple way to do this, after having turned the pudding on to a hot serving dish, is just to warm the brandy in a small saucepan, pour it over the pudding and then put a match to it. A sprig of holly on top will then complete the picture.

If you have not made your own Christmas Puddings, still use your pressure cooker for reheating the bought one. If it is in a container with an airtight cover, have 1 pint of boiling water in the cooker and reheat for 40 minutes at **H**igh pressure; if the cover is taken off and the pudding covered with a double thickness of greased greaseproof paper, only 30 minutes would be required.

BEFORE CHRISTMAS

THE CHRISTMAS HAM

This can be pressure cooked according to the instructions given on p. 116 at least two days before Christmas and kept in a cool place or a refrigerator in foil or a plastic bag.

CHESTNUTS AND GIBLETS FOR STUFFING

These should be prepared on Christmas Eve.

GIBLET STOCK

Clean the neck, crop, liver, heart thoroughly and leave to soak in salted water for an hour. Lift the trivet from the cooker, put in 1 pint water, a sliced carrot and onion, a few peppercorns and a little salt and the rinsed giblets, bring to pressure in the usual way, cook for 30 minutes and reduce the pressure with cold water. Keep the liver to add to the stuffing and put the stock on one side for making the gravy next day.

CHESTNUTS

Put ½ pint water in the cooker, the trivet and ½ lb chestnuts, each slit with a pointed knife on both sides, bring to pressure in the usual way, cook for 3 minutes and allow the pressure to reduce at room temperature. Peel the chestnuts while still warm and take off the inner skins.

CHESTNUT STUFFING

½ lb chestnuts; 2 tablespoons fine breadcrumbs; 2 tablespoons margarine; grated rind of a lemon; salt, pepper, a pinch of mixed herbs, 1 egg.

Mash or sieve the chestnuts, stir with the other ingredients and bind with the egg to a crumbly consistency, using a little giblet stock if necessary to obtain the correct consistency. If the bird is not being stuffed overnight, store the stuffing in a plastic bag in a cool place.

CRANBERRY SAUCE

¼ lb cranberries; ¼ pint water; 6 oz sugar.

Lift the trivet from the cooker, put in the water and sugar, stir until dissolved, allow to boil, put in the washed fruit, bring to pressure in the usual way, lift off the cooker immediately and allow the pressure to reduce at room temperature. This sauce may be served cold with the turkey or hot when 1 dessertspoon of blended cornflour should be added and the sauce cooked, stirring very gently for 2 to 3 minutes.

AFTER CHRISTMAS

TURKEY SOUP

The stock should be prepared overnight.

Pressure Cooking Time: 45 minutes

The carcass of a turkey; 3 or 4 stalks of celery, 2 sliced carrots, 2 sliced onions, bouquet garni, a few pieces of lemon rind, for the stock; 1 tablespoon diced turkey meat and 1 hardboiled egg per person; 2 tablespoons butter, 2 tablespoons flour, seasoning, sherry to flavour if available, for soup; melba toast or cream crackers to hand separately.

Remove all the meat from the carcass and break it up to fit into the cooker. Add the rest of the ingredients and sufficient water to half fill the pan—approximately 2 pints. Bring to the boil in the open pan, skim well, bring to pressure in the usual way, cook for 45 minutes and allow the pressure to reduce at room temperature. Strain and leave in a cool place overnight. Next day, have ready the diced turkey meat and the hard-boiled eggs; carefully lift off the fat from the stock. In a medium-sized saucepan, melt the butter, add the flour and cook until it turns slightly brown. Away from the heat add a little of the stock, return to the stove and bring to the boil, stirring all the time, gradually adding the rest of the stock to give a soup consistency. Add the seasoning to taste, put in the diced meat and leave to simmer gently for 5 minutes. Cut a slice from the centre of each egg for garnish, chop the rest and just before serving add to the soup for reheating and stir in the sherry. Pour the soup into individual cups and put the slices of egg in the centre of each. Hand the melba toast or crackers separately.

TURKEY AND CHESTNUT SPECIAL

Pressure Cooking Time: 5 minutes and 5 minutes

1 large cup of rice, ½ lb chestnuts, ½ pint water for the cooker; 1 tablespoon margarine or butter; 1 tablespoon flour; 2 onions; 2 tomatoes; 2 oz mushrooms; ½ green pepper if available; ½ pint thinned gravy from turkey or ½ pint turkey stock; 1 teaspoon Worcester Sauce; dark leg meat from turkey sufficient for 4; seasoning; 1 tablespoon redcurrant or cranberry jelly; chopped parsley.

Put the rice with two cups of water into a container, cover and stand on trivet with water in cooker and the chestnuts, prepared as for stuffing, around it. Bring to pressure in the usual way, cook for 5 minutes and allow the pressure to reduce at room temperature. During the cooking, dice the meat, onions and pepper, slice the mushrooms and cut the tomatoes in four, preheat the oven for the rice. Lift out the rice; peel and skin the chestnuts and cut into four. Lift the trivet from the cooker and throw away the water. Heat the fat and cook the onions until golden brown. Add the tomatoes, onions and pepper if used and cook for a further 2 to 3 minutes. Add the gravy and sauce, stir well, put in the meat and seasoning, bring to pressure in the usual way, cook for 5 minutes, reduce the pressure with cold water. During this cooking, finish off the rice as given in the instructions on p. 146 and just before serving the turkey form into a ring on a hot serving dish. Taste and correct the seasoning for the turkey, reheat with the jelly and pour into the centre of the rice ring, sprinkling thickly with chopped parsley. An attractive garnish for the rice would be lemon baskets (p. 299) filled with a little more jelly.

If stock has been used instead of gravy, lift the turkey and vegetables into the rice ring with a straining spoon and thicken the gravy, after correcting the seasoning, with blended flour adding a little gravy colouring if necessary.

If you are looking for a thoughtful and luxury Christmas gift for a member of the family for whom it is difficult to choose a present, for something to add to a Christmas hamper for an old-age pensioner, as your contribution to a Christmas Bazaar, as an extra for the Christmas tea, here are some inexpensive yet quickly made sweets which, in pretty papers, could make up a charming home-made box of goodies.

RUM TRUFFLES

Pressure Cooking Time: $1\frac{1}{4}$ hours

1 tin sweetened condensed milk, $1\frac{1}{2}$ pints water with a little lemon or vinegar for the cooker; a few drops of rum essence or 2 dessertspoons of rum, drinking chocolate or cocoa, a little sieved apricot jam, 2 packets of chocolate vermicelli.

Put the water, trivet and tin of milk in the cooker. Bring to pressure in the usual way, cook for $1\frac{1}{4}$ hours, allow the pressure to reduce at room temperature. When the tin is quite cold, turn out the caramelised milk, add the rum and beat well. Put a small amount of the chocolate or cocoa powder on one plate, the just warmed sieved jam in a small basin and the vermicelli on another plate. Dip your fingers in the powder and form the mixture into small truffles, put each in turn on a skewer, dip in the jam and roll in the vermicelli. Allow to set and put into sweet papers. For variety, some of the truffles could be coated with green or pink sugar strands.

CHOCOLATE CREAM FUDGE

Pressure Cooking Time: 5 minutes

1 tin sweetened condensed milk; 6 oz plain chocolate; 6 oz milk chocolate; 3 oz chopped nuts, can be almonds, hazels or walnuts; 1 teaspoon vanilla; $\frac{1}{2}$ pint water with lemon or vinegar for the cooker.

Put half the milk in one bowl with the grated plain chocolate and the other half in another bowl with the grated milk chocolate. Put the water in the cooker, then one bowl covered with a double thickness of greaseproof paper, the trivet and then the other bowl also covered. Bring to pressure in the usual way cook for 5 minutes and reduce the pressure with cold water. Lift out the bowls, add half the chopped nuts and vanilla to each, stir well. Pour into small greased pans and cut in squares when cold and firm or drop in spoonfuls on to waxed paper and remove when hardened.

If the condensed milk is not sweetened, dissolve 1 lb granulated sugar in the milk before putting in the basins with the chocolate.

SECTION XII

Preservation of Fruit and Vegetables

This is a section that perhaps you will consider wasted on you, feeling that you would never have time to make your own marmalade, jam or chutney, or that living in a town as so many of us do it would not be economical to bottle fruit. But here pressure cooking can open up a new world for you in which you will find it is so easy and quick to make a batch of marmalade, to do a couple of bottles of strawberries or pears, that the small amount of trouble involved is well worth while, particularly when you tell your visitors and guests that you did them yourself and can show them your cupboard of home-made preserves. Even in these days of high-quality shop produce there is a certain glow of pride for a housewife in home preserving and it is perhaps a good thing to continue to practise this craft oneself and pass it on to the next generation.

With modern pressure cookers, it is not of course possible to make preserves or to do bottling on the grand scale; if you live in a town a simple system is to start in the Spring and then right through the Summer to Autumn to obtain small quantities of fruit just when it is at its best and most reasonably priced in your local shop, when you are out driving in the country or through the kind offers of friends with gardens. When you think of all the fruits which follow on one after the other, you will realise that even using just 2 lb at a time, and with your pressure cooker, by the season's end you could have 30 lb or so of marmalade and jam made and prepared, just while you are in the kitchen about the ordinary daily cooking and work.

Whether you have a small or a large garden, you are still sure to find your pressure cooker invaluable for preservation. Fruit and vegetables retain their colour, flavour and vitamin content at the highest level if they can be preserved as soon as possible after picking: it is therefore very convenient to have available a means of preserving small quantities just as they are ripe and ready, doing this daily perhaps in the season, rather than to keep them over for a day or two to have enough for one big, all-out effort by which time some may have passed their best.

No elaborate equipment or years of experience is necessary to be successful; just an understanding of the principles, careful following of the instructions—and a little bit of luck—and you will be surprised how clever everyone will think you when they see and taste the results.

In the following sections this principle of through-the-year preserving has been followed, hoping this will be of help to you and that you will take advantage of these special uses of your pressure cooker.

Among the different methods of preserving fruit are the following:

Jams: With fresh or dried fruits.

Jellies: With fresh fruits cooked to a pulp and strained through a jelly bag, the juice only being used or, with thin shreds of peel in marmalades.

Cheeses and Butters: With fresh, acid fruits, sieved to a pulp. As they require a large amount of fruit in proportion to the end product they are usually made only by those who have plenty of fruit available or when there is a glut. They are usually served as an accompaniment with meats.

Marmalades: Using citrus fruits, either thick or jelly types.

Pickles and Chutneys: Using certain firm and sound fruits, but as these need not be necessarily of good quality it is a useful method for keeping rough or windfall fruit.

Sauces: Using ripe tomatoes with spices, etc.

Bottling: Almost every fruit can be satisfactorily preserved in this way.

Deep-freezing: This is dealt with in a separate section, p. 277.

FRUIT	SEASON	TYPE OF PRESERVE
Seville or Bitter Oranges	January, February, March	Thick or jelly marmalade
Gooseberries	April–May	Jam, jelly, chutney, bottled, canned
Rhubarb	April–June	Bottled, canned
(Forced Garden)	May onwards	Jam, chutney, sauce, bottled, canned
Apricots (imported)	May–July	Rather expensive but make excellent jam, bottled, canned
(dried)	All the year round	Jam
Cherries	June onwards	Most varieties not suitable for jam; some varieties good for bottling and canning but others tend to lose colour
Currants		
Black	June and onwards	Jam, jelly, bottled, canned, syrup
Red	June and onwards	Jam, jelly, bottled, canned
Raspberries	June onwards	Jam, but not using a pressure cooker; bottled, canned
Strawberries	June onwards	Jam, but not using a pressure cooker; bottled, canned
Loganberries	June onwards	Jam, jelly, bottled, canned
Peaches (imported)	June onwards	Expensive and not too satisfactory for jam; bottled and canned if special varieties are used, or do not keep a good colour, chutney
Mulberries	July and August	Jam and jelly
Greengages	July to September	Not easily set for jam, tend to cloud when bottled or canned
Plums	August onwards	Jam, chutney, bottled and canned
Tomatoes		
Ripe	August onwards	Jam, chutney, sauce, juice, bottled, canned
Green	August onwards	Chutney
Pears (home-grown)	August onwards	Chutney, bottled, canned.
Damsons	September and October	Jam, jelly, cheese, bottled, canned.

FRUIT	SEASON	TYPE OF PRESERVE
Blackberries		
Cultivated	August and September	Jam alone or with apple, jelly, bottled, canned
Wild	September and October	Jam with apple, jelly
Crab Apples	September and October	Jelly
Whortle- and Elder-berries	September and October	Jam with apple or blackberries
Tangerines	November onwards	Jelly marmalade
Grapefruit	All the year round	Marmalade
Lemons	All the year round	Thick and jelly marmalade
Oranges (sweet)	All the year round	Marmalade with lemons and grape-fruit
Limes	May to June	Jelly marmalade
Apples (cooking)	All the year round	Jam, jelly, cheese and butters, chutney; jelly for adding to other jams; bottled and canned as pulped, purée or in quarters.

GENERAL INSTRUCTIONS FOR JAMS, JELLIES AND MARMALADES

The most important point to remember is that these preserves are meant to keep and, if they are to remain in good condition during storage, care must be taken in the choosing of the fruit and in making sure that the essential ingredients—sugar to preserve, acid to improve the colour and flavour and help prevent crystallisation of the sugar and pectin to obtain a set—are present in the correct proportions. A good recipe should have decided all this for you, but it is as well to know something about the principles involved so that every stage of the process is understood.

First, about the pressure cooker itself: made of aluminium it is perfectly suitable for jam and marmalade making and indeed recent tests have shown that preserves cooked in this material, or in stainless steel, keep a higher proportion of their vitamin C content.

The pressure cooker's role is to soften the fruit in the required amount of water, before the sugar is added. Once the sugar has been put in, the preserve has to be allowed to boil in an open pan—that is, in the pressure cooker without the cover, so that it can thicken and the setting point be tested.

The recommended pressure for the precooking of fruit for jams and marmalades is 10 lb. While a fixed **High** pressure (15 lb) can be used for marmalades as these contain a high proportion of acid and pectin and it is therefore easy to obtain a good set, it is rather too high a pressure and temperature for the softer fruits and its use may result in a lower yield and a slight loss in colour and flavour. If your model of pressure cooker has only a fixed weight you may find that, on application to the manufacturer, a variable set of weights can be supplied at a reasonable cost.

The pressure cooker should not be more than two thirds full when the sugar has been added and is dissolved. At this point the preserve should be boiled as fast as possible and if enough room is not left in the pan to do this the jam will either boil over or will have to boil slowly which will darken it in colour and probably spoil its flavour. For this reason, the recipes are for 2 or 3 lb of fruit only at a time; if a large saucepan is available it is quite a good idea when making jam or marmalade to pressure cook several lots one after the other, adding each into the big pan and then all the sugar, as this will still save a considerable amount of time and fuel.

The fruit chosen should be of good quality, as fresh as possible, under rather than over-ripe, and without any sort of blemish. All fruits except the very soft varieties should be cooked first to soften the skins and to break down the cell walls to extract the pectin before the sugar is added. It is here that the pressure cooker comes into its own as most fruits require no more than a few minutes to be reduced to a pulp and, because there is little loss by evaporation, only a minimum of water need be added. This keeps the fruit and juice concentrated so that a shorter boiling time is necessary after the addition of the sugar, leading to a jam with the best possible colour and flavour. Fruits which do not require presoftening such as strawberries and raspberries are therefore not included among these recipes. A certain amount of water must be added with the fruit and the quantity given in these recipes is correct for pressure cooking and is approximately one-third of the amount given for normal cooking.

The **acid** necessary is present in many of the fruits from which preserves are made, but if there is none or too little, then more must be added and the easiest to use and most readily available is lemon juice. While there can be no hard-and-fast rule about how much is needed, an average amount would be one tablespoon to each 2 lb of fruit. Not only does the acid content vary according to the fruit itself, but it can also be affected by the ripeness of the fruit and how dry it is, so the condition of the fruit is very important. Fruits with little acid are late blackberries (which is why apples are usually added to this jam or jelly) and pears and cherries, from which a satisfactory jam cannot really be made as adding lemon or apple juice overrides their own flavours. When additional acid is required in jam it is added for the softening process.

Pectin is a natural setting property found in the cell walls of fruits and is released when fruit is cooked. Like acid, it is present in varying quantities and quality and, if a fruit is very deficient in it, there is no point in trying to make it into jam unless one is prepared to add a commercial pectin or it is possible to use the juice of apples, lemons or redcurrants without spoiling the original flavour. Fruits deficient in pectin are usually those also lacking acid such as blackberries, cherries and pears; neither rhubarb though acid, nor marrow will set without the addition of lemon juice, for example.

Sugar is added to preserves to ensure their keeping qualities. Preserving sugar is the most easily dissolved and so it is the easiest to use when available, but lump or granulated sugar will do equally as well and will make no difference to the jam in storage. It is a help if the sugar is warmed first before being added to the jam as it will dissolve more quickly and cool the jam down less so that boiling point is more quickly reached. The jam must be stirred over a low heat until the sugar is dissolved, then brought to the boil as quickly as possible and boiled rapidly until setting point is reached without further stirring. Again, there is no hard-and-fast rule about how much sugar should be added but an average is 1 lb to each 1 lb of fruit or fruit juice; however, if a fruit is known to be rich in pectin, for example blackcurrants, $1\frac{1}{4}$ lb can be added for each 1 lb of fruit. There is no need to skim the jam during cooking; if necessary it can be removed after setting point is reached.

Setting point, providing that the fruit has been well softened before the addition of the sugar, should be between 5 to 10 minutes but seldom longer than 20; prolonged boiling when the jam shows no sign of setting after this time, will not necessarily produce a set. The easiest way to test for a set is to dip a wooden spoon in the jam, lift it out and twist it for a moment or two to allow the jam to cool. Then holding the spoon edge side down the jam will run off; if it is ready, the last drop left on the spoon will stay as a blob of jelly hanging from the edge. Lift the pan from the heat immediately and skim if necessary, using a skimmer or perforated spoon dipped in hot water and wiped just before use.

Finishing the jam is also very important. It should be poured or filled with a ladle, into clean, dry, warm jars; if it has whole fruit in, it must be left until a skin forms to show that the jelly is thickening slightly otherwise the fruit will rise to the tops of the jars giving a very uneven jam. Because preserves shrink as they cool, each jar must be filled literally to overflowing, a waxed circle be gently pressed on to cover the whole surface and the rim of the jar be wiped with a clean cloth dipped each time in hot water. The final cellophane circle should be put on immediately each jar has been filled or else be left off until the jam is quite cold, during which time the jars should be covered with a piece of greaseproof paper just laid over the tops. If preserves are covered when only warm, moulds may grow in the warm pocket of air between the waxed circle and the top cover.

A simple method of testing whether your jam making has been successful is to work out an easy sum based on the amount of sugar used and the number of pounds of jam resulting. This can be done as soon as you know how much sugar you are going to use so that you have some idea of what quantity of jam you are aiming for and a little experience of using your cooker as a preserving pan will enable you to judge whether you have about the right amount. What you have to remember is that an average yield is $\frac{5}{3}$ of the amount of sugar: i.e., if you are adding 3 lb of sugar, your sum will be

$$\tfrac{5}{3} \times 3 = 5 \text{ lb or } \tfrac{5}{3} \times 2 = 3\tfrac{1}{3} \text{ lb}$$

If you have much more than this, then the jam will be too runny, and if much less, then the jam will probably be much too thick. It is not always worth while to try and correct either of these; your family are sure to think it delicious either way and you will know better next time.

Storage of the jam should be in a dry place to prevent moulds growing, in a cool place to prevent fermentation and shrinkage and in a dark place to preserve the colour. Label the jam with its contents and the date and be sure that you keep your preserves on the move, putting the latest made to the back and bringing the earliest forward so that they are used while still at their best.

To summarise the process of jam making:

The fruit chosen should be firm, sound, without blemish and as dry as possible.

Acid, pectin and sugar should be present in the correct proportions and this has been worked out as accurately as possible in the following recipes.

All fruit, except the very soft varieties such as strawberries and raspberries should be precooked to soften the skins and break down the cell walls to release the pectin. This is the pressure cooker's job.

The sugar should be added, warm if possible, to the boiling fruit and stirred over a low heat until dissolved, when the jam must be allowed to boil as rapidly as possible until setting point is reached. For this reason, the pressure cooker here is used as an open pan and must not be more than two-thirds full.

The jam should not be skimmed during boiling; do this, if necessary, just before potting the jam.

Setting point is when the last drop on a wooden spoon, held edgeways, does not drop off but stays as a blob of jelly.

The jam should be potted immediately into clean, dry, warm jars unless it contains whole fruit or peel, when it should be left until a thin skin forms.

Each jar should be filled to the very top and covered immediately with a waxed disc.

The final covering should be put on immediately or left until the jam is quite cold.

Jars should be stored in an airy, cool, dry and dark space.

Faults which occur may be due to:

Overboiling, which can cause a sticky jam, dark in colour and with a burnt flavour.

Underboiling, when the preserve will be runny even when cold.

Insufficient pectin or acid or too high a proportion of sugar to fruit when the preserve does not set and there is no sign of a jell.

Fermentation giving a fizzy taste because too little sugar has been used.

Mould because the jar was not filled right to the top and has been stored in a warm damp place. This will not be harmful as long as every little bit is carefully lifted away before the jam is used.

Crystallisation, due to insufficient acid if the crystals are like rice grains or too much acid if it is a solid mass. To get rid of it, just take off the cover and stand the jar in a gently boiling saucepan of water, then allow the jam to set again and use at once.

Shrinkage caused by being kept in too warm a place or too long.

Cloudy because the scum has been stirred in during the cooking or not removed entirely after cooking.

Fruit rising in the jars because the preserve has not been allowed to cool a little before potting or was put in when the jars were too hot.

JAMS

Medium (10 lb) pressure is recommended. The trivet is not used. The pressure is allowed to reduce at room temperature.

GOOSEBERRY JAM

Pressure Cooking Time: 3 minutes

2 lb gooseberries still green; $\frac{1}{2}$ pint water; $2\frac{1}{2}$ lb sugar.

Top, tail and wash gooseberries. Put the water and fruit in the cooker and continue as given in the instructions. The colour of the finished jam will depend on the type and ripeness of the fruit; the longer the boiling, the pinker the jam will be.

Yield: approx. $4\frac{1}{2}$ lb.

RHUBARB JAM WITH GINGER

Pressure Cooking Time: to pressure only

$2\frac{1}{2}$ lb rhubarb; 2 oz root or 4 oz preserved ginger; juice and rind of 2 lemons; 2 lb sugar.

Wash the rhubarb, cut into 2-inch lengths, run cold water over and put into cooker without allowing to drain; add the finely chopped peel and juice of the lemons. Bring to the boil, press down well with a potato masher. Bring to pressure only, add the bruised root ginger in a piece of muslin loosely tied, or the preserved ginger cut into dice and the sugar. Before potting, lift out the muslin bag.

Yield: approx. $3\frac{1}{3}$ lb.

FRESH APRICOT JAM

Pressure Cooking Time: 4 minutes

2 lb of apricots, after the stones have been removed; $\frac{1}{2}$ pint water; 2 lb sugar.

Wash the fruit, halve and remove the stones. If liked, some of these can be cracked, then the kernels be blanched by dipping in boiling water and halved. Put the water, fruit and kernels in the cooker and continue as given in the instructions.

Yield: approx. $3\frac{1}{2}$ lb.

FRESH PEACH JAM

Pressure Cooking Time: 4 minutes

3 lb of peaches after the stones have been removed; ½ pint water; strained juice of 2 lemons; 3 lb sugar.

Prepare and cook as for **Fresh Apricot Jam**, adding the lemon juice to the cooker with the water and fruit.

Yield: approx. 5 lb.

DRIED APRICOT JAM at 15 lb (fixed) pressure

Pressure Cooking Time: 10 minutes

1 lb dried apricots; 2 pints boiling water; juice of 1 large lemon; 3 lb sugar; 2–3 oz blanched, shredded almonds if liked.

Cut the apricots into small pieces and put in the cooker, pour over the boiling water and leave, covered, for about 1 hour. Bring to pressure, cook for 10 minutes and allow the pressure to reduce at room temperature. Add the lemon juice, almonds if used and the warmed sugar and continue as given in the instructions. This will be a thick jam, more of a purée than a jelly and is excellent for cooking with steamed puddings, serving with rice puddings, as a filling for tartlets and flans or as a sauce over ice-cream.

Yield: approx. 5 lb.

BLACKCURRANT JAM

Pressure Cooking Time: 3–4 minutes

2 lb blackcurrants; 1 pint water; 3 lb sugar.

String the fruit and wash well. Put the water and fruit in the cooker and continue as given in the instructions.

Yield: approx. 5 lb.

LOGANBERRY JAM

Pressure Cooking Time: to pressure only

3 lb loganberries; 3 lb sugar.

Pick over the fruit, put in a colander and run cold water over. Put straight into the cooker without allowing to drain. Bring to the boil and press down well with a potato masher. Bring to pressure only and continue as given in the instructions.

Yield: approx. 5 lb.

PLUM JAM

Pressure Cooking Time: 5 minutes

About $2\frac{1}{4}$ lb of plums to weigh 2 lb when stoned; $\frac{1}{4}$ pint water; 2 lb sugar.

Wash and stone the fruit, holding the fruit over the cooker so that no juice is lost. If a lot of the fruit is left on the stones tie these loosely in a piece of muslin and cook them with the fruit but add a little more water as some will be taken up by the cloth. Squeeze the bag well by pressing it against the side of the cooker before lifting it out. Continue as given in the instructions. If the plums are of a sweet variety, a tablespoon of lemon juice should be added before the cooking to help to obtain a good set.

Yield: approx. $3\frac{1}{2}$ lb.

RED TOMATO JAM at 15 lb (or fixed) pressure

Pressure Cooking Time: 3 minutes

$3\frac{1}{2}$ lb tomatoes; $\frac{1}{2}$ lb cooking (Bramley) apples; 2 small lemons; $2\frac{1}{4}$ lb sugar. A small stick of cinnamon may be added for the pressure cooking, if liked.

Pour boiling water over the tomatoes, allow to stand for a moment, then skin and cut into quarters. Remove the peel and core from the apples and put these with the thinly peeled rind of lemon in a piece of muslin, loosely tied. Cut up the apples roughly and squeeze the lemons. Put the tomatoes and apples in the cooker and heat gently, mashing down well to extract the juice. Add the muslin bag and lemon juice, and continue as given in the instructions, lifting out the muslin bag and squeezing well, before adding the sugar.

Yield: approx. 4 lb.

DAMSON JAM

Pressure Cooking Time: 5 minutes

$2\frac{1}{4}$ lb of damsons; $\frac{1}{4}$ pint water; 3 lb sugar.

Wash the fruit. Put the water and the fruit in the cooker and continue as given in the instructions (p. 241 etc). Remove as many of the stones as possible during the cooking, straining back any jam that may be taken out as well; a small piece of butter put on the surface after setting point has been reached and before potting will help to bring the last ones to the top.

Yield: approx. 5 lb.

BLACKBERRY AND APPLE

Pressure Cooking Time: 7 minutes

2 lb blackberries; ¾ lb green cooking apples when peeled and cored; ¼ pint water; 3 lb sugar.

Pick over blackberries, wash and drain. Remove peel and cores of apples and put these in a muslin bag. Put the blackberries, cut up apples and water in the cooker and continue as given in the instructions. Lift out the muslin bag and squeeze well before adding sugar.

Yield: approx. 5 lb.

If **Blackberry Jam** is preferred on its own, then use 2 lb of fruit, 2 lb of sugar, ¼ pint of water and 2 tablespoons of lemon juice, adding this for the pressure cooking. Continue as given in the instructions.

If the **Blackberry Jam** is preferred seedless, then sufficient blackberries must be pressure cooked to give at least 2 lb of pulp when sieved. Using the strained juice, pressure cook the apples as for **Blackberry and Apple**, on their own. Weigh the combined pulps and use an equal weight of sugar. Continue as given in the instructions.

APPLE GINGER

Pressure Cooking Time: 5 minutes

3 lb apples; ¼ pint water; rind and juice of 1 large lemon; ground ginger; sugar.

Wash the apples, cut in quarters, put into cooker with the water and the rind and juice of lemon, bring to pressure in the usual way, cook for 5 minutes and allow the pressure to reduce at room temperature. Sieve the pulp, measure, add one level teaspoon of ground ginger and 1 lb of sugar to each 1 pint of sieved apple, bring to the boil and continue as given in the instructions.

MARROW AND GINGER JAM

Pressure Cooking Time: 2 minutes

2 lb of marrow after preparation; rind and juice of 2 lemons; 1 oz root ginger; 2 lb sugar.

Peel the marrow, remove seeds and cut the pulp into 1 inch squares. Tie the brushed ginger and lemon rinds loosely in a piece of muslin. Put the lemon juice and marrow into the cooker, heat gently until enough liquid is extracted from the marrow to just cover the bottom of the cooker, put in the muslin bag and pressure cook for 2 minutes. Allow the pressure to reduce at room temperature, add the sugar, stir and leave in a covered bowl for 24 hours. Lift out the bag and squeeze well; continue as given in the instructions. This jam may require up to 30 minutes boiling, when the marrow should be transparent and the syrup have thickened. It will not set as jam does.

Yield: approx. 3 lb.

UNUSUAL JAMS

FRUIT SALAD JAM

Pressure Cooking Time: 4 minutes

This can be an excellent preserve, using any mixture of fresh fruits particularly if one has been making other jams or fruit bottling. The fruit used should still be of good quality, firm, etc, and not just the throw-outs. Do not use too high a proportion of any one fruit or colour. Add sufficient of pectin rich fruits such as gooseberries, blackcurrants, apple with others such as cherries, strawberries, pears, in the proportion of:

2 lb mixed fruit; ½ pint water; 2 lb sugar and a little lemon juice if the jam should have too sweet a taste after the sugar has been added and is dissolved.

Yield: approx. 3½ lb.

JAPONICA PRESERVE

Pressure Cooking Time: 4 minutes

2–3 lb fruit; 1½ pints water; ½ teaspoon (or more to taste) cloves or allspice; sugar.

Wash the fruit and cut into eight, being careful to remove any soft or bruised parts. Put all the fruit, including pips into the cooker with the water, bring to pressure, cook for 4 minutes and allow the pressure to reduce at room temperature. Sieve the fruit, add the juice and measure the pulp. Return to the cooker, bring to the boil, add the spices and ¾ lb of sugar for each 1 pint of pulp. Continue as given in the instructions (p. 241 etc).

MEDLAR JAM

Pressure Cooking Time: 7 minutes

This fruit must be over-ripe before eating or making into jam.

Medlars; ¼ pint water; sugar; vanilla pod or vanilla essence.

Skin and remove the crowns from sufficient medlars to weigh about 2½ lb. Put into the cooker with the water, allow to boil first and press down with a potato masher before bringing to pressure. Cook for 7 minutes, allow the pressure to reduce at room temperature, sieve and weigh the pulp. Return to the cooker, reboil, add $\frac{3}{4}$ lb sugar for each pound of pulp, the vanilla pod or essence to taste and cook, stirring all the time until thick. Remove the vanilla pod before potting.

MELON AND PINEAPPLE

Pressure Cooking Time: 10 minutes

2 lb melon, $\frac{1}{2}$ lb pineapple when prepared; juice of 3 lemons; 3 lb sugar.

Cut skin from melon, taking off as much of the fruit as possible. Slice the pineapple, core it, cut off the skin and remove all the black bits. Cut melon and pineapple into small cubes. Continue as given in the instructions (p. 241 etc).

Yield: approx. $4\frac{1}{2}$ lb.

MULBERRY JAM

Pressure Cooking Time: 3 minutes

2 lb mulberries; 2 tablespoons water; 2 lb sugar; 2 tablespoons lemon juice.

Carefully remove any blemished fruit, all small twigs and leaves. Put water and fruit in cooker, allow to boil in the open pan and mash the fruit gently to extract a little juice. Continue as given in the instructions (p. 241 etc).

Yield: approx. $3\frac{1}{2}$ lb.

This is a very pippy jam and it is easier and perhaps better to make it into jelly. As the pips tend to rise in the jars after potting quite a lot can be lifted off then, but this must be done with a teaspoon dipped each time in water kept boiling in a small saucepan.

PINEAPPLE PRESERVE

Pressure Cooking Time: 10 minutes

Pineapple; lemon juice; loaf sugar.

A pineapple weighing 3 lb will give approximately $1\frac{1}{2}$ lb pulp. Cut the pineapple into $\frac{1}{2}$-inch slices, remove skin and core and tie this loosely in a piece of muslin. Cut the fruit into small pieces doing this in a dish to contain the juice. Weigh the fruit and juice, put into the cooker with two teaspoons of lemon juice per pound of pulp and allow to boil, pressing down well to extract some more juice. Put in the muslin bag, bring to pressure in the usual way, cook for 10 minutes and allow the pressure to reduce at room temperature. Lift out the bag and squeeze gently, mash the fruit to a pulp, add 14 oz sugar for each pound of pulp and continue as given in the instructions (p. 241 etc).

PINEAPPLE AND APRICOT JAM

Pressure Cooking Time: 10 minutes

This is a standby jam which can be made at any time in the year if the jam cupboard is bare and there is no suitable fresh fruit to replenish it with.

1 lb dried apricots; $1\frac{1}{2}$ pints water for soaking and cooking; 1 small tin of pineapple; 4 lb sugar; juice of 1 lemon.

Cut the apricots into small pieces, put into the cooker, pour over the boiling water and allow to soak, covered, for at least one hour. Add the pineapple juice and pressure cook. Add the pineapple cut into small pieces, the lemon juice and sugar and continue as given in the instructions (p. 241 etc).

Yield: approx. 7 lb.

JELLIES

The principles and instructions as given for Jams apply equally to Jelly making, but the fruit chosen must be plentiful as only the juice is used, it must be rich in pectin and acid or else must be combined with another which has these properties and should have a distinctive flavour. Such fruits as cherries, pears, strawberries would not therefore be suitable as so much pectin and acid would have to be added that they would lose their own flavour.

Fruit for jelly making should be washed and carefully looked over but does not require any other preparation in the way of peeling, stalking and so on, as all this will be left behind when the juice is strained. This makes it a quick and easy process, particularly with gooseberries and currants, and is excellent for windfall fruits, though apples usually need another fruit with them as they may tend to be insipid; this, however, makes them a good source of acid and pectin for setting other fruits which may be slightly deficient by themselves.

When making jelly it is essential that the fruit be completely broken down to release the acid and pectin into the water and so your pressure cooker will be just the thing for this. After pressure has been reduced, mash the fruit up well until it is a complete pulp before putting it into a jelly bag.

This is an essential piece of equipment for jelly making; you may be able to buy one of these locally and then it will be made of felt or flannel; if not you could make one yourself, using a smooth but thick tea-towel and sewing tapes at each corner. An upturned chair or stool with the tapes tied to the legs and a large bowl into which the juice can drain will then be quite satisfactory. The jelly bag must have a kettle of boiling water poured through it just before the pulp is put in.

It is not possible to give the exact proportions of fruit, water or sugar for jelly making; with a pressure cooker the fruit should not more than half fill the base, the water should be $\frac{1}{2}$ to 1 pint, depending on the type of fruit, and the sugar be measured according to the amount of strained juice obtained.

With fruits very rich in pectin, such as blackcurrants and apples, a second extract of juice may be made by returning the fruit to the cooker after the first straining, adding half the amount of water originally used and giving the same pressure cooking time, adding the second extract to the first.

The pulp should be allowed to drain for about 1 hour and the bag must never be squeezed, otherwise the jelly will be cloudy.

The warmed sugar is added, as for jam, and then the jelly must boil rapidly until setting point is reached. At this moment which may be as little as 1 minute for redcurrant jelly and certainly no more than 10 minutes after a jelly first begins to boil, quick action is necessary, otherwise the jelly will start to set in the pan and its appearance in the jars will be spoiled. All scum should be quickly removed with a spoon dipped in boiling water if there is a lot or with pieces of kitchen paper torn with ragged edges, drawn along the surface if there is only a little.

The jelly should then be poured into the warmed jars at once and quickly covered with a wax disc. For jellies, small containers are the best as jelly is better eaten as soon as possible after it is opened.

To summarise the process of jelly making:

The fruit should be ripe, well picked over and washed, but does not need any other preparation.

It should be thoroughly cooked and well broken down before being strained.

The pulp should be allowed to drain for about an hour, the jelly bag should not be squeezed and the jelly should be finished off the same day.

A second extract may be made from those fruits known to be rich in pectin and acid.

The warmed sugar should be added to the strained juice when it is at boiling point, except for pale extracts such as apple and gooseberry when the longer cooking while the sugar dissolves tends to give a deeper colour.

After setting point has been reached, the scum should be quickly removed and the jelly poured into small containers as quickly as possible.

The jars should not be moved until the jelly has set.

Faults which may occur may be:

Air bubbles in the jar because the jelly has been stirred during boiling or not poured into the jars quickly enough.

Cloudy jelly because the texture of the jelly bag was not fine enough or the bag was squeezed.

Weepy jelly because there was too much acid in the fruit.

Only a few samples of jellies are given here because there are so many that can be made from fruits on their own or combined with others that it is rather fun for the housewife to try out her own 'mixtures', depending on the fruit available; in fact, as long as a good jelling-juice is obtained there is no limit to the varieties that can be made and which will soon become special family favourites. No yield is given as this will depend on the amount of juice obtained but it should still be $\frac{5}{3}$ approximately, of the amount of sugar added.

BLACKCURRANT JELLY

Pressure Cooking Time: 5 minutes

About 3 lb blackcurrants; 2 pints water; sugar in the proportion of 1 lb to each pint of strained juice.

Be sure and mash the fruit well before straining.

CRAB APPLE JELLY

Pressure Cooking Time: 8 minutes

About 3 lb of crab apples; water; sugar in the proportion of 1 lb to each pint of strained juice.

Cut the apples across and when they are in the cooker add sufficient water to just show through the top layer.

GOOSEBERRY JELLY

Pressure Cooking Time: 5 minutes

3 lb gooseberries; 1 pint water; sugar in the proportion of 1 lb to each pint of strained juice.

A delicious combination is **Gooseberry and Strawberry**, replacing 1 lb of gooseberries with 1 lb of strawberries.

Two recipes are given here for **Mint Jelly**. The first is really delicious and, as gooseberries are in season when the mint is at its youngest and best, you may find you prefer it to the more usual one made with apples, available when the mint is getting towards the end of its season's growth.

MINT JELLY WITH GOOSEBERRIES

Pressure Cooking Time: 5 minutes

2 lb gooseberries; $\frac{1}{4}$ pint water; sugar; bunch of fresh mint; chopped mint; a little green colouring.

Make the strained gooseberry juice following the instructions (p. 252), return to the cooker, add 1 lb of sugar per pint and when dissolved and the jelly is boiling again put in a good bunch of bruised mint tied loosely together with string. After 5 minutes or so, or when the jelly looks nearly ready to set, lift out the mint and continue boiling until setting point is reached. Allow to stand until a thin skin forms, then gently stir in the finely chopped mint and the colouring. Pour into small containers and cover as usual.

MINT JELLY WITH APPLES

Make in the same way as the preceding recipe but use 2 lb of really green cooking apples and 2 tablespoons of lemon juice in place of the gooseberries.

You might also try this with parsley instead of mint if you have a plentiful supply. In this case, cook the sprigs of parsley with the apples and have plenty of finely chopped parsley to add to the finished jelly. A tablespoon of vinegar can take the place of the lemon juice.

Parsley Jelly is delicious with fish and with hot and cold meats.

REDCURRANT JELLY

Pressure Cooking Time: 1 minute

About 3 lb redcurrants; water to just show through the top layer; sugar in the proportion of $1\frac{1}{4}$ lb to each pint of juice.

Be sure to mash the fruit well before straining. After adding the sugar, no more than 1 to 2 minutes' quick boiling, stirring all the time, will be necessary to reach setting point and then it must be potted immediately. A second extract can certainly be made from the same fruit.

A proportion of raspberries will make a delicious **Raspberry and Redcurrant Jelly**.

APPLE JELLY

Pressure Cooking Time: 5 minutes

About 3 lb of apples of a good flavour; 1 pint of water; sugar in the proportion of 1 lb of sugar to each pint of strained juice.

If to be on its own, flavourings such as lemon peel, ginger or cloves may be added for the pressure cooking.

Variations of **Apple Jelly** could be made with equal quantities of **Mulberries, Elderberries, Whortleberries, Cranberries** and so on.

If a fruit juice (apple, gooseberry or redcurrant) is required for adding to jams with a poor set, pressure cook the fruit as for making jelly and use the strained juice in the proportion of 2 tablespoons to 2 lb of fruit.

MARMALADES

Here again, the principles and general instructions are the same as for jams and jellies, the thick peel needing thorough cooking, a job the pressure cooker will do in a fraction of the normal time necessary. It must be remembered that with citrus fruits the pectin required to obtain a set is mostly contained in the white pith and the pips and it is for this reason that the best oranges for marmalade making are Sevilles as those are mostly what they consist of. If the pith is not wanted in the finished product it can be cut off the peel but must be tied loosely with the pips in a muslin bag and added during the cooking, being lifted out and well squeezed before the sugar is added.

It really is not necessary to remove the pulp when you have a pressure cooker as it is so thoroughly cooked that it is never unpleasant in the finished product. If your family prefer a marmalade with less fruit, then one of the jelly types could be chosen.

With other citrus fruits such as lemons, grapefruit and sweet oranges, so many now reach us with thin skins and seedless that it is not easy to obtain a marmalade with plenty of jelly round the fruit; it is quite a good idea therefore when you have in mind to make one of these marmalades to start saving the pips a while in advance—from oranges squeezed for juice, from lemons used in cooking and from grapefruit prepared for breakfast. Put them as you get them into a small cup or egg-cup and just cover them with water, adding them and the extract in a muslin bag to the fruit, just before pressure cooking.

Using a pressure cooker, there is no need whatever to soak the fruit overnight; this will have no effect in the way of better flavour or setting as is often thought.

Even though one may think of citrus fruits as being very acid, a little lemon juice is usually added as marmalade fruits are bulky, rich in pectin and can take twice as much sugar as other fruits and therefore the proportion of acid is considerably less than in jams.

To summarise the process of marmalade making:

Either **M**edium (10 lb) or **H**igh (15 lb) pressure can be used.

The fruit should be fresh and must be well washed.

All pith must be included with the pips in the cooking.

Only half the amount of water should be used for the cooking, adding the rest with the sugar. This will prevent the fruit and juice boiling out during the cooking.

The fruit must be soft before the sugar is added.

The lemon juice can be added either for the cooking or with the sugar.

The scum should be removed after setting point has been reached.

The marmalade should be allowed to stand a little before potting otherwise the fruit will rise in the jars.

The waxed circle should be put on as each jar is filled, the final covering when the marmalade is really cold.

THICK MARMALADES

SEVILLE ORANGE MARMALADE

Pressure Cooking Time: 10 minutes

2 lb of Sevilles; juice of 2 lemons; 2 pints water; 4 lb sugar.

Wash the fruit. Depending on the type of marmalade wanted the fruit can be:

(1) Cut in quarters, the pips removed and tied loosely in a muslin bag, the fruit be cut, chopped or minced after the cooking and the bag be squeezed and lifted out before the sugar is added.

(2) The fruit can be peeled, the pith be cut off with a knife and roughly chopped up and added with the pips in a muslin bag as above. The fruit should be roughly chopped up too and the peel cut up, chopped or minced after cooking.

(3) The fruit can be skinned, the pith removed and the peel be cut as required before cooking. The peel, cut up fruit and the chopped pith and pips, in a muslin bag as above, are then all cooked together.

Put the fruit, peel and muslin bag with *half* the water into the cooker, bring to pressure in the usual way, cook for 10 minutes and allow the pressure to reduce at room temperature. Lift out the muslin bag and squeeze well; strain the fruit putting the juice back into the cooker and cut up the peel. Add this to the cooker with the other *half* of the water and the lemon juice, bring to the boil on a high heat, add the sugar and stir until dissolved over a low heat, bring to the boil quickly again and boil rapidly until setting point is reached. Skim if necessary, allow to stand until a skin has formed, pot, cover at once with a waxed disc. Allow to get cold, cover and tie down, label and store.

Yield: approx. 6½–7 lb.

LEMON MARMALADE

Pressure Cooking Time: 7 minutes

2 lb of lemons; 1 pint water; 4 lb sugar.

As for **Seville Orange Marmalade**.

Yield: approx. 6½–7 lb.

GRAPEFRUIT MARMALADE

Pressure Cooking Time: 10 minutes

Grapefruit weighing 1½ lb; lemons weighing ½ lb; 1 pint water; 4 lb sugar.

As for **Seville Orange Marmalade** (p. 257), but use all of the lemon and not just the juice.

Yield: approx. 6½–7 lb.

SWEET ORANGE MARMALADE

Pressure Cooking Time: 8 minutes

1½ lb sweet oranges; ¾ lb lemons; 1 pint water; 4 lb sugar.

As for **Seville Orange Marmalade**, but use all the lemons, not just the juice. This marmalade may have a cloudy appearance when potted, depending on the kind of oranges used.

Yield: approx. 6½ lb.

THREE FRUIT MARMALADE

Pressure Cooking Time: 10 minutes

2 oranges, 1 grapefruit, 2 lemons to weigh 2 lb; 1½ pints water; 4 lb sugar.

As for **Seville Orange Marmalade**.

Yield: approx. 6½–7 lb.

JELLY MARMALADES

ORANGE SHRED

Pressure Cooking Time: 8 minutes

2 lb Seville oranges; juice of 2 small lemons; 1¼ pints water; 3 lb sugar.

Peel four of the oranges finely, remove the pith very carefully, shred the peel finely and tie loosely in a muslin bag. Chop the rest of the fruit and all the pith roughly, put into the cooker with the water, the lemon juice and the muslin bag, bring to pressure in the usual way, cook for 8 minutes and allow the pressure to reduce at room temperature. Lift out the muslin bag, put the shreds into a strainer and pour a kettle of boiling water over them. Strain the rest through a jelly bag and continue as for jelly making (p. 251 etc) until just before setting point, then skim the marmalade, add the shredded peel and continue boiling until setting point is reached. Continue as given in the instructions (p. 257).

Yield: approx. 5 lb.

LEMON SHRED

Pressure Cooking Time: 8 minutes

2 lb lemons; 1¼ pints water; 3 lb sugar

As for **Orange Shred** (p. 258).

LIME JELLY MARMALADE

Pressure Cooking Time: 10 minutes

1 lb of limes (about 8); juice of 1 lemon; 1½ pints water; 1½ lb sugar.

Although the colour of the marmalade will not be good, it will be less bitter and with a better set if the limes are used when they are beginning to turn yellow.

Wash the limes, peel off the rind with a potato peeler and shred it finely. Take off as much pith as possible from the fruit, cut the fruit in half, take away the pips which should not be cooked, squeeze out the juice and add it to the peel with the strained lemon juice and leave overnight. Cut up the pulp, tie in a muslin bag, put in the cooker with the peel, juice and water, bring to pressure in the usual way, cook for 8 minutes and allow the pressure to reduce at room temperature. Lift out the muslin bag, squeeze very gently, add the sugar and continue as given in the instructions (p. 257).

Yield: approx. 2½ lb.

TANGERINE JELLY

1½ lb tangerines; ½ grapefruit and 1–2 lemons to weigh ½ lb; 1½ pints water; 2¼ lb sugar.

As for **Orange Shred** (p. 258).

FRUIT CHEESES AND BUTTERS

CRANBERRY CHEESE

Pressure Cooking Time: 3 minutes

2 lb of cranbrerries; ½ pint water; sugar.

Wash the cranberries, put into the cooker with the water, bring to pressure in the usual way, cook for 3 minutes and allow the pressure to reduce at room temperature. Sieve the fruit, weigh the pulp and juice, return to the pan and boil until it is really thick. Add 12 oz sugar for each pound of pulp and continue cooking, stirring all the time until the fruit holds on the spoon without dropping off. Pot and cover at once.

This is an excellent preserve to serve with Roast Turkey and dishes made from it such as Turkey Pilaff or Curried Turkey.

DAMSON CHEESE

Pressure Cooking Time: 8 minutes

2 lb damsons; $\frac{1}{4}$ pint water; sugar.

Make as for **Cranberry Cheese** (p. 259).

LEMON CURD OR CHEESE

Pressure Cooking Time: 10 minutes

2 large or 3 standard eggs; $\frac{1}{2}$ lb caster sugar; finely grated rind of 2 lemons; strained juice of 1 lemon; 2–3 oz unsalted butter; $\frac{1}{2}$ pint water and $\frac{1}{2}$ squeezed lemon for the cooker.

Beat the eggs lightly and strain into a china, earthenware or oven-proof bowl that will fit into the cooker. Add the sugar and stir until well mixed. Put in the lemon rind and juice and lastly the butter in small knobs and stir well again. Put the water and trivet in the cooker, stand in the bowl and cover with a double thickness of greaseproof paper. Bring to 15 lb (fixed) pressure, cook for 10 minutes and allow the pressure to reduce for 10 minutes. Lift out the bowl, stir the curd well, pour into a warm jar and cover with a waxed disc. Seal when cold. Lemon curd should have the consistency of thick cream and coat the back of the spoon with a thin film when it is cooked. It will thicken as it cools. This quantity will make a 1 lb jar and no more should be made at one time as Lemon Curd does not keep for more than 5 to 6 weeks as it has no preservative added to it.

ORANGE CURD

Use the same method as for **Lemon Curd** but with the grated rind of two oranges and two tablespoons of mixed orange and lemon juice. As orange peel does not grate as finely as lemon, the curd when cooked should be put through a sieve if a smoother consistency is preferred.

PICKLES AND CHUTNEYS

These are very simple to make and again there is a wide choice of recipes, almost any combination of available fruits or vegetables being suitable. Your pressure cooker will once more be invaluable for the rapid and complete softening of the ingredients, though the thickening to reduce the contents to the correct consistency must always be done in the open pan, stirring all the time. These preserves require **High** (15 lb) pressure.

For storage, care must be taken that the jars are well sealed or else the vinegar will evaporate, but it must not be allowed to come into direct contact with metal, otherwise it will lead to rusting. A cover of greaseproof paper will not be sufficient. If jars with metal screw or push-on tops are chosen, a waxed disc should go on first, then a circle of cardboard and, if possible the inside of the metal tops should be given, a few days previously, a coating of clear lacquer. It is possible to buy plastic push-on covers now to fit 1-lb or 2-lb jars, and these are both suitable and practical as they can be used over and over again. A form of synthetic skin which can be purchased is excellent too as a cover over a waxed disc.

MUSTARD PICKLE

Pressure Cooking Time: 1 minute

3 lb vegetables made up of cucumber, marrow, French or runner beans, small onions or shallots, cauliflower, unripe green tomatoes; ½ lb kitchen salt; 4 pints water.

Prepare the vegetables by dicing, leave the cauliflower in flowerets and cut the tomatoes into eight. Dissolve the salt in the water and put this brine and the vegetables into a large bowl and leave overnight. A weighted plate should be put into the bowl to make sure all the vegetables remain covered. The next day, rinse the vegetables well.

Prepared vegetables; 1 pint white vinegar; 4 oz brown sugar; 1½ level tablespoons of dry mustard; 2 level tablespoons ground ginger; 2 tablespoons ground turmeric; 2 tablespoons of flour.

Put the strained vegetables into the cooker with ¾ pint of the vinegar, the sugar, mustard and ginger, bring to pressure in the usual way, cook for 1 minute and reduce the pressure with cold water. During the cooking blend the flour and turmeric with the rest of the vinegar. Carefully lift a selection of each vegetable into the jars with a straining spoon, add the thickening to the liquid in the cooker, bring to the boil, cook for 2 minutes until really thick, then pour into the jars, using a round-bladed knife to make sure the sauce gets round, down and through the vegetables. Cover immediately.

Yield: approx. 4 × 1-lb jars.

If liked the vinegar can be boiled separately for about 5 minutes with a tablespoon of pickling spice and then be strained before being put in the cooker.

This is an expensive chutney but it would be excellent to make and keep for that special occasion when you are really looking for something different to serve your family or impress your guests. It would go well with curries, game or turkey or a home-made Galantine for a summer meal.

APRICOT CHUTNEY

Pressure Cooking Time: 20 minutes

2 lb apricots; 1 lb onions; 1 lb seedless raisins; 1¼ pints white wine vinegar; 1 tablespoon salt; 1 dessertspoon cayenne pepper, 2 tablespoons ground ginger, 1 oz coriander seed, tied in muslin; 2 tablespoons made mustard; 1 lb white sugar.

Halve, stone and chop apricots, chop onions and raisins. Lift the trivet from the cooker, put in the vinegar and onions and allow to simmer on a low heat for 10 minutes. Add the apricots, raisins, salt and spices, bring to pressure in the usual way, cook for 20 minutes and allow the pressure to reduce at room temperature. Lift out the bag of spices. Stir well, add the sugar and made mustard and continue boiling, as necessary, until the required thick consistency is reached. Taste and correct seasoning, bottle while still boiling and seal immediately.

GREEN TOMATO CHUTNEY

Pressure Cooking Time: 10 minutes

2 lb green tomatoes; 2 onions; 2 apples; 4 oz sultanas or seedless raisins; 1 tablespoon salt; 3 heaped teaspoons of pickling spice tied in muslin; ½ lb brown sugar; 1 tablespoon ground ginger; 1 teaspoon cayenne pepper; 1 pint vinegar.

Cut up the tomatoes, the peeled and cored apples and the onions and chop the raisins. Put these with the pickling spice, the salt, and ½ pint of the vinegar in the cooker, bring to pressure in the usual way, cook for 10 minutes and reduce the pressure with cold water. Put in the rest of the vinegar, lift out the bag of spices, add the sugar, the pepper, the ginger and stir until boiling, cooking until the chutney thickens. Pour into the jars and cover immediately.

MARROW CHUTNEY

Pressure Cooking Time: 8 minutes

3 lb marrow; 1 tablespoon salt; 1 lb green apples; ½ lb onions or shallots; 1 heaped tablespoon pickling spice; 1 tablespoon salt; 1 pint malt vinegar; ¾ lb brown sugar; 1 teaspoon powdered turmeric.

Peel the marrow, remove the pips and cut into small pieces. Leave to soak overnight in layers sprinkled with the salt. Next day, drain well, then put into the cooker with the peeled and chopped apples and onions, the spices tied loosely in muslin, the salt and half the vinegar. Bring to pressure in the usual way, cook for 8 minutes, reduce the pressure with cold water and lift out the muslin bag. Add the sugar and the rest of the vinegar and cook, stirring frequently until the consistency of thick jam. Pot and seal immediately.

BEETROOT RELISH

Pressure Cooking Time: 15–20 minutes and 5 minutes

Beetroots to weigh 1 lb; 1 lb chopped cabbage; 1 heaped tablespoon horseradish sauce or freshly grated horseradish; 1 tablespoon dry mustard; 1 teaspoon salt; a pinch of cayenne pepper; ½ pint vinegar; ½ lb white sugar.

Pressure cook the beetroots whole, according to their size, between 15 to 20 minutes. Peel and chop into fine dice; throw away the water. Return to the cooker with all the other ingredients except the sugar, bring to pressure again, cook for 5 minutes and reduce the pressure with cold water. Add the sugar and cook, stirring frequently until the relish thickens. Pot and seal immediately.

SWEET APPLE CHUTNEY

Pressure Cooking Time: 10 minutes

3 lb sour apples; ¼ lb crystallised ginger; 1 level teaspoon cayenne pepper; 2 crushed cloves of garlic; 1 level teaspoon salt; 2 level teaspoons mixed spice; 1 pint malt vinegar; 12 oz brown sugar; ½ lb sultanas.

Peel, core and cut up the apples and put into the cooker with the garlic and half the vinegar. Bring to pressure in the usual way, cook for 10 minutes and allow the pressure to reduce at room temperature. Add the chopped ginger, the pepper, salt, spice, sugar and sultanas and cook, stirring frequently until the consistency of thick jam. Pot and seal immediately.

PEAR CATSUP

Pressure Cooking Time: 10 minutes

3 lb of hard, cooking but well flavoured pears; $\frac{1}{2}$ pint white vinegar; 6 oz brown sugar; a heaped teaspoon each of pepper, cinnamon, ground cloves and salt.

Wash the pears, peel them if the skins are marked, cut up roughly, put into the cooker with the vinegar, bring to pressure in the usual way, cook for 7 minutes and reduce the pressure with cold water. Rub through a sieve, return to the cooker, add all the other ingredients and boil, stirring frequently until the catsup thickens. Pot and seal immediately.

SAUCES AND KETCHUPS

If these are to be kept for any length of time they should be poured, while still boiling, into heated 1 lb Kilner jars which can be sealed, leaving 2-inch headspace. The instructions for sealing fruit purées, p. 271, should then be followed. If for immediate use, well washed and dried sauce bottles can be used, the sauce being poured while still boiling into the hot jars, each one as filled being capped immediately with the original bottle caps, scrupulously clean and dry and tied down with a double thickness of greaseproof paper.

TOMATO SAUCE

Pressure Cooking Time: 3 minutes

4 lb ripe red tomatoes; $\frac{1}{4}$ pint white vinegar; $\frac{1}{2}$ teaspoon each ground ginger, ground cloves, ground mace; a pinch of cayenne pepper; salt; 8 oz white sugar.

Slice the tomatoes, put into the cooker with the vinegar, bring to pressure in the usual way, cook for 3 minutes and allow the pressure to reduce at room temperature. Rub the tomatoes through a fine sieve, return to the cooker, add all the other ingredients and cook, stirring frequently until the desired consistency. Bottle as given in instructions (p. 271).

Yield: approx. 2 pints.

TOMATO KETCHUP

Pressure Cooking Time: 10 minutes

2 lb well-ripened tomatoes; 1 large cooking apple; 1 medium onion; $\frac{1}{4}$ pint white wine vinegar; 1 dessertspoon pickling spice, tied in muslin; $\frac{1}{4}$ lb white sugar; a good pinch of cayenne pepper and salt.

Put the quartered tomatoes, cored and quartered apple and chopped onion into the cooker with the vinegar and spices, bring to pressure in the usual way, cook for 10 minutes and reduce the pressure with cold water. Put through a sieve, return to the cooker and boil, stirring all the time until thick. Add the seasonings and sugar and cook a further 10 minutes. Taste and correct seasoning and bottle at once according to the instructions given on p. 271.

ROSE HIP SYRUP

Pressure Cooking Time: 2 minutes

2 lb ripe rose hips; 2 pints of water; $\frac{1}{2}$ lb sugar.

Put the rose hips through a coarse mincer and then directly into 1 pint of fast boiling water in the cooker. Bring to pressure in the usual way, cook for 2 minutes and allow the pressure to reduce at room temperature. Strain through a jelly bag. Rinse out the cooker, put back the syrup, add 1 pint of boiling water then the sugar and allow to boil for 5 minutes. This syrup must now be treated like bottled fruit if it is to keep, so pour immediately into clean, hot, 1-lb Kilner jars leaving at least 2 inches headspace and continuing as given in the instructions on p. 271, bringing to pressure only and allowing the pressure to reduce at room temperature before tightening the jars.

This syrup will not keep for more than a week or so once it is opened.

FRUIT STERILISATION

The bottling of fruit, contrary to what many housewives may think, is a very simple process; now that you have a pressure cooker you can be sure it will also be quick and completely safe. Its purpose is to allow you, when fruit is at its best or if it has to be bought, at its cheapest, to preserve it for the times when fresh fruit is scarce and expensive. It requires very little equipment, so little time that a couple of jars can be processed in a matter of minutes and the satisfaction of having a lovely shelf of home bottled fruit is out of all proportion to the time and effort involved. Even though a wide choice of frozen and tinned fruit is now readily available and the town housewife would not find it economic to go out and buy large quantities of fruit for bottling, there will always come a day in the season when, on the way home she may see lovely peaches, apricots, pineapple even, at just the right price and asking to be 'put away' for that special recipe. Or perhaps a friend will offer some raspberries and there are the redcurrants in the local shop so that the family can look forward to delicious home-made tarts in the depths of winter. For the country housewife it will be a comfort to know that her pressure cooker is just waiting to deal with a sudden surplus of fruit when even the family cannot eat another gooseberry or strawberry and if just sufficient is picked daily, at its best, for one lot of bottling at a time, it need never become a chore.

The theory behind fruit bottling is simply that fruit must be brought to a certain temperature high enough to kill the moulds and yeasts on it and to arrest the agents in it which normally would cause it to become over-ripe and then to rot. This particular temperature can be reached in a pressure cooker in a matter of minutes so that the fruit is sterilised in only a fraction of the time which used to be necessary; quick, simple, effective, just what the busy housewife expects of her pressure cooker.

GENERAL INSTRUCTIONS

THE PRESSURE COOKER

As most fruits are soft it is important that they should not be overcooked in the processing, so the recommended pressure for fruit bottling therefore is **Low** (5 lb); if **High** (15 lb) pressure is used the same bottling times must be kept to, so as to ensure complete sterilisation even though this may mean that not quite such a good result is obtained.

As it is important that your pressure cooker should be working completely efficiently for this purpose, now might be a good time to check that neither the gasket nor the safety plug are showing any signs of leakage.

THE BOTTLING JARS

The most usual types of vacuum jars sold in this country are:

Screw-top, such as the Kilner with a specially surfaced metal cover fitted with a plastic ring and a screw-band. After the cover has been put on the screw-band is tightened down and then turned back a mere quarter turn to allow for any expansion of the jar during heating. After processing, the band is screwed down again as tightly as possible until the jar is ready to have the seal tested.

Clip-top jars have similar metal or glass covers with a separate rubber ring placed on the neck of the jar before the cover is positioned. The clip-top secures the cover allowing it to lift slightly during the processing and then holding it firmly while cooling to form the vacuum.

Clip-tops are also available for use on 1-lb and 2-lb jam jars and are entirely satisfactory, though it must be remembered that jam jars are not designed for this purpose and may crack because of the higher temperature required for bottling.

All equipment must be carefully looked at each year before being used again: check that the jars have no cracks or chips round the neck that could prevent a seal forming and see that the covers are in good condition and the rings have not stretched or perished. It is essential that the clips should still have plenty of spring in them; if they appear to be loose a good tip is to put a coin on the cover before putting on the clip, though this should be only a temporary remedy until new ones can be bought. Screw-bands should also be a good fit and, to prevent them rusting they should, after the seal has been tested, be washed, dried, wiped over with a little oil and put back loosely on the jars for storage.

THE FRUIT

Choose fresh, firm but ripe fruits with the exception of gooseberries which must be green and hard otherwise they will overcook. Do not be tempted to bottle damaged or over-ripe fruit just to save it.

The fruit in each jar should be as near the same size and ripeness as possible to ensure even cooking and be sure to prepare enough to fill the number of jars you have decided to do, remembering that there is always a certain amount of wastage from peeling, stoning and stringing.

Those fruits such as apples and pears which discolour when peeled should be dropped into a solution of 1 teaspoon of salt to 1 pint of water and just before packing be thoroughly rinsed in cold water.

As the bottling time is so short, hard fruits such as cooking pears may not be softened enough during the processing so they should be brought up to pressure in the cooker before being packed into the jars.

Fruits that need skinning such as tomatoes and peaches should be left in boiling water for about half a minute so that they can be easily peeled.

Soft fruits such as strawberries which shrink a lot when heated are best preserved according to the special instructions given as this ensures a good colour and a properly filled jar.

Bulky fruits or those which are over-plentiful such as apples, tomatoes, may be economically packed, following the instructions given, as purées or pulps.

THE SYRUP

While it is possible to bottle fruit in water it does not give such a good flavour or colour to fruit which is to be stored for any length of time and as fruit is acid, it is more economical in the end to use a syrup as the fruit then takes up the sweetening in the jars and requires less sugar to be added before serving. If a very heavy syrup is used this may cause the fruit to rise in the jars, but this is only a matter of looks and can often be avoided in any case by careful packing of the jars. Syrups may be average or thick and a good suggestion is to decide when bottling what the fruit is likely to be used for and let this decide the strength of the syrup. For instance, Pie fruit, using an average syrup of 6 to 8 oz per pint of water would be fruit that is to be cooked again, in pies, tarts, suet puddings, so that it can be further sweetened if necessary.

Dessert fruit, using a heavy syrup of 10 to 12 oz per pint of water would be fruit that could be turned straight out of the jars for serving.

Granulated or loaf sugar can be used and should be dissolved in the water in a small saucepan with a lip to make it easy to pour out and be allowed to boil for at least 1 minute just before use. Do not leave it boiling away madly for any length of time or it will evaporate.

If strawberries have been presoaked or pears precooked the syrup should be strained and reboiled before filling into the jars.

SPECIAL INSTRUCTIONS

CANNING

Use the same method for preparation of the fruit and syrup and the same pressure cooking time, following the canning machine manufacturer's instructions for closing the cans. These may be laid on their sides when packing into the cooker if this allows more to be processed at one time.

ADJUSTMENTS FOR ALTITUDE

If fruit bottling or canning at an altitude of more than 3,000 feet above sea-level use **M**edium (10 lb) pressure instead of **L**ow (5 lb), or increase the timings by 4 minutes if using **H**igh (15 lb) pressure.

INSTRUCTIONS FOR FRUIT BOTTLING

Check that the jars are clean, heat by filling with a little warm water and stand them, ready for packing in a large bowl half filled with boiling water.

Have ready in the cooker, the trivet, $1\frac{1}{2}$ pints of water to which has been added a spoonful of vinegar and put to boil.

Make the syrup and put to boil.

Put the covers and rubber rings into a small bowl and cover with boiling water.

Pack the jars firmly with the prepared fruit, layer upon layer working around the edges but always remembering to keep the centre filled in and just a little higher than the outsides. Except for very small or soft fruits such as currants and raspberries, each piece should be put in separately and always manage to get just one more in than you thought you possibly could. Only a tight pack with firm fruits such as cherries, halved apricots and peaches, pears, gooseberries, rhubarb in lengths will ensure a full, good-looking result which is the kind that will give the most satisfaction.

Soft fruits such as berries and apples, cannot be tightly packed and will therefore always tend to float in syrup.

Tomatoes in brine may squash a little during the processing so the jar may show some space at the top.

When the jars are packed to the very top, fill with the boiling syrup leaving at least $\frac{1}{4}$ inch headspace. To remove the air bubbles which may get caught among the fruit, only pour a little in at a time and twist the jar sharply from side to side before adding any more. Space must be left above the syrup as the fruit will make some juice of its own and if the jar is completely filled, the syrup may boil out and be wasted.

Wipe the rim of the jar before putting on the covers and adjust the screw-bands or clips. After screwing the bands down tightly, unscrew a mere quarter turn.

Lift the packed jars, filled with the boiling syrup, from the boiling water in the bowl into the boiling water in the cooker. This preheating of the jars will prevent them cracking when being heated quickly as the cooker is brought to pressure. The jars should not be allowed to touch each other or the sides of the cooker.

Bring to pressure on a medium heat, cook for the time given and leave the pressure to reduce at room temperature for at least 5 minutes.

Lift the jars out and if screw-bands have been used, screw them down as tightly as possible, doing this again at least once more before leaving the jars on one side to cool.

The next day, test the jars to make sure the seals have taken. Unscrew the bands or remove the clips and see if the covers can be lifted. If they are firm, the jars are ready for storage. If a vacuum has not been formed and the cover can be taken off, use the fruit at once and check the jar, cover and screw-band or clip before using again.

For storage, wipe the jar and cover, wash the screw-band and clip, dry, then smear them and the cover with a little oil to prevent rusting. The clips should be put away; the screw bands can be put back just resting on the jars but should not be screwed down in case any deterioration of the fruit should take place, when this will allow the covers to lift instead of the jars bursting. Label the jars with the date of bottling so that they are used in the right order and keep in a cool place and preferably in the dark to conserve the colour of the fruit.

Cans should be treated as given in the manufacturers' instructions.

INSTRUCTIONS FOR SOLID PACK FOR BERRIES

Prepare the fruit and lay in a single layer in a large bowl.

Boil a heavy syrup, pour over the fruit, cover and leave overnight.

Next day, lift the fruit carefully into the jars, packing them as given in the general instructions (p. 269) and leaving as much syrup behind as possible.

Reboil the syrup, fill the jars slowly and with plenty of twists to get rid of any air bubbles.

Continue as given in the general instructions, processing for 3 minutes.

These fruits will keep a good colour for 3 to 4 months if each jar is stored individually in a brown paper bag to be sure that the light is kept out. For longer storage, add a little artificial colouring to the syrup before boiling.

INSTRUCTIONS FOR BOTTLING FRUIT PULP OR PURÉE

For Pulp, prepare the fruit as for stewing, put into the cooker with $\frac{1}{2}$ pint of water but no sugar, bring to pressure in the usual way, cook for the required time (see Table, p. 182) and allow the pressure to reduce at room temperature. During the cooking, have the jars, etc, ready as given in the general instructions. Mash the fruit to a pulp and pour the pulp immediately, while still boiling hot into the jars. Be sure that the rim is wiped before putting on the covers, then continue as given in the general instructions (p. 269), processing for 1 minute.

For Purée, follow instructions for pulp but when the pressure is reduced, sieve the fruit then reboil the purée and pour at once into the jars leaving at least $\frac{1}{2}$ inch headspace. Be sure that the rim of the jar is wiped clean before putting on the cover. Continue as given in the general instructions, processing for 3 minutes for fruit, 5 minutes for tomato purées.

Citrus fruits such as Seville oranges, grapefruit, lemons, for marmalade making may be in season or at their cheapest when the housewife has still sufficient marmalade from previous years or is too busy to spare the time to make more. To preserve these fruits for later use weigh, prepare and cut them up in the usual way and pack loosely into the jars, leaving a 1 inch headspace and do not add any liquid. Process for 15 minutes according to the instructions. Label each jar with its actual weight of fruit and when making into marmalade, add sufficient water to bring the juice up to the required quantity and add the correct proportion of sugar, as given on pages 257, 258. The pulp will not require further softening.

DIRECTIONS FOR FRUIT BOTTLING

The times given are for 1-lb and 2-lb jars and for 1-lb cans.

FRUIT	PREPARATION	MINUTES AT LOW PRESSURE
Apples	Peel, core, cut in quarters or slices. Put in brine solution, until packed, then rinse well with cold water	1 minute
Apricots	Rinse fruit in cold water. If left whole, prick with fork once or twice; if halved, remove stones	1 minute
Blackberries	Wash if necessary. May be packed with sliced apples ready for pies or tarts	1 minute
Blackcurrants	String, rinse in cold water, drain	1 minute
Cherries	Wash and stalk; whole; if stoned add juice from fruit to syrup and reboil	1 minute
Damsons	Rinse in cold water; leave whole, prick once or twice with a fork	1 minute
Greengages	Rinse in cold water; leave whole, prick once or twice with a fork	1 minute

FRUIT	PREPARATION	MINUTES AT 5 LB PRESSURE
Gooseberries	Rinse in cold water. Must be hard and green or will burst in the cooking	1 minute
Loganberries	Pick over very carefully, and rinse, drain. Follow instructions for soft fruit pack	3 minutes
Mulberries	As above	3 minutes
Peaches	Peel by leaving in boiling water $\frac{1}{2}$–1 minute. Halve and stone. If large, cut in quarters or slices	3 minutes (halved) 1 minute (sliced)
Pears	Peel and core and put in brine solution until ready for packing, rinse with cold water	3 minutes
	If hard-cooking variety, pressure cook in syrup at 15 lb for 1–3 minutes, reboil the syrup before pouring over the fruit in the jars	3 minutes
Pineapple	Cut in $\frac{1}{2}$-inch slices, cut away skin, remove eyes, leave in slices or cut in cubes	3 minutes
Plums	Remove stalks, wash in cold water. If left whole, prick once or twice with fork. If halved, remove stones	1 minute
Raspberries	Follow instructions for soft fruit pack	3 minutes
	Unless being bottled with redcurrants, when use equal quantity of the fruits and pack loosely	1 minute
Redcurrants	Stalk, rinse with cold water and drain	1 minute
Rhubarb	Cut off leaves and base of stems. Wipe and cut into even lengths just to reach the shoulders of the jar for the outside pieces and the top of the jar for the centre pieces. Squeeze in as many lengths as you can as rhubarb shrinks a great deal when cooked	1 minute (forced) 2 minutes (garden)
Strawberries	Follow instructions for soft fruit	3 minutes
Tomatoes	Small, whole, unpeeled. Add boiling brine, 1 level teaspoon salt, pinch of sugar per pint of water instead of syrup	3 minutes
	Peeled by leaving in boiling water for $\frac{1}{2}$ to 1 minute; pack small ones whole, large may be halved or quartered. Do not add liquid; sprinkle each layer with a little salt and a pinch of sugar	
Fruit Salad	If several different fruits have been bottled and there are enough pieces left over to make up one or two jars, these can be processed as fresh fruit salad giving the time for the fruit which requires the longest cooking	

FAULTS IN FRUIT BOTTLING

If a jar has not sealed: the jar, cover and band or clip should be checked; care should be taken to tighten the screw-band immediately after processing.

Poor colour of fruit: it may have been under- or over-ripe, have been processed too long or the jars may not have been stored in the cool and the dark.

Discoloration of fruit at the top of the jar: while the jar may have sealed all the air has not been expelled—just what would happen if the fruit was left peeled or cut and uncovered in the kitchen. Care must be taken to get rid of the air bubbles when filling with syrup, the screw-bands must be loosened slightly for processing and the correct cooking time must be given. Check, too, that the inside of the cover, against the fruit, is not rusted or corroded.

Fruit rising in the jar: the fruit was over-ripe and has over-cooked; the jar was not packed tightly enough or, if a very heavy syrup has been used, the fruit itself is lighter and just simply floats.

Air bubbles in tight packs such as strawberries: this can be avoided by adding the syrup as the jar is packed, covering each layer in turn.

Cloudy fluid in the jars: the fruit was dirty or over-ripe.

Sediment in the jars: probably the water used for the syrup was very hard. This will not be harmful.

Mould on fruit or fermentation: jars not processed for long enough or at the full, correct pressure; a slight leak round the jar which will eventually loosen the cover. Open the jar at once, being careful when doing this if it has fermented because it will open like a bottle of pop, and discard the contents.

VEGETABLE BOTTLING

Unless the town housewife is able to obtain freshly picked vegetables and can get them from garden to bottling jar in a very short space of time, it is not recommended that vegetable bottling should be undertaken for, as fresh vegetables are now obtainable all the year round and with the wide selection of frozen vegetables also to be found in the shops this process, which must be very carefully done and almost scientifically carried out, would not really be worth while. Even for the country housewife with her own garden it is usually the very young or luxury vegetables or those with a very short season such as asparagus, peas, sweet corn for which, if she has plenty, she may want to carry out this lengthy process.

Vegetables, unlike fruit, are non-acid foods and therefore do not contain in themselves the acids which will prevent bacteria forming. Unless these are destroyed by exposure to a much higher temperature than that obtainable in an ordinary saucepan these heat-resistant bacteria may cause spoilage of vegetables in jars or cans which cannot be detected by sight, smell or taste. For these reasons, safety when bottling vegetables can only be assured if a pressure cooker is used and this is the only method recommended at present by the Ministry of Agriculture, Fisheries and Food for domestic preservation. It must be carried out exactly and to the letter, and if there is any doubt at all about the contents of the jar when it is opened they should be discarded and kept away from pets.

GENERAL INSTRUCTIONS

THE PRESSURE COOKER

The only recommended pressure for vegetable bottling is **M**edium (10 lb). If **L**ow (5 lb) pressure were used the temperature reached would not be high enough to ensure the complete destruction of all bacteria, while **H**igh (15 lb) pressure, having regard to the length of the processing, would tend to lower the quality of the vegetables in appearance and flavour.

Provided that your pressure cooker has been checked that it is in good working order to register 10 lb pressure and that the instructions are carefully followed, this process will be satisfactory and safe and can be completed with absolute confidence.

THE BOTTLING JARS

Information as to these will be found under the same heading in the Fruit Bottling section (pp. 266/7) and applies equally here except that, owing to the necessary prolonged heating of the jars it is not recommended that jam jars be used.

VEGETABLES

All vegetables should be young, fresh and in prime condition; leafy ones such as brussels sprouts, spinach, are too difficult to be processed in the home and are not recommended. All should be thoroughly washed and cleaned in several changes of water and root vegetables should be well scrubbed before peeling.

It is necessary to scald vegetables before packing them into the jars as this ensures their cleanliness, shrinks them and helps to set their colour. This is done by plunging them in a large pan of boiling water for a given time, then rinsing them under cold water to facilitate handling.

Vegetables, unlike fruit, should not be packed tightly; the jars should be well filled but the vegetables should not be pressed down or crammed in.

THE BRINE

This is prepared in the proportion of 1 level tablespoon of kitchen, not table, salt per pint of water and must be poured, boiling, into the jars to fill them. For green vegetables, such as peas and French or runner beans, artificial colouring brighter than will be required in the finished jar as it too will be affected by the cooking, should be added to the brine and if liked, 1 level tablespoon of sugar per pint can be put into the brine for peas.

GENERAL INSTRUCTIONS FOR BOTTLING

Having prepared and blanched the vegetables, the instructions for fruit bottling should now be followed right through (pp. 269/70), using 10 lb pressure and giving the processing times as set out in the following table.

Almost all bottles of vegetables show a considerable loss of liquid at the end of the processing. This is due to the long time for processing leading to rapid boiling of the liquid in the jars; it would not interfere with the keeping quality, even if the jars were to be completely empty of liquid and under no circumstances must the jars be opened and filled up to replace the liquid lost unless the whole sterilising process is gone through again.

FOR SERVING

The vegetables should be reboiled in their own brine and any left will make an excellent base for soups, stews, etc.

CANNING

Complete instructions for canning vegetables, including those for pressure cooking, will be found in the canning machine manufacturer's manual and must be followed to the letter.

If more than two jars of vegetables are being bottled at one session it will save time and fuel if all are blanched, using the pressure cooker, according to the time-table given on p. 277, at one time.

DIRECTIONS FOR VEGETABLE BOTTLING

VEGETABLE	PREPARATION	BLANCHING TIME (MINUTES)	MINUTES AT 10 LB PRESSURE
Asparagus	Trim, scrape off scales, cut in even lengths, tie in bundles and pack upright, stalks uppermost	2–3	35
Beans			
Broad	Varieties recommended which will not turn brown are Green Windsor and Triple White	3	40
French	String if necessary, break off ends, pack whole. Green Refugee is the recommended variety	3	40
Runner	Scarlet Emperor is the recommended variety. String and slice	3	40
Beetroot	Choose young small ones and leave whole or slice or dice	15–20	40
Carrots	If young, leave whole; if older slice or dice	5	40
Celery	Use the hearts only. Pack head down	6	35
Mushrooms	Field varieties. Cut off nearly all stalk, wash, peel, put on trays in oven and sprinkle with salt and pepper and leave until juice has been extracted. Pack hot into jars and cover with own juice	15–20	35
Peas	Onward, Laxton, Lincoln are the recommended varieties. If very dry season or unless picked fresh and young, peas may tend to burst and leave a starchy deposit in the jar	2	45
Potatoes	Only new ones at the beginning of the season are worth home-bottling	5	45
Sweet Corn	Golden Bantams, Evergreen, recommended. Shuck, silk, wash. Cut from cob to obtain whole kernels	3	50
Vegetable Macedoine	Diced mixed vegetables of any kind. Blanch and process according to the longest-timed vegetables		

POULTRY AND MEAT BOTTLING

This again requires the use of a pressure cooker, but as this is a very specialised process and not of general interest the instructions are not given here. Those set out in the pressure cooker manufacturer's manual or the complete booklet issued by the Ministry of Agriculture, Fisheries and Food, Bulletin No 21 obtainable from HM Stationery Office should be consulted and followed.

INSTRUCTIONS FOR BLANCHING VEGETABLES READY FOR DEEP-FREEZING

When undertaking deep freezing of vegetables, the first process must be blanching or scalding, otherwise the vegetables may develop unpleasant flavours from the action of the enzymes which they contain and they may not retain a good colour in storage. After the young, tender vegetables have been cleaned and picked over they are blanched, in the normal way in a large quantity of boiling water for a given time, then are plunged into cold water to prevent overcooking and to cool them as quickly as possible so that they can be handled and the process be continued.

For full instructions, follow those given by the manufacturers of your deep-freezer, but, for certain of the larger, longer-cooking vegetables blanching can be done quickly and satisfactory with your pressure cooker saving time and fuel, as large quantities of boiling water are not necessary and this will also mean much less steam in the kitchen.

Only vegetables which are suited to blanching with the pressure cooker are included in the following table: have ½ pint of hot water in the cooker before putting in the vegetables and use the trivet.

	PRESSURE	BLANCHING TIME
Asparagus (thick stems)	Low (5 lb)	1 minute
Beans		
Broad	„ (5 lb)	To pressure only
French or Runner	„ (5 lb)	To pressure only
Beetroot (unskinned)	High (15 lb)	5–15 minutes, according to size
Broccoli	Low (5 lb)	To pressure only
Brussels Sprouts	„ (5 lb)	1 minute
Carrots (unpeeled)	High (15 lb)	2 minutes
Corn-on-the-Cob	„ (15 lb)	2 minutes
Peas	Low (5 lb)	To pressure only

Reduce pressure immediately as soon as the blanching time is up.

SECTION XIII

Other Uses for the Pressure Cooker

It must not be forgotten that a pressure cooker is also a very efficient small steriliser and as such can be used in the home if required for sterilising syringes, small instruments, bandages, rubber gloves and by chemists, doctors, veterinary surgeons and others who need to sterilise small quantities of eye-drops for example, or phials, surgical instruments, etc. All these have been tested under laboratory conditions and complete sterilisation has been achieved and can be fully recommended. Examples of methods and times are as follows:

STERILISATION OF MEDICAL INSTRUMENTS

20–30 minutes at 15 lb (fixed) pressure

If the instruments are put directly into the cooker the shorter time, at the equivalent temperature of 250° F or 120° C will be sufficient.

If the instruments are wrapped, perhaps to be carried some distance after sterilisation, or are put into a container to facilitate handling, the longer time should be given to allow for the steam and heat to penetrate the covering.

The pressure should be allowed to reduce at room temperature for at least 10 minutes at the end of the sterilising time.

STERILISATION OF EYE-DROPS

20 minutes at High (15 lb) pressure

The pressure cooker has been recommended by the Pharmaceutical Journal for the purpose of sterilising the distilled water, the containers and all measures used in the preparation of eye-drops.

STERILISATION OF DRY CLOTHS, BANDAGES, ETC.

20–30 minutes at High (15 lb) pressure

These must be laid on a flat dish standing on the trivet and be covered over completely with a piece of nylon film to prevent the steam as it condenses when the pressure is reducing, from moistening them.

STERILISATION OF RUBBER GLOVES

20 minutes at High (15 lb) pressure

These can be done on the trivet and this process does not in any way cause quicker deterioration of the material than the use of other forms of sterilisers.

STERILISATION OF ADHESIVE FLOUR PASTES

10 minutes at High (15 lb) pressure

This method may be found convenient for such pastes, to be used under laboratory or particularly, tropical conditions, to ensure a uniform consistency and the absence of moulds.

The mixed paste should be put into an enamel bowl and after pressure has been reduced be beaten until smooth with a fork.

SECTION XIV

Your Pressure Cooker Out and About

When you reach this chapter, I am sure you will not need to be convinced that for those who are considering an outdoor holiday, camping, caravanning, boating, a pressure cooker is a must and the first item to be included on the equipment list. Just think of all the advantages its use will bring: complete meals in the one pan so handy when a small stove or one burner is all that is being taken along: so sparing of fuel when this has to be carried and might take up too much space if large cans or containers were necessary; so economical on food bills allowing for less expensive foods to be bought yet cooked satisfactorily, which is important if one is holidaying on a budget; so safe on small stoves or on tossing boats as everything is sealed in the pan and even if the cooker is toppled over it will not spill; so light on water supplies which may have to be carried or fetched a distance as it requires only the minimum for pressure cooking—indeed, in these and many other ways the pressure cooker has proved itself and found its way to many strange places such as the Himalayas with the Everest expedition, a lone Atlantic crossing in a rowing boat and overland to the Far East and Australia.

Wherever you go you will find your pressure cooker arousing interest, encouraging people to talk to you about it and what you are doing—a real friend, in every sense.

The recipes given here are mostly composite ones, to serve a substantial dish for four as a first course, out of the one pan and could most suitably be followed by fresh fruit, bought pastries, etc, or by a pudding, pressure cooked first and kept hot in a bowl or pan of boiling water or to be served cold.

Where tinned foods are to be served, meat and pastas are best turned into a solid container for reheating putting at least $\frac{1}{2}$ pint water in the cooker itself, bringing to pressure in the usual way and cooking for 1 to 3 minutes according to the type of food and the time recommended. Vegetables should be opened, strained and be heated through in a perforated container for the larger ones such as potatoes, carrots, etc, or in a solid container for peas, beans, etc, when they will be less likely to become overcooked if being done with other foods. It is not essential to turn out of the tins, which can be successfully reheated unopened allowing about one-third of the time given on the tin but this way they take up quite a lot of room and probably not enough could be reheated at once to satisfy the family. If using two containers, put a solid one first in the bottom of the cooker in the water using the trivet as a platform on which to stand the second container. The top one, if solid, should then be covered with a piece of greaseproof paper (from round the butter or margarine would be fine) to prevent the steam falling back into the container as liquid when pressure is reduced.

Nowadays there are so many easily carried and packed cooking aids to save extra work and saucepans that it is a good idea to take a selection of them with you. Among these would be packets of bouquet garni, white and various sauces, gravy powder, grated cheese, suet crust mixes, dehydrated vegetables and a selection of packet soups which, by their various flavours, can make a basic stew or dish seem different every day.

These could be added or substituted for ingredients given in the following recipes.

As a final bonus for those cooking out and about—if the cooker is stood in a bowl of water to reduce the pressure it will heat the water which will then be most useful for the washing up.

BAKED BEAN SOUP

Pressure Cooking Time: 5 minutes

2 tins of butter beans; 1 tin of tomatoes; 1 large onion sliced; 1 pint of water with a little meat extract added; 2 tablespoons flour, 2 tablespoons butter or margarine creamed together; salt, pepper, Worcester Sauce if available; any left over meat, cut up small, if available; fresh rolls to accompany.

Lift the trivet from the cooker, put in the strained beans, the tomatoes, onion, liquid and seasoning, bring to pressure in the usual way, cook for 5 minutes and reduce the pressure with cold water. During this cooking, beat the flour and fat together in a cup until creamy. Stir the soup well, breaking the beans up into smaller pieces, add a little more water or the liquid from the beans if the soup is now very thick, put in the diced meat, then beat in, a little at a time as the soup is reheated, the creamed thickening. Retaste and correct seasoning and serve with rolls or chunks of French bread.

BAKED BEANS WITH PORK OR HAM

Pressure Cooking Time: 20 minutes

$\frac{1}{2}$ lb small haricot beans; 1 large peeled and sliced onion; 2 tablespoons of green diced pepper if available; 4 thick slices of fat bacon or salt pork cut into 1-inch pieces; 3 tablespoons of brown sugar; 1 teaspoon of dry mustard; 1 pint of water; salt and pepper.

Overnight or in the morning after breakfast, boil the water, pour over the beans, cover and leave to soak. Lift the trivet from the cooker and fry the meat until golden brown. Add the onion and mustard and leave for a minute or two, then put in the beans with the soaking water, the sugar, green pepper and the seasoning. Bring to pressure in the usual way, cook for 20 minutes and leave the pressure to reduce of its own accord. Serve piping hot.

CHICKEN WITH DUMPLINGS

Pressure Cooking Time: 5 minutes
Ordinary Cooking Time: 10 minutes

1 boiling chicken; 1 pint of water with chicken cube if available; seasoning; 1 packet of frozen peas or a tin; dumplings made from 8 tablespoons of flour, 4 tablespoons of shredded suet, salt, cold water to mix (or a packet of suet pudding mixture bought before leaving); 2 tablespoons of flour blended with a little milk or stock for thickening.

Joint the chicken; lift out the trivet, put in the liquid, the chicken pieces and the seasoning, bring to pressure in the usual way, cook for 5 minutes and reduce the pressure with cold water. During this cooking, prepare the dumplings and shape into eight balls. Put in the peas, return the pan to the heat and allow the liquid to boil, add the dumplings and boil for 10 minutes during which time the cooker should be just covered with a plate. Lift out the dumplings and the chicken pieces, add the thickening, reboil, taste and correct seasoning and cook for a minute or two. Serve with some of the sauce poured over the chicken, the rest kept hot in the cooker until required.

GIPSY STEW

Pressure Cooking Time: 10 minutes or 10 minutes to the pound

$1\frac{1}{2}$ lb veal pieces or a piece of veal on the bone weighing $2\frac{1}{2}$–3 lb; 1 onion; 2 slices of streaky bacon; 1 pint of water; seasoning; 1 small tin of tomatoes or tomato purée or paste; 1 tin or packet of frozen peas; sufficient potatoes cut to cook in 4 minutes; a little butter; flour for thickening if necessary.

Toss the veal pieces in seasoning or sprinkle seasoning over the joint. Dice the onion and bacon. Lift the trivet from the cooker. Melt the butter and gently cook the diced onion, put in the veal and the water, bring to pressure in the usual way and cook for all but 4 minutes of the cooking time. If the meat is on the bone, lift out, take off the meat and cut into large dice. Put back into the cooker with the peas and potatoes, bring to pressure again, cook for the remaining 4 minutes and reduce the pressure with cold water. Lift out the meat and potatoes, add the tomatoes or purée to taste, correct the seasoning, add the thickening if necessary, reboil and cook for a minute or two and pour over the meat and vegetables.

If you are staying long enough to have anywhere to store things, the veal bone could be cooked again with 1 pint of water, some vegetables and seasoning to make some good stock for another soup or meat dish.

LAMB AND KIDNEY STEW

Pressure Cooking Time: 12 minutes

1–2 lb shoulder of lamb cut into 2-inch cubes (keep bone to go in with the ingredients to give a good stock); 2 kidneys; 2 tablespoons fat; 2 onions; 2 carrots; 2 turnips or any other vegetable available; whole potatoes for four; ½ pint water; seasoning; thickening and gravy colouring as required.

Cut the meat from the bone and into 2-inch dice, toss in seasoned flour, slice the onions, carrots and other vegetables, peel the potatoes. Lift the trivet from the cooker, heat the fat and brown the onions well. Add the meat and brown on all sides. Take the cooker from the heat, allow to cool slightly, add the water and stir to take any brown bits off the bottom of the pan. Put in the bone, the vegetables and seasoning, bring to pressure in the usual way, cook for 12 minutes and reduce the pressure with cold water. Lift out the bone; add the thickening and colouring as necessary, reboil, taste and correct seasoning, cook for 2 to 3 minutes and serve piping hot. If you have any redcurrant or mint jelly or sauce with you, a teaspoonful can be added just before serving.

MACARONI PICNIC

Pressure Cooking Time: 6 minutes

½ lb macaroni; 1 pint water with salt; 1 tablespoon butter or margarine, 1 level tablespoon flour; 1 small tin of tomato soup; pepper and a teaspoon of sugar; grated cheese.

Lift the trivet from the cooker, put in the salted water, allow to boil, throw in the macaroni, bring to pressure in the usual way, cook for 6 minutes and reduce the pressure with cold water. Strain the macaroni, saving the water and keep hot by covering with the cooker lid. Melt the fat in the pan, add the flour and cook without colouring, add the tomato soup, reboil and cook until it thickens if necessary adding a little of the macaroni water to obtain the correct consistency of a pouring sauce. Taste and correct seasoning, stir in the macaroni, reheat and serve sprinkled thickly with cheese.

If there was any meat or cooked sausages left over from another meal or a small tin of corned beef could be spared this, chopped, could be added with the macaroni for the reheating.

MEAT LOAF DINNER

Pressure Cooking Time: 15 minutes

This loaf is best made early in the day so that it has time to become firm before cooking.

1 lb of minced beef; 2 slices of dry bread soaked in hot water; 2 onions; pinch of mixed herbs; seasoning; egg; 2 tablespoons of fat; ½ pint water; sufficient potatoes, carrots or other vegetables for the family, to cook in 5 minutes; thickening and colouring as required for the gravy.

Press the excess water from the bread; dice the onions finely and combine thoroughly with the meat, seasonings, herbs and bread. Bind firmly but not too moistly with egg, roll tightly in a piece of greaseproof paper and allow to stand. Lift the trivet from the cooker, heat the fat and fry the meat roll all over until really brown. Lift out and roll again loosely in the paper. Put the water and trivet in the cooker, then the roll, bring to pressure in the usual way, cook for 10 minutes and reduce the pressure with cold water. Lift out the roll, pile in the potatoes, carrots, etc, and season well. Put back the roll, bring to pressure again, cook for 5 minutes and reduce the pressure with cold water. Lift out the roll, serve the vegetables, take out the trivet, thicken and colour the gravy as required, reboil, taste and correct seasoning and cook for 2 to 3 minutes. Unwrap the roll and serve with some of the gravy poured over or, cut into slices, put a portion on each plate with a little gravy and keep the rest hot, until required, in the cooker.

PORK CHOPS, AMERICAN STYLE

Pressure Cooking Time: 7–8 minutes

4 pork chops about ¾ inch thick; 2 tablespoons dripping or fat; 2 onions; ½ pint stock or water; 4 hard eating apples; 2 tablespoons ready-made stuffing; 4 cloves; sufficient medium potatoes for 4; packet of frozen peas (thawed out); flour for thickening; seasoning; gravy colouring if necessary.

Wipe, trim the chops and season well. Peel and slice the onions; wash, peel and core the apples and fill the centres two-thirds full with stuffing and stick each with a clove. Prepare the potatoes. Lift the trivet from the cooker, heat the fat, brown the chops well on both sides and lift out. Brown the onions, add the hot liquid (if cold, allow the cooker to cool), the trivet, then the chops and on top again, the potatoes in a perforated container. Bring to pressure in the usual way, cook for 7 to 8 minutes, reduce the pressure with cold water. Put in the thawed-out peas in a perforated container, cover with a piece of foil or greaseproof paper, put in the apples, bring to pressure again, remove immediately and allow the pressure to reduce of its own accord. Lift out the apples and peas; serve a portion of potatoes and a chop with an apple on top surrounded with peas on each plate. Lift out the trivet, add the blended flour and colouring if necessary, reboil the gravy, taste to correct seasoning and cook a few moments. Pour a little carefully round the chops and leave the rest in the cooker to keep hot until required.

SCALLOPED POTATOES WITH HAM

Pressure Cooking Time: 8 minutes

8 medium potatoes; 4 portions of raw ham slices; a little made mustard; ½ pint thin white sauce (this could be bought in packets before leaving); seasoning; golden crumbs; a large bowl or dish which will fit in the cooker; ½ pint water for the cooker.

Wash, peel and slice the potatoes thickly; spread the ham slices thinly with the mustard. Grease the bowl with a little butter. Put in the sliced potatoes seasoning each layer well. On top put the prepared slices of ham and pour the white sauce over—remember this dish must be large enough for there to be at least 1 inch spare above the sauce or it will boil over. Put the water, trivet and covered bowl in the cooker, bring to pressure in the usual way, cook for 8 minutes and allow the pressure to reduce of its own accord. Serve sprinkled with golden crumbs or grated cheese if available.

If you cannot put a large enough bowl into the cooker for the family appetites you may be able to use two shallow ones and stand one on top of the other with the trivet in between, covering the top one with greaseproof paper or foil.

SHORT CUT RISOTTO

Pressure Cooking Time: 10 minutes

2 tablespoons margarine or oil; 1 medium onion, sliced; 1 large cup (8 oz) rice; 1 small tin mushrooms; 2 or 3 bacon rinds or slices streaky bacon; 1 pint of water (liquid from mushrooms could be included); 1 small, sliced apple; ½ lb skinned, quartered tomatoes; 2 tablespoons tomato or other sauce; 2 tablespoons sultanas; a bay leaf if available; seasoning; 1 small tin of spam or luncheon meat; seasoning; 2 tablespoons grated cheese.

Lift the trivet from the cooker, heat the fat and fry the bacon rinds or chopped bacon until golden. Add the onion, mushrooms and rice and allow to cook a moment or two in the fat. Add the liquid, apple, tomatoes, sultanas, sauce, seasonings and the meat cut into $\frac{1}{2}$-inch dice. Stir well, bring to pressure in the usual way, cook for 10 minutes and reduce the pressure with cold water. Lift out the bacon rinds and bay leaf, taste and correct seasoning, and serve, piping hot, handing the grated cheese separately or sprinkled over the top.

FROZEN PRECOOKED MEALS OF MEAT, CHICKEN, ETC.

Where it is recommended that these should be reheated for 15 to 30 minutes you will find it a great help, particularly if living alone, out and about or in a great hurry, that this can be done in the pressure cooker with, or without, accompanying vegetables. If you were going to pressure cook vegetables, put these in the cooker as you usually do, put the precooked meal in its container stood in a pie dish or something suitable to collect any gravy should it run out and stand on top of the other foods, or if being reheated on its own put the dish on the trivet. A pressure cooking time of 3, 4 or 5 minutes will thoroughly reheat these foods, whether they are started from frozen or thawed, and they will not mind whether pressure is reduced at once or at room temperature.

COFFEE DESSERT

Even on an outdoor holiday, one may still have visitors and want to put on a special meal. This recipe will make a really extravagant dessert and can be served even round the camp fire. The basis of caramelised milk must be prepared overnight.

Pressure Cooking Time: $1\frac{1}{4}$ hours

1 tin of sweetened, condensed milk; $1\frac{1}{2}$ pints water with a little vinegar or lemon juice for the cooker; $\frac{1}{4}$ pint hot, very strong coffee; 2 tablespoons of chopped nuts if available; sweetened whipped cream for decoration with a few pieces of crystallised cherry if available.

For the crumb pastry shell: 20 rich tea biscuits; 3 tablespoons melted butter; 2 tablespoons sugar.

Put the water, trivet and the unopened tin of condensed milk into the cooker. Bring to pressure in the usual way, cook for $1\frac{1}{4}$ hours, allow the pressure to reduce at room temperature, lift out the tin and leave overnight. Next morning, make the pastry shell, mixing the finely crushed biscuits and sugar in a basin with the melted butter. Press this mixture evenly on to a deep plate or pie dish and leave to set while making the filling. Turn the caramelised milk out of the tin into a large bowl, slowly stir in the hot coffee, add the chopped nuts and beat until quite smooth. Pile on the pastry shell, allow to cool and just before serving, decorate with the whipped cream, cherries, etc.

If a coffee flavour is not liked, concentrated fruit juice can be used instead, or, after beating, sliced bananas can be stirred in, a few being reserved for decoration.

If your housekeeping does not include crystallised cherries, take three or four of the children's fruit jellies, halve them and set them in the cream, cut side up to give colour.

TOPPED APPLE PUDDING

Pressure Cooking Time: 5 minutes steaming;
15 minutes at 15 lb

This is a real camping way to make a pudding, which can be served direct from the cooker.

4 large cooking apples; 3–4 oz sugar to taste; $\frac{1}{2}$ teaspoon grated nutmeg, 2 or 3 cloves or strip of lemon rind for flavouring; 3 tablespoons cold water; 8 oz suet crust.

This pudding should be made following the instructions for **Sea Pie**, p. 122, putting the water, sugar, sliced apples and flavouring into the cooker instead of the meat.

MADELEINES

Pressure Cooking Time: 5 minutes steaming;
10 minutes at 15 lb

Here is a quick way of having your own home-made cakes for tea.

3 eggs and their weight in butter, sugar, flour; a little vanilla essence; some red jam diluted with a very little water, desiccated coconut, glacé cherries and angelica if available; $\frac{3}{4}$ pint water with lemon juice or vinegar for cooker.

Use small greased teacups and fill each only half full. This quantity should make eight to ten madeleines and they can be cooked with four standing in the water in the cooker covered with a double thickness of greased greaseproof paper, then the trivet, then four more cups, covered as before. Make the madeleines as given for **Canary Pudding,** and cook as given in the instructions on pp. 159/60. When the cakes are cold, trim them so that they stand level and are of even height (any cake trimmings could be used for the **Golden Crumble** recipe). Warm the jam with the water in a small saucepan, put each cake in turn on a skewer and dip into the jam, turning round to coat all over evenly, then roll in the coconut. Dip halved cherries and little angelica leaves in the jam and decorate the top of each madeleine.

SECTION XV

Miscellaneous

SAUCES

However much care and attention has gone into the preparation of a dish it can always be improved in flavour and food value by a well-made sauce. Very often it is indeed 'the sauce that makes the dish'. Nowadays, there is a large selection of ready-made sauces which are invaluable if time is short, but it is much more satisfying to make one's own and so easy to become a sauce expert, particularly using the concentrated stocks and juices from pressure cooking which form such an ideal base and should never be wasted.

Even the plainest food can be made more appetising by the clever choice of a sauce, while others, which may be traditional, are served as an aid to digestion, to bring out a particular flavour or to improve the appearance of the main dish.

Accompanying sauces are prepared separately in an ordinary saucepan as they require stirring during the cooking. When made, they may be kept hot by standing in a larger saucepan or dish one-third filled with hot water, over a low heat, so that they will not overcook or burn. To prevent a skin forming, just lay a circle of dampened greaseproof paper over the top until required for serving.

Sauces may be divided for easy reference into groups: white, brown, mayonnaise, sweet and miscellaneous and examples of these, following a basic foundation sauce for each type, are given here.

As a general rule, sauces are made in two consistencies, either a coating sauce requiring 1 tablespoon of flour to a ½ pint of liquid or pouring sauce requiring 1 level tablespoon of flour to a ½ pint of liquid. Thickened gravies to accompany pot roasts, stuffed joints, hot meat rolls and so on require 1 dessertspoon flour to a ½ pint of liquid. Other thickening agents, for special sauces, are cream and yolks of eggs.

For all sauces accompanying savoury dishes, the liquid used should include some of the stock or liquid from the food cooked, so as to make sure that none of the goodness of the food is wasted.

FOUNDATION WHITE SAUCE

1 tablespoon butter or margarine; 1 tablespoon flour; salt and pepper; ½ pint liquid (milk and liquid from the cooking).

In a small saucepan, allow the fat to melt but without colouring. Add the flour and cook gently, stirring over a low heat for a minute or two, again without allowing to colour. Remove from the heat, add the liquid gradually, stirring all the time, return to the heat, bring to the boil and cook for 2 to 3 minutes still stirring. Add the seasoning, taste to check and keep hot until ready to serve.

In many of the preceding recipes the sauce is begun during the pressure cooking, using milk or stock as half the liquid and the cooking liquid being added, after pressure has been reduced, to give the required consistency.

Variations of this sauce are:

Anchovy: With fish stock and anchovy essence added to taste.
Caper: With fish stock and one tablespoon of chopped capers.
Egg: With one finely chopped hard-boiled egg.
Mustard: With one teaspoon dry mustard added with the flour. A little vinegar may also be added for sharpness.
Parsley: With one to two dessertspoons finely chopped fresh parsley.

BECHAMEL

A slightly richer white sauce requiring that, before addition to the white roux, the milk is boiled with an onion stuck with two cloves and a piece of carrot for 20 minutes or so, in a covered saucepan. The rest of the liquid may be fish, meat, poultry or game stock or from the cooked dish; 1 tablespoon of cream is added just before serving.

Variations of this sauce are:

Celery: With ½ lb celery purée and ¼ pint of the celery stock.

Mornay or Cheese: With the addition of two to three tablespoons of grated or Parmesan cheese. A little dry, white wine may also be added.

Soubise or Onion: With two large sliced or puréed boiled onions, a little nutmeg and cream.

Suprême or Mushroom: With sliced fresh, cooked mushrooms and their liquor or sliced tinned mushrooms and the juice of a quarter of a lemon.

QUICK TOMATO CREAM SAUCE

½ pint white sauce; 1 small tin of tomatoes or tomato purée; a little cream.

Make the white sauce and keep hot. If using tinned tomatoes, drain and sieve to give a thick purée. Heat this but do not boil then stir in one or two spoonfuls of cream. Add this to the white sauce, whisk well together, reheat but do not allow to boil.

This sauce is excellent with fish for an invalid or infant dish, with savoury meat rolls and balls and for cereal and pasta dishes.

FOUNDATION BROWN SAUCE

1 tablespoon dripping; 1 small onion; 1–2 tablespoons flour; ½ pint stock or cooking liquid; salt and pepper.

In a small saucepan, melt the dripping and fry the onion until golden. Add the flour and cook, over a low heat, stirring all the time until dark brown but not burnt. Remove from the heat, gradually add the liquid, stirring all the time, return to the heat and cook for 2 to 3 minutes until thick, still stirring. Add the seasoning, taste to check and keep hot until required.

For use with fish, add one teaspoon of vinegar.

Variations of this sauce are:

Espagnole: A piece of streaky bacon, a tomato and a pinch of herbs should be allowed to cook gently with the onion for 5 minutes or so. Sieve the sauce before serving, add one or two tablespoons of sherry, reheat, but do not allow to boil.

Madeira: With two tablespoons tomato purée, reheat and add two tablespoons Madeira instead of the sherry, but do not allow to boil.

Reforme: With only one tablespoon of sherry and with one dessertspoon of red-currant jelly, one tablespoon of port wine and a pinch of cayenne added while the sauce is simmered for 10 minutes or so before serving.

EGG SAUCES

The basis of these sauces is yolk of egg and butter whisked together, the volume increasing as more butter is added. Great care must be taken with them as curdling can easily occur and patience is needed to achieve the correct result, which is well worth while. At least half an hour must be allowed for making a sauce of this kind and all one's attention must be given to it. A small milk saucepan, a small heat-proof basin or one of the boilable plastic bowls and a small wire whisk are the equipment required, and it is best to make only small quantities as these sauces are very rich and it is difficult to reheat them to serve a second time.

HOLLANDAISE

Have ready a small saucepan about half full of hot, not boiling, water, and over a very low heat. Throughout the cooking the water must not boil and this may be found easier if an asbestos mat is used. Put into the bowl 1 dessertspoon of strained lemon juice, 1 teaspoon of cold water and 1 tablespoon of butter. When this is melted, whisk in a beaten yolk of a large egg and continue whisking until the sauce begins to thicken slightly. Then add another 2 tablespoons of butter piece by piece and whisking continuously in between each addition until the sauce thickens and will leave a trail and is shiny like mayonnaise. Remove the basin from the heat and continue stirring while adding salt, pepper and more strained lemon juice to taste until the bowl is just warm. Cover, stand on one side until required when give a final stir.

MOUSSELINE

For savoury dishes: add 1 tablespoon of thick whipped cream and beat in, just before serving.

For sweet dishes: use 1 dessertspoon of maraschino instead of the lemon juice, 1 dessertspoon of sugar instead of seasoning and a whipped white of egg can be beaten in with the cream just before serving.

If any Hollandaise or savoury Mousseline Sauce is left over, stir in some chopped chives, parsley, gherkins as available and allow to get cold. If put into a screw-top jar and kept in the refrigerator it will make a delicious substitute for mayonnaise with meat, fish or vegetable salads.

MAYONNAISE

Most of us take fright at the thought of making our own mayonnaise as we have heard of the difficulty and hard work involved but it is not really as bad as all that—a good recipe and a little care and one's trouble is well rewarded. If you have a refrigerator, decide to do double or triple quantity while you are at it and store it in an airtight container on the bottom shelf. If you have an electric mixer, then follow the manufacturer's instructions. Remember that fresh, good-quality oil is essential for a perfect tasting result.

1 yolk of egg; ½ teaspoon of dry mustard; a little salt and pepper; ¼ teaspoon caster sugar; ¼ pint salad or olive oil; 2–3 teaspoons of vinegar or lemon juice.

Put the yolk of egg in a small bowl, add the dry ingredients and mix together well with a wooden spoon. Add a bare half teaspoon of vinegar to moisten and then the oil, literally drop by drop, stirring steadily all the time so that the mayonnaise turns and thickens. As this keeps both hands busy and one cannot hold the bowl stand it on a cloth to prevent it turning. Should the mayonnaise show signs of curdling because the oil has been added too fast, quickly stir in a drop or two of cold water or, if very bad, beat another yolk of egg in another bowl and stir the mayonnaise into it. Once the mayonnaise has thickened, the rest of the oil can be added in a thin stream with a little vinegar added from time to time to keep the correct consistency. A tablespoon of cream may be added at the last, for extra richness.

VARIATIONS

Tartare: Stir in one dessertspoon each of capers, parsley, chives and red pepper if available and 1 teaspoon each of finely chopped gherkins and shallots.

Chaudfroid: This should be mayonnaise of a flowing consistency and to make it set when cold a ¼-oz packet of gelatine must be dissolved in a ¼ pint of slightly warm aspic jelly (this can be bought), and be added to 1 pint of mayonnaise which also must be slightly warm. The sauce should then be put through a sieve and one tablespoon of cream be added. To prevent the sauce setting if not used at once it should be stood in a bowl of hot water.

MISCELLANEOUS SAUCES

TOMATO SAUCE

Pressure Cooking Time: 5 minutes

½ oz butter; 1 small rasher of streaky bacon; 1 sliced onion and carrot; ½ lb fresh or ½ pint tinned tomatoes; 1 bay leaf; 1 teaspoon tomato purée; salt and pepper; ½ pint white stock; pinch of sugar if liked; 2 teaspoons cornflour blended with a little more stock.

If the pressure cooker is not in use, the sauce can be made in this as follows: lift out the trivet, melt the butter and gently fry the chopped bacon. Put in the onion and carrot and cook without allowing to colour. Add the tomatoes, stirring well to mash them if they are fresh ones. Put in the tomato purée, the seasonings and sugar and lastly the stock. Bring to pressure in the usual way, cook for 5 minutes and reduce the pressure immediately. If the sauce is to be made while other foods are being pressure cooked, do exactly the same but leave to simmer in a covered saucepan for 30 minutes. Sieve the sauce, return to the pan, add the blended cornflour and stir until boiling. Taste and correct seasoning. If the sauce is to be served with fish leave out the bacon and use fish stock.

APPLE SAUCE

This can be made loose in the pressure cooker by cooking the apples with ¼ pint water for 2 to 3 minutes, without the trivet or can be done in a solid container without any water being added, and at the same time as the accompanying vegetables such as potatoes and sprouts to be served with the meat. Two cloves to four apples can be added for the cooking if liked. When pressure has been reduced the apples should be beaten until smooth with a tablespoon of butter and a little sugar to taste.

BREAD SAUCE

Simmer one onion stuck with two cloves, in ½ pint milk with a blade of mace added, for half an hour. The flavoured milk should then be poured over four tablespoons fresh white breadcrumbs, one tablespoon of butter, salt and pepper be added and left to stand for at least half an hour. A little more milk may be added if too thick, taste and correct seasoning and reheat just before serving.

MINT SAUCE

Chop one small handful of washed and dried fresh mint leaves with one heaped teaspoon of sugar. Put in a small jug or dish, pour over one dessertspoon of boiling water and add a $\frac{1}{4}$ pint of vinegar. Mint sauce should stand on one side for at least an hour and be well stirred before serving.

VINAIGRETTE DRESSING

Mix a quarter teaspoon each of salt, pepper and mustard in a small basin with three tablespoons of olive oil, then whisk in one tablespoon of vinegar. This dressing should be kept in a stoppered or screw-top bottle so that it can be well shaken each time before use. A squeeze of lemon juice may be added to taste.

QUICK PIQUANT SAUCE

1 tablespoon butter; 1 diced onion; 1 crushed clove of garlic; $\frac{1}{2}$ diced green pepper; a small bay leaf; 1 tin of tomatoes or tomato purée.

Heat the butter in a frying pan, cook the onion for a few minutes until transparent, add the garlic, pepper and bay leaf and allow to cook gently. If using the tin of tomatoes, strain and sieve to give a purée. Add this to the rest of the ingredients, allow to boil. Add water or stock to give the correct consistency, a little meat or vegetable extract if liked, for extra flavouring, taste and correct seasoning, lift out bay leaf and serve.

This sauce would be just right to serve with stuffed vegetable dishes such as marrow, onions or tomatoes, or could accompany rice and pasta dishes, or for vegetarians be a change with the **Butter Bean Ring, Lentil and Tomato Cutlets** and so on.

SWEET SAUCES

WHITE SAUCE

Use the foundation white sauce with two teaspoons of sugar instead of seasoning and a little vanilla or other flavouring to taste.

CHOCOLATE SAUCE

2 oz plain chocolate or 1 level tablespoon of cocoa; 1 tablespoon of caster sugar; $\frac{1}{2}$ pint water; 2 teaspoons cornflour blended with a little water; a taste of sherry if liked.

Melt the chocolate and sugar in the water and boil for a moment or two stirring until smooth. Add the blended cornflour, stir until boiling; cook for 2 to 3 minutes and add sherry before serving.

CUSTARD SAUCE

$\frac{1}{2}$ pint milk with a strip of lemon peel; 1 egg; 1 teaspoon of cornflour; 1 teaspoon of sugar.

Blend the cornflour with a little of the milk, boil the rest and pour over the blended flour. Return to the pan, add the sugar and bring to the boil stirring all the time. Take from the heat, add the beaten egg, then stir over a low heat until the custard thickens but do not allow to boil.

To make this custard into a mousse-like sauce a stiffly beaten white of egg may be folded in when the custard has cooled a little.

JAM SAUCE

2 tablespoons jam; $\frac{1}{4}$ pint water; 1 teaspoon cornflour blended with a little water; a few drops of lemon juice.

Boil the water with the jam gently for a few minutes, add the blended cornflour, stir until boiling, and while cooking for 2 to 3 minutes add lemon juice and colouring if necessary.

ORANGE OR LEMON SAUCE

Thin shreds of orange or lemon rind; $\frac{1}{4}$ pint of water; juice of the half fruit; 1 teaspoon of blended cornflour; 1 tablespoon of sugar.

Boil the shreds of fruit in the water until tender. Add the blended cornflour, stir until thickened, add the sugar and strained juice and serve.

GARNISHES AND ACCOMPANIMENTS

BACON ROLLS

Use thin slices of streaky bacon. Stretch each slice by running the back of a kitchen knife along it, cut into three or four pieces, roll and put on skewers. Can be grilled, turning once, fried in fat in the cooker, before putting in other ingredients or cooked in a roasting tin in the oven, as with a chicken, when it is being browned after pressure cooking.

BOUQUET GARNI

This is a mixture of dried herbs which can now be bought, in muslin bags or sachets from most grocers, but if you wish to make your own so that the selection can be varied or fresh herbs can be used a basic selection would be: 1 bay leaf, 1 blade of mace, 1 pinch of mixed herbs, a few black or white peppercorns, a sprig of parsley; tied into a small square of butter muslin, put in for the cooking and lifted out before serving.

BRANDY BUTTER

For serving with Christmas Pudding: cream 4 oz unsalted butter until white, beat in 6 oz of finely sieved icing sugar, then brandy, four to eight dessertspoons, to taste. Put in a refrigerator or cool place to harden.

BROWNED CRUMBS

For garnishing cauliflower and the tops of savoury dishes: melt about 1 oz of butter or oil in a frying pan, add three tablespoons of fresh white breadcrumbs and stir with a metal spoon until golden brown. Only a medium heat should be used and care must be taken that they do not get dark or burnt. Season with salt and pepper before using.

FRENCH BREAD

As an accompaniment to any savoury dish: cut 6-inch pieces diagonally from a long French loaf and slit diagonally at 1-inch intervals almost through to the bottom crust. Spread these cuts with butter, place the bread on a baking tray and leave in a slow oven, Gas No 2, 300° F, for about 5 minutes until warmed through.

FRIED CROÛTONS

Use white bread, slice thinly and cut off the crusts. Dice into small squares by cutting $\frac{1}{4}$-inch strips in one direction and then across or into triangles by cutting diagonally from corner to corner. Have hot fat ready in the frying pan, throw in the croûtons and keep turning them so that they brown evenly on all sides. They should be a gingery brown and crisp but not brittle. Lift on to kitchen paper to drain. They may be served plain on a savoury doily and handed separately, or if in triangles be half dipped in chopped parsley and be used to garnish the dish.

FRIED ONION RINGS

To garnish fish and other savoury and made-up dishes: use large onions, peel, cut into thinnish slices and separate each into its separate rings. Toss in seasoned flour and fry in hot fat until golden brown. Drain on kitchen paper.

FRIED PARSLEY

For garnishing fish, grilled and made-up dishes: pick over fresh, bushy parsley sprigs, pinching off the stems; wash and toss in a teatowel to dry. Fry in hot fat before it reaches hazing point, until the spluttering ceases. Fried parsley should be crisp but still bright green.

GHERKIN FANS

To garnish fish, boiled rice: make parallel cuts down almost the full length of each gherkin, then spread out like a fan.

LEMON BASKETS

As a garnish for fish, joints or pasta dishes, very effective for special occasions: place the lemon sideways to you, cut a slit about $\frac{1}{8}$ inch off centre to half-way down, then cut across from the end to meet this, thus taking away a quarter wedge of the lemon. Repeat on the other side; the $\frac{1}{4}$ inch left in the centre will now be the handle of the basket. Clean this and the basket itself of the lemon pulp and fill with cooked peas to garnish fish, mint jelly to garnish lamb or cranberry jelly for turkey and poultry dishes.

LEMON BUTTERFLIES

To garnish fish and cheese dishes: cut thin slices of lemon in half, remove any pips, make a cut almost to the centre and spread to form a butterfly. When on the dish lay flat or twist and put a small sprig of parsley in the centre.

LEMON SHELLS

Cut thin slices of lemon, remove any pips, make a slit to the centre, take hold of each edge and move them in opposite directions so that they overlap to form a cone. When on the dish, put a small sprig of parsley in each.

VARIOUS STUFFINGS

When using stuffing for pressure-cooked foods, a dry texture will be best as excess moisture will not have the chance to be driven off as when in the oven. This should apply particularly when packet stuffing is being used; add less than the recommended quantity of liquid.

PLAIN STUFFINGS FOR MEATS AND FISH

Four tablespoons of fresh breadcrumbs or 2 slices of bread, crusts cut off, soaked in hot water and then pressed in a strainer to take away all excess liquid; $\frac{1}{2}$ oz chopped suet, 1 tablespoon finely chopped parsley, a pinch of mixed herbs, a little grated lemon rind mixed well together with sufficient milk or beaten egg to bind but with a dry not moist consistency.

When using stuffing, pack loosely as it will swell during the cooking.

CHEESE OR MEAT STUFFING

For vegetables such as onions and tomatoes: 2 oz grated cheese or minced, cooked meat, 2 tablespoons of fresh breadcrumbs or soaked bread, 2 tablespoons of crisp, chopped fried bacon, plenty of seasoning and a little egg to moisten. To this should be added the chopped centre of the vegetables themselves.

RICE STUFFING

For red or green peppers, marrows, cucumbers: fry 1 small diced onion in a little butter, add 2 peeled, chopped tomatoes, cook for a minute or two, add 2 oz cooked diced meat or ham and 1 large tablespoon of rice with plenty of salt and pepper. Pack loosely to allow for the expansion of the rice.

UNCLASSIFIED RECIPES

MARINADE

Used for meats, pieces of poultry and game to enrich the flavour before cooking. Mix together in a deep bowl, $\frac{1}{4}$ pint red wine, 2 tablespoons vinegar, 1 tablespoon olive oil, a crushed clove of garlic, a medium sliced onion, a few peppercorns, a bay leaf, a pinch of thyme or mixed herbs and seasoning. Put in the meat, cover the bowl and turn the meat at least once and preferably more often, while leaving it to soak for 12 to 24 hours. Before cooking, the meat should be dried with kitchen paper.

A MIREPOIX

A bed of vegetables on which the food to be braised is placed. Melt a tablespoon of butter and fry one slice of chopped bacon until the fat runs out. Add 2 to 3 large carrots and turnips, 2 large onions, 2 to 3 sticks of celery cut into large pieces, fry until brown. Pour off the fat, add sufficient stock to come halfway up vegetables but not less than $\frac{1}{2}$ pint, a bouquet garni and plenty of seasoning. Place meat or food to be braised, on top.

SOUR CREAM

For special dishes such as **Beef Strogonoff** (p. 94) or **Pork Fillets** (p. 155) or as a sauce coating for carrots, parsnips, beetroots, etc: to $\frac{1}{4}$ pint double cream add 2 teaspoons of strained lemon juice, stir well and allow to stand for at least 3 to 4 hours in a warm place. Sour cream with chopped chives or capers is excellent as a coating for green beans, cucumbers or tomatoes.

TO HARD-BOIL EGGS

Pressure Cooking Time: 3–5 minutes

If a number are required for salad, for Scotch eggs or just for a picnic in-the-hand, put $\frac{1}{2}$ pint water in the cooker without the trivet, put in the eggs (which should not just have been lifted from the refrigerator, or they may crack), bring to pressure in the usual way, cook for 5 minutes, reduce the pressure with cold water, take out the eggs and drop into cold water until cool.

If one or two are required for an accompanying sauce, or as garnish they may be wrapped in greaseproof paper or aluminium foil and cooked in with the dish, then be dropped, unwrapped into cold water until cool. For curries where they are to be served in a sauce, allow cold water to run over the wrapping, then take out, shell and put straight back.

For dishes where the egg is cooked with tomatoes, ham, a little cheese to be served to babies and invalids and may need to be a little softer, the egg may be broken into a cup and can then be cooked with accompanying vegetables. Recipes for this are given in the appropriate sections.

FOOD FOR PETS

Although there are now so many prepared and canned foods for dogs and cats, many people still like to have fresh foods as part of their pet's diet but the cheap cuts of meat, horseflesh, coarse fish require a lot of cooking and often make for unpleasant, hanging-around odours in the house. Be sure and use your pressure cooker for this purpose, increasing cooking times as experience will soon show you is necessary, saving fuel and cooking smells and still being quite certain that, with the high temperatures reached, your pressure cooker will be safe and sterile for the family meals as well.

COMPARABLE CONVERSION OF WEIGHTS, MEASURES AND TEMPERATURES

	ENGLISH	AMERICAN	NEAREST METRIC EQUIVALENT
Solids			
Butter and other fats	8 ozs	1 cup	200 g
Flour	8 ozs	2 cups	,,
Sugars (white)	8 ozs	1 cup	,,
Sugars (brown)	8 ozs	1¼ cups	,,
Syrup or Treacle	4 ozs	¼ cup	100 g
Rice	8 ozs	1 cup	200 g
Dried Fruit	8 ozs	1 cup	,,
Meat (minced)	8 ozs	1 cup	,,
Split Peas, Lentils	8 ozs	1 cup	,,
Flour	1 oz	1 heaped measuring tablespoon	25 g
Sugar	1 oz	1 level measuring tablespoon	25 g
Butter	1 oz	1 smoothed level measuring tablespoon	25 g
Liquids	½ pt	½ cup	250 ml

OVEN TEMPERATURES	GAS REGULO	FAHRENHEIT	CENTIGRADE
Cool	½	250°	121°
Slow	2	300°	150°
Moderate	4	375°	190°
Hot	6–7	450°	233°

Pressures (1 metric bar = 1 kg per sq cm) at sea-level

5 lb per sq inch	=	0·35 kg per sq cm
10 lb ,, ,,	=	0·70 kg ,, ,, ,,
15 lb ,, ,,	=	1 kg ,, ,, ,,

QUICK CHECK TIME-TABLE FOR MEATS

JOINTS SUITABLE	PREPARATION	PRESSURE COOKING TIME	ACCOMPANIMENTS
Pot-roasting (with trivet) joints weighing 3 lb or under			
Beef: topside, brisket, rolled rib	Trim, remove fat, tie securely. Weigh. Brown lightly in hot fat, in open pan over medium heat. Lift out, season with salt and pepper. Drain off fat. Add required amount of hot liquid	12–15 minutes per lb	Thin gravy, horseradish sauce
Veal: stuffed shoulder, loin		12–14 minutes per lb	Thickened gravy, bacon rolls, lemon
Mutton or Lamb: stuffed, rolled breast		10–12 minutes per lb	Thickened gravy, mint or onion sauce
Boiling (without trivet) joints weighing 3 lb or under			
Beef: brisket, silverside	Sufficient water to half fill cooker	15 minutes per lb	Mustard sauce, garnish of vegetables
Veal: knuckle	Sufficient water to half fill cooker	10 minutes per lb	Boiled rice, bacon rolls, lemon
Mutton: leg	Sufficient water to half fill cooker	15 minutes per lb	Caper sauce
Pork: pickled leg, hand, belly	Sufficient water to half fill cooker	18 minutes per lb	Thickened gravy, haricot beans
Ham: gammon, hock, collar, flank	Sufficient water to half fill cooker	12 minutes per lb	Cooking liquor or parsley sauce, hot
	On trivet, water according to cooking time	12 minutes per lb	Coated with golden crumbs, salad, cold
Pig's, Sheep's, Calf's Head	Prepare in usual way (see recipe, p. 104), 1 pint boiling water	35–45 minutes	Sliced tongue, diced brain, white sauce
Pig's Trotters	Use $\frac{1}{4}$ pint vinegar, $\frac{1}{4}$ pint water	30 minutes	Garnish of vegetables, brown

Beef: chuck, rump	Brown in hot fat, over medium heat in open pan. Prepare mirepoix (see recipe, p. 300). Drain off fat. Add liquid to just show through vegetables	10 minutes	Mashed vegetables from mirepoix, thickened gravy
Oxtail	Fry onions, then joints in hot fat; $1\frac{1}{4}$ pints boiling liquid	40 minutes	Redcurrant jelly, thickened gravy
Veal: rolled, stuffed breast	Stuff, roll tightly, tie or skewer, weigh; continue as for Beef stew	12 minutes per lb	Brown quickly under hot grill, thickened gravy, bacon rolls, lemon
Mutton or Lamb: chops and cutlets	As for Beef stew	10 minutes	As for Beef stew
Hearts	Clean out, three-quarter fill with stuffing, secure loosely, continue as for Beef stew	30 minutes	As for Beef stew
Liver	As for Beef stew	5 minutes	As for Beef stew
Kidneys	Brown in bacon fat, add $\frac{1}{2}$ pint hot liquid	7 minutes	Brown sauce, with red wine added
Pork: chops, plain	As for Beef stew	10–12 minutes	As for Beef stew, apple sauce or rings
Stuffed	As for Beef stew; brown small, whole onions, after lifting out chops	12–15 minutes	Browned whole onions, thickened gravy
Ham: 1-inch-thick gammon slices	Brown in hot fat, top with pineapple rings, use juice as liquid	10 minutes	Parsley sauce, peas
Stewing (without trivet)			
Beef: stewing steak cut into 1-inch cubes	Toss lightly in seasoned flour; fry gently in hot fat, over medium heat, in open pan. Add vegetables and required amount of liquid	15–20 minutes	Thickened gravy
Mince	Fry gently as above	7 minutes	Triangles of toast, chopped parsley

QUICK CHECK TIME-TABLE FOR MEATS—*continued*

JOINTS SUITABLE	PREPARATION	PRESSURE COOKING TIME	ACCOMPANIMENTS
Stewing (without trivet)—contd.			
Tripe	Add onions; sufficient water to cover	15 minutes	White sauce, fried croûtons
Veal pieces	Seal in a little hot butter but without browning; add vegetables and $\frac{1}{2}$ pint hot liquid	12 minutes	White sauce, bacon rolls, lemon, slices of hard boiled egg, chopped parsley
Sweetbreads	See recipe, p. 105	6–8 minutes	Triangles of fried bread, lemon, parsley
Mutton or Lamb: best end of neck	Cut into chops or pieces	10–12 minutes	Thickened sauce, chopped parsley
Meat and Pastry dishes			
Steak and Kidney Pudding	See recipe, p. 120	Steam 15 minutes Pressure cook 55 minutes	Mixed vegetables, extra gravy
	With pre-cooked meat, see recipe, p. 121	Steam 15 minutes Pressure cook 35 minutes	Mixed vegetables, extra gravy
Suet Roll	See recipe, p. 122	Steam 10 minutes Pressure cook 35 minutes	Mixed vegetables, extra gravy
For Steak and Kidney Pie	Add $\frac{3}{4}$ pint liquid	Pressure cook 10 minutes Oven bake 30 minutes	Mixed vegetables, extra gravy
Cold Meats			
Brawn: pig's head	See recipe, p. 138	35 minutes	Green salad, hard boiled egg, gherkin
Galantine of Beef	See recipe, p. 139	35 minutes	Press, coat with golden crumbs; salad
Pressed Tongue	Tie in muslin; sufficient water to half fill cooker	15 minutes per lb	Press; new potatoes, salad

INDEX

STOCKS AND SOUPS

VEGETABLES

FISH

CEREALS, RICE AND PASTAS

PUDDINGS, BREAD AND CAKES

FRUITS AND DESSERTS

Regional and Continental

Vegetarian and Invalid Dishes

Infant and Child Feeding

Complete and Special Meals

Preservation of Fruit and Vegetables

Out and About

Miscellaneous